Representing Abortion

Representing Abortion analyses how artists, writers, performers, and activists make abortion visible, audible, and palpable within contexts dominated by anti-abortion imagery centred on the fetus and the erasure of the pregnant person, challenging the polarisation of conversations about abortion.

This book illuminates the manifold ways that abortion is depicted and narrated by artists, performers, clinicians, writers, and activists. This representational work offers nuanced and complex understandings of abortion, personally and politically. Analyses of such representations are urgently needed as access to abortion is diminished and anti-abortion representations of the fetus continue to dominate the cultural horizon for thinking about abortion. Expanding the frame of reference for understanding abortion beyond the anti-abortion use of the fetal image, contributors to this collection push beyond narrow abstractions to examine representations of the experience and procedure of abortion within grounded histories, politics, and social contexts.

The collection is organised into sections around seeing (and not seeing) abortion; fetal materiality; abortion storytelling and memoir; and representations for new arguments. These themes cover a range of topics including abortion visibility, anti-abortion discourse, pro-choice engagements with the fetus, personal experience, and media representations. The analyses of such representations counteract anti-abortion rhetoric, carving out space for new arguments for abortion that are more representative and inclusive and asking audiences to envision new ways to advocate for safe abortion access through reproductive justice frameworks.

This is an innovative and challenging collection that will be of key interest for scholars studying reproductive rights and reproductive justice, as well as women's and gender studies. *Representing Abortion* is organised to structure upper-year undergraduate and graduate courses on reproductive rights and reproductive justice in a new and engaging way.

Rachel Alpha Johnston Hurst is Associate Professor of Women's and Gender Studies at St Francis Xavier University in Antigonish, Nova Scotia. Her research is concerned with the relationships between power, embodiment, and (visual) culture, from the perspectives of psychoanalysis and decolonial thought. She is author of *Surface Imaginations: Cosmetic Surgery, Photography, and Skin* (2015) and co-editor of *Skin, Culture, and Psychoanalysis* (2013). Her most recent essays have been published in *History of Photography*, *Feminist Studies*, *Configurations*, and *Body & Society*.

Interdisciplinary Research in Gender

www.routledge.com/Interdisciplinary-Research-in-Gender/book-series/IRG

Representing Abortion

Edited by Rachel Alpha Johnston Hurst

Routledge
Taylor & Francis Group

LONDON AND NEW YORK

First published 2021
by Routledge
2 Park Square, Milton Park, Abingdon, Oxon OX14 4RN

and by Routledge
52 Vanderbilt Avenue, New York, NY 10017

Routledge is an imprint of the Taylor & Francis Group, an informa business

British Library Cataloguing-in-Publication Data
A catalogue record for this book is available from the British Library

Library of Congress Cataloging-in-Publication Data
Names: Hurst, Rachel Alpha Johnston, 1977– editor.
Title: Representing abortion / edited by Rachel Alpha Johnston Hurst.
Description: Abingdon, Oxon; New York, NY : Routledge, 2021. |
Series: Interdisciplinary research in gender |
Includes bibliographical references and index.
Identifiers: LCCN 2020022734 (print) | LCCN 2020022735 (ebook) |
ISBN 9780367860417 (hardback) | ISBN 9781003016595 (paperback) |
ISBN 9780367540029 (ebook)
Subjects: LCSH: Abortion. | Abortion in art. |
Abortion in literature. | Abortion in motion pictures.
Classification: LCC HQ767 .R357 2021 (print) |
LCC HQ767 (ebook) | DDC 362.1988/8—dc23
LC record available at https://lccn.loc.gov/2020022734
LC ebook record available at https://lccn.loc.gov/2020022735

ISBN: 978-0-367-86041-7 (hbk)
ISBN: 978-1-003-01659-5 (ebk)

Typeset in Sabon
by Newgen Publishing UK

Contents

Figures

Contributors

Michele Byers is Professor of Women and Gender Studies at Saint Mary's University in Halifax, Nova Scotia. She has published widely in the areas of television, media, youth culture, and identity and has held several Social Sciences and Humanities Research Council (SSHRC) grants for the study of Canadian television. She is editor or co-editor of four edited collections, including *Growing Up Degrassi: Television, Identity and Youth Cultures* (2005).

T.L. Cowan is Assistant Professor of Media Studies (Digital Media Cultures) in the Department of Arts, Culture, and Media and the Faculty of Information at the University of Toronto. T.L.'s research/creation focuses on cultural and intellectual economies, networks, and methods of trans-feminist and queer digital media and performance practices. She is currently completing a monograph, *Transmedial Drag and Other Cross-Platform Cabaret Methods*. T.L.'s performance practice draws from cabaret, spoken word, costume-based and alter-ego performance, agit-prop theatre, stand-up comedy, video and sound art, installation, and intervention.

Kelly Gordon is Assistant Professor in the Department of Political Science at McGill University. Her research focuses on North American party politics, and in particular the role that women and representations of gender play in structuring conservative political persuasion in Canada and the United States. Kelly's book, *The Changing Voice of the Anti-Abortion Movement: The Rise of "Pro-Woman" Rhetoric in Canada and the United States* (2015, co-authored with Dr Paul Saurette), received several academic awards, including the Canadian Political Science Association (CPSA) 2016 Donald Smiley Prize for the best book published in the field of Canadian politics and the American Political Science Association (APSA) Lipset Award for making a significant contribution in the field of Canadian political science. Her current book manuscript, tentatively titled *Gendering Political Persuasion: Gender, Victimhood, and Conservative Activism and Politics in Canada*, examines the rise of new forms of discourses of victimisation within the contemporary Canadian conservative movement.

Lena Hann is Assistant Professor of Public Health at Augustana College in Rock Island, IL and an Abortion Conversation Projects grant partner. She previously worked in the reproductive health and abortion care fields as a pregnancy options counsellor, laboratory technician, and education programmes coordinator. Her best practices guide, *Patient-Centered Pregnancy Tissue Viewing: Strategies and Best Practices for Independent Abortion Providers*, was published in 2020 through the Abortion Care Network.

Melissa Huerta is Associate Professor of Spanish at Denison University, where she teaches courses on Latino/a and Latin-American literature and Spanish language. Her research is focused on the intersections of identity and praxis in Latina cultural productions. She has published on Teatro Luna and Tanya Saracho. She holds a PhD from the University of Illinois, Chicago. She has published in *Chicana/Latina Studies* and *HowlRound*.

Rachel Alpha Johnston Hurst is Associate Professor of Women's and Gender Studies at St Francis Xavier University in Antigonish, Nova Scotia. Her research is concerned with the relationships between power, embodiment, and (visual) culture, from the perspectives of psychoanalysis and decolonial thought. She is author of *Surface Imaginations: Cosmetic Surgery, Photography, and Skin* (2015) and co-editor of *Skin, Culture, and Psychoanalysis* (2013). Her most recent essays have been published in *History of Photography*, *Feminist Studies*, *Configurations*, and *Body & Society*.

Claire L. Kovacs is Curator of Collections and Exhibitions at the Binghamton University Art Museum. Her research practice grapples with the ways that art history can support "The Common Good" (to borrow a phrase from the National Endowment for the Humanities (NEH)), using curatorial practice and writing as a mechanism by which to amplify under-told stories. Her chapter on the SisterSerpents is part of a larger project on the collective, begun at the NEH/Newberry Library Summer Institute on Art and Public Culture in Chicago. More information about her curatorial practice and scholarship can be found on her website, clairekovacs.org.

Heather Latimer is Assistant Professor of Gender and Women's Studies at the University of British Columbia, Okanagan. Her research focuses on reproductive politics, fiction and film, and feminist theories. Her first book is *Reproductive Acts: Sexual Politics in North American Fiction and Film* (2013). Recently she has published essays in the *Journal of Intercultural Studies* (2019) and *Feminist Theory* (2020).

Jeannie Ludlow is Professor of English and Women's, Gender, and Sexuality Studies at Eastern Illinois University. She has worked as an abortion patient advocate at Whole Woman's Health of Peoria, Illinois and at the Center for Choice in Toledo, Ohio, and is an anti-racist advocate. Recent publications include "Graphic Abortion: The Grotesque in Diane Noomin's 1990s Abortion Comics" in *Feminist Formations* (summer 2019) and "Inappropriate/d Generations: Artifactual Pregnancy and Diffracted Choice in Comic Narratives" in *Monstrous Women in Comics*, edited by Elizabeth Coody and Samantha Langsdale.

Manon S. Parry is Professor of Medical History at the Vrije Universiteit Amsterdam and Senior Lecturer in American Studies and Public History at the University of Amsterdam. She was previously Curator in the History of Medicine Division of the National Library of Medicine, National Institutes of Health, Maryland, USA, where she curated gallery and online exhibitions on a wide range of topics, including global health and human rights, disability in the American Civil War, and medicinal and recreational drug use. Her latest book project is titled "Human Curiosities: Expanding the Social Relevance of European Medical Museums."

Dagmara Rode is Assistant Professor in the Department of New Media and Digital Culture, University of Łódź, Poland. She has published a book on Derek Jarman's work titled *First Person Politics: The Oeuvre of Derek Jarman* in Polish (2014), and several articles on feminist art and activism, experimental film, and video art. Currently she is working on a book on feminist activist filmmaking in Poland. Rode is also a member of Manifa Łódź – a feminist activist collective.

Sucharita Sarkar is Associate Professor of English at D.T.S.S. College of Commerce, Mumbai, India. Her doctoral thesis investigated mothering narratives in contemporary India. Her research explores intersections of maternity with body, cultures, religion, media, and self-writing, from a South Asian perspective. Her recent published works include chapters in *Thickening Fat: Fat Bodies, Intersectionality and Social Justice* (2019); *The Politics of Belonging in Contemporary India: Anxiety and Intimacy* (2019); *Breastfeeding and Culture: Discourses and Representations* (2018); *Motherhood(s) and Polytheisms* (2017); and *Farm to Fingers: The Culture and Politics of Food in Contemporary India* (2017), among others.

Paul Saurette is Associate Professor at the School of Political Studies, University of Ottawa where he researches and teaches on a variety of topics, including ideology and rhetoric, political communication, populism, the conservative and progressive movements in North America, and a wide range of social and political theory. The recipient of several teaching and research awards, his books include *The Kantian Imperative* (2005) and *The Changing Voice of the Anti-Abortion Movement: The Rise of "Pro-Woman" Rhetoric in Canada and the United States* (2015, co-authored with Kelly Gordon). He is currently writing a new book titled *Climate Populism* with Mat Patterson, Shane Gunster, Simon Dalby, and Bob Neubauer.

Jennifer Scuro, PhD, is the author of *The Pregnancy ≠ Childbearing Project: A Phenomenology of Miscarriage* (2017) as well as *Addressing Ableism: Philosophical Questions via Disability Studies* (2017) and a recently published article titled "Thoughts on the Postpartum Situation" in *Frontiers in Sociology*, Special Issue on Birth (2018). Her books have been reviewed in *Hypatia Reviews Online* and *The International Journal of Feminist Approaches to Bioethics* (IJFAB). She has exhibited some of the original artwork from her graphic novel with the award-winning organisation, *The ART of Infertility*.

Yoonha Shin earned her PhD in English at the State University of New York at Buffalo. Her research interests include reproductive rights/justice, fictional imaginations of feminist activism, postfeminist popular culture, and feminist pedagogy. She currently teaches as an Assistant Professor of English and advises the Feminist Book Club at the County College of Morris in New Jersey.

Katherine Side is Professor, Department of Gender Studies, Memorial University, Newfoundland. She is author of *Patching Peace: Women's Civil Society Organizing in Northern Ireland* (2015) and co-editor of *Grenfell's Medical Mission and American Support in Newfoundland and Labrador, 1890s–1940s* (2019). Her research examines visual representations and images and she has published about abortion access in the Republic of Ireland and Northern Ireland in *Social Politics, International Feminist Journal of Politics, Gender, Place and Culture, Feminist Studies*, and *Human Rights in Ireland*.

Rachel Marie-Crane Williams earned an MFA in Studio Art and a PhD in Art Education from Florida State University. She has been employed since 1999 as a tenured faculty member at The University of Iowa in the Gender, Women's and Sexuality Studies (GWSS) Department and in the School of Art and Art History. Currently, she is the University Faculty Ombudsperson. Her scholarship related to incarcerated women, comics, qualitative research, and visual art has been published in the *Journal of Arts Law and Management, Visual Arts Research, Studies in Art Education, Southern Cultures, International Journal of Comics Art, Journal of Art Education, Feminist Studies*, and *Meridians*. She is working on two graphic novels, one about the Detroit Race Riot of 1943 and the other about the murder of Mary Turner.

Aurore Yamagata-Montoya obtained her PhD on the representation of Japanese children and the construction of national identity in photographs from the University of the West of England (UK). Her research interests are at the junction of photography, childhood and family, and Japanese and cultural studies. She is a co-founder and the president of the Mutual Images Research Association, an independent entity that has organised workshops on the relations between Japan and other countries since 2013. She is also manager of the open-access, blind peer-reviewed *Mutual Images Journal*.

Acknowledgements

This book is dedicated to the cultural workers, abortion providers, and activists whose creative insight enables us to think about abortion in a more expansive and meaningful way through a reproductive justice lens. Their work produces new representations of abortion which engender arguments and activism for safer abortion access that encompass a larger array of abortion experiences and responses. The process of bringing an edited book into being is notorious for long delays, shiftless contributors or editors, and occasionally temper tantrums; this edited book involved none of these elements, even though many of us were writing chapters through the personal and professional nadirs that are a part of living life. I suspect that one reason our collective work on this book was so smooth and dynamic is that we all felt the urgency of our project in a global context where safe abortion access is under threat and anti-abortion activism expands. Working on this project has been enormously pleasurable and generative, and I am appreciative of the new relationships that were formed and more established relationships that were strengthened through this process. I have much gratitude and admiration for the contributors to this volume – thank you. This book received a great deal of support in addition to the authors' contributions. Riley Wolfe provided superb research assistance for this book; I enjoyed hearing their insights into the chapters, and their work to get the manuscript ready for submission was invaluable. My editor, Alex McGregor, enthusiastically supported this project from my initial book proposal. She provided excellent advice and direction at crucial moments. Eleanor Catchpole-Simmons shepherded the book to the submission stage and beyond, offering gentle prompts and giving useful information along the way. Nicola Howcroft is a skilled project manager who guided the book through the production process in an impressively efficient and responsive manner. Sally Evans-Darby carefully copyedited the manuscript, improving its flow while maintaining the authors' singular voices. As always, I am thankful for Mary Newberry's incisive reading and analysis, which produced the beautiful index. A final thanks is owed to the St Francis Xavier University Council of Research, which provided research funding in support of this book.

1 Representing abortion

Rachel Alpha Johnston Hurst

How is abortion visualised, heard, and felt – particularly in ways that support safe abortion access? *Representing Abortion* intervenes in scholarly, cultural, and activist conversations about abortion to expand how we think about abortion. The chapters in this book challenge the continued predominance of anti-abortion images and descriptions of the fetus as the primary signifier of abortion in the public sphere, understandings that are fortified by the personification of the fetus through diagnostic medical imaging. Contributors to this collection offer in-depth analyses that highlight the artistic, performative, literary, clinical, and activist efforts to represent abortion outside of this narrow vision and, significantly, to centre the pregnant person as the subject of abortion.[1] This imaginative intellectual-political work reclaims images and narratives about abortion from anti-abortion rhetoric, but it also creates new images and narratives while destabilising anti-abortion attempts to fix the meaning of the fetal image. Contributors explore the ramifications of these acts of creativity and reclamation for how abortion is understood beyond the binary of the fetus-as-person (pro-life) and individual choice (pro-choice). A central objective of this book is to build on these expanded frameworks to imagine abortion differently. *Representing Abortion* proposes and inspires new arguments for abortion access grounded in reproductive justice frameworks. The chapters and examples analysed in this book incorporate images and narratives that resonate with a wider range of abortion experiences, particularly those that are ordinary and non-sensational (in contrast to, for example, the rhetorical use of unwanted pregnancy resulting from rape or incest as a difficult-to-dispute justification for abortion access). Thus, the chapters in this book contribute to a popular surge in abortion storytelling as well as the uptick in recent scholarship on abortion and reproductive justice.

This introduction outlines three key areas of scholarship that help situate the chapters and the book's contribution overall. I begin with a truncated discussion of representation in feminist theory that emphasises how intersections with Black cultural theory and psychoanalysis have shaped feminist understandings of representation as a site of struggle and additionally as psychically complex and generative. This discussion of representation sets the scene for a consideration of feminist scholarship about the fetal image over the past thirty-five years, which helps demonstrate how and why the fetal image has come to occupy its status as the primary representation of abortion. Following this discussion, I provide a brief overview of reproductive justice approaches, which are centred in the contributions to this collection. Here I define reproductive justice, discuss the uneasy position of abortion within reproductive justice, and explain why reproductive justice offers us the best framework from which to consider representations of abortion. And finally, I discuss contemporary abortion studies. I give a brief gloss of scholarship and creative work about abortion narratives, and the connections between activists and lawmakers, abortion legislation, the anti-abortion movement today, and analyses of abortion produced by providers that reflect on the clinical context. The introduction ends with an outline of the book and a synopsis of its contributions.

Feminist theory, representation, and fetal images

Lisa Disch astutely observes that in feminist theory and practice since the mid-twentieth century, representation occupies a place of significance eclipsed perhaps only by the concept of gender (2016, 781). Feminist analyses of representation have drawn attention to the paucity of women as legitimate subjects of culture, history, and politics; this book focuses on cultural representation and the roles of language and image in shaping meaning through interpretation. Feminist analyses have not materialised in isolation, and have benefitted enormously from exchange with critics who challenge prevailing cultural representations that fortify oppressive structures of power like white supremacy, heterosexism, ableism, classism, and transphobia. The scholarship of Black cultural theorists, particularly Stuart Hall and bell hooks, has been invaluable to feminist thought because this work incisively critiques the relationship between representation, ideology, and domination (Hall 1990; hooks 1992). Rooted in a discussion of Frantz Fanon's psycho-analytic inquiry into the psychical violence of colonisation, Hall's brilliant insights that "dominant regimes of representation were the effects of a critical exercise of cultural power and normalisation," and that these regimes possess the "power to make [Black people] see and experience ourselves as Other," provide a rich ground from which to consider the ideological use of representation as central to domination (1990, 225). Writing about the generative capacity of film to do something more than simply "unearthing that which the colonial experience buried and overlaid, bringing to light the hidden continuities it suppressed," but rather to produce identity through "*retelling* the past," Hall claims representation as a process that is additionally illustrative and imaginative (1990, 224). For these reasons, bell hooks names representation as a "site of struggle," a field in need of intervention and transformation "in our political movements of liberation and self-determination … be they anti-imperialist, feminist, gay rights, black liberation, or all of the above and more" (1992, 3–4). Throughout this volume, contributors are invested in representation as a site of political struggle for improved abortion access; a field that is in need of critiques that dismantle dominant ideas, maxims, and images about abortion, but also of creative and liberatory retellings.

Psychoanalytic theory also intersects with feminist considerations of representation and Black cultural studies in imaginative ways. A common second-wave feminist assumption that continues to hold authority is the idea that dominant images of women in popular culture have a straightforward negative effect on women, and that solving this problem is as simple as creating more realistic or empowering images (Hollows 2000, 21–4). Indeed, while "what we can see is in every way related to what one can say," feminist efforts resulting in an endless proliferation of new images can be co-opted by the dominant culture as a way of capturing the "other" as knowable and containable (Phelan 1993, 2). Psychoanalysis is rooted in an acknowledgement of the unconscious, or the notion that our psychical life is not fully conscious but also motivated by unconscious mental representations. Psychoanalysis offers a way to think through another logic – one of fantasy and desire – that embraces what might appear nonsensical when understood through consciousness. Psychoanalytically inflected feminist thought considers representation as following "two laws," according to Peggy Phelan: "it always conveys more than it intends; and it is never totalizing" (1993, 2). Representation always contains ruptures and absences because it can never replicate the real, and Phelan argues that close readings of this excess and failure to totalise can engender "psychic resistance and, possibly, political change" (1993, 2). As Kaja Silverman argues, the "aesthetic text can help us to do something collectively which exceeds the capacity of the individual subject to effect alone" because it can destabilise and forge new identifications that are not directed by dominant cultural ideals that reinforce domination; representation is thus an imperfect way of creating more expansive psychical space (1996, 5). What is exciting about so many of the representations of abortion discussed in this book is their capacity to tease out the excess meaning in dominant representations, to resist dominant understandings of abortion that intend to be totalising, and, through this work, to inspire more complex conversations about abortion as an experience and as a central element of healthcare.

Visual representations of the fetal body are central to anti-abortion discourse. Karen Newman carefully traces images of the pregnant female body and the fetus from the ninth century to the present, and argues that they share a "core schema" whose meaning changes through time alongside the history of ideas; these modes of visualisation have "profoundly determined 'fetal politics' " in the present (1997, 2). Ultrasound images of the fetus *in utero* and photographs of the mutilated fetal body are the most tangible representations of what abortion *is* in public contexts, reaching far outside of anti-abortion discourse into popular culture. Although this use of images began with American anti-abortion activism in the 1960s, this strategy has been taken up internationally. For over three decades, feminist scholars have analysed the contemporary cultural significance of images of the fetus, particularly the fetal ultrasound but also photographs like the notorious series by Lennart Nilsson published in the April 30, 1965 issue of *Life* under the title "Drama of Life Before Birth." Although schoolchildren commonly receive media literacy education and there is widespread awareness and reportage about the existence of deepfakes and the manipulative power of photo editing, the fetal image maintains its status as truth even in the present day. Fetal images continue to be understood as capturing the real of bodily interiority and are employed in public and private settings as confirmation of the fetus's personhood – its life. Faye Ginsburg referred to this as the "conversion power of the fetus" in 1989 – the belief held by anti-abortion activists that there is an integral "truth" of the fetal image that cannot be rationally denied after viewing ultrasound images of the fetus *in utero* or magnified photographs of mutilated fetal remains (1998, 104–5). The fetal image is imbued with two logics generated within anti-abortion discourse, according to Janelle S. Taylor: the creation of an aura through ultrasound that confirms both the singularity and universality of the fetus's humanity, and the manufacture of trauma through photography that suspends language, particularly the stories, reasons, and justifications for having an abortion (1992, 70–4). The creation of fetal personhood and traumatic experience are fundamental to anti-abortion ideology and would be impossible without the manipulation of the fetal image.

Nilsson's photographs frequently appear as a reference point from which to begin analysis of anti-abortion uses of fetal images (Duden 1993; Stabile 1992), and for good reason. His composition of the photographs translates fetuses and embryos tenderly into tiny personas that swim through shadowy space and suck their thumbs like babies. The warm colours, rendered more vivid through contrast against the black background, belie the reality that these fetuses and embryos were dead specimens obtained through legal abortion in Sweden and posed by Nilsson (Buklijas and Hopwood 2014). The ideological possibilities of the fetal image were seized early on by anti-abortion activists. Floating in darkness, the fetus occupies a space that is prior to the social and, importantly, independent of the pregnant person's body. Drucilla Cornell notes that such images create "a vision of the pregnant mother and her fetus that artificially separates the two," deployed by anti-abortion activists to argue for separate rights held by the fetus and mother, obscuring the reality that the fetus's life is "inseparable from the physical and mental well-being of the woman of whose body *it is a part*" (1995, 32; emphasis in original). This separation facilitates an understanding of the rights of women and of fetuses as oppositional, and as advances in medical imaging produce even finer and more detailed fetal images for public consumption, access to such images is also conceived of as the right for citizens to know and see the "reality" of abortion (Palmer 2009, 174). Fetal images have nimbly traversed from anti-abortion placards into the courtroom. The expansion of legislation in the United States that compels pregnant women to view an ultrasound scan prior to obtaining an abortion is publicly framed as "Right to Know Acts" that force a confrontation with the fetal image in order to sow doubt in the mind of the woman seeking an abortion and dissuade her from proceeding (Sanger 2017, 109). Mandatory ultrasound viewing shrewdly capitalises on the private understandings that intentionally pregnant people hold about fetal images as a way of confirming the pregnancy, bonding with the fetus, or as simply a diagnostic procedure (Mitchell 2001, 6) as well as the activist work of the women's health movement and patients' rights organisations that resulted in an improved awareness of informed consent. It is also a crystallisation of how the fetus becomes a fetish object that must be considered outside of the pregnant person's body.

Feminist scholars of the 1980s and 1990s describe this representation as the "public fetus," to use Barbara Duden's keen phrasing, arguing that it shapes the psychical and physical perception of pregnant women (1993, 52). The interior of women's bodies has been "publicised" since the nineteenth century, according to Duden – transformed paradoxically into the subject of administration, the law, and medicine while the exterior of her body is privatised ideologically and culturally (1992, 336). Scientific and medical interventions into pregnancy diminish the significance of quickening – feeling fetal movement – by subordinating it to a new continuum of technological practices that "discover" the fetus by "recognizing it as a public fact" (Duden 1992, 343). In her ground-breaking essay "The Power of Visual Culture in the Politics of Abortion," Rosalind Pollack Petchesky observes that anti-abortion activism over the past fifty years has struggled to control the symbolic meaning of the fetus through the image (1987, 263). Consequently, the fetal image comes to be *the* signifier of abortion, and because "feminists and other pro-choice advocates have all too readily ceded the visual terrain," we are left with an empty abyss in place of representations of abortion that are positive and support abortion access (Petchesky 1987, 264).

Cultural producers like writers, visual artists, and performers, as well as healthcare workers and advocates like abortion providers and reproductive justice activists, have directly responded to anti-abortion representations of abortion through their work. Curiously, however, feminist scholarship has not adequately taken up the critical call to systematically analyse the significant theoretical and political work of representing abortion accomplished by these cultural workers, abortion providers, and activists – an absence that this book addresses. This kind of feminist scholarly investigation is urgently needed, as it provides alternatives to the preponderance of anti-abortion fetal imagery and addresses the impasse of the "pro-choice" and "pro-life" binary through providing more complex understandings that address feelings and ideas presently not accepted within the rhetoric of "choice." Contributors' chapters argue for safe and legal access to abortion, and their analyses are aligned with reproductive justice approaches that locate abortion rights within a complex web of relations of land, class, race, colonialism, and bodily sovereignty.

Abortion and reproductive justice approaches

Reproductive justice frameworks bring together the theories and movements of reproductive rights and social justice, and are organised around three central principles: "(1) the right *not* to have a child; (2) the right to *have* a child; and (3) the right to *parent* children in safe and healthy environments" (Ross and Solinger 2017, 9; emphasis in original). The SisterSong Women of Color Reproductive Justice Collective formed out of the Women of African Descent for Reproductive Justice, and amongst their many impressive accomplishments, they coined the now widely used principle of reproductive justice (SisterSong n.d.). Bodily autonomy is central to reproductive justice, as well as a recognition of the limitations of movements or arguments based on the impoverished foundation of "choice" and individual rights. Reproductive justice facilitates an analysis of reproduction that acknowledges the harm wrought by mainstream feminist reproductive rights organising through its alliances with white supremacist ideology and the eugenics movement, as well as by centring the perspectives of white, middle-class, heterosexual women to determine a reproductive healthcare agenda. Instead, reproductive justice centres the interrelationship of reproduction with racism, colonialism, classism, ableism, homophobia, and transphobia, and offers expansive, creative inquiry into the politics of reproduction that exceeds "choice." Thus, in addition to exposing the racist logics that informed, and continue to inform, family planning, sterilisation, and contraception programmes as well as the benefits that white, middle-class women reap from such programmes, police violence and environmental racism – to give two examples – are central topics in reproductive justice scholarship and activism. A significant strength of reproductive justice as an activist and analytic framework is that it situates abortion within social and historical contexts and it acknowledges a range of responses to abortion that are not easily categorised as "pro-choice" or "pro-life" (Smith 2005).

Reproductive justice is an important organising framework for expanding abortion access. It is critical to ensure that its complexity is not erased as the language of reproductive justice is adopted by mainstream pro-choice organisations, and it is equally important to recognise that the American context from which reproductive justice emerges is not universal. For example, the Ontario Coalition for Abortion Clinics (OCAC), founded in 1982 by the Immigrant Women's Health Centre, Hassle Free Clinic, and the Birth Control and VD Information Centre in Toronto, was critical of the language of "choice" and situated the ability to determine whether or not to have children as also shaped by class and race, as well as access to social programmes like childcare and parental leave throughout the 1980s (Egan and Gardner 2016, 133). Shannon Stettner suggests that this was because

OCAC adopted a socialist feminist framework, rather than the liberal feminist framework so often associated with arguments for individual choice (2016, 335). Additionally, the insistence that reproductive justice is "not just about abortion" (SisterSong n.d.) can have an unintentionally stigmatising effect, as scholars like Carly Thomsen argue. Abortion is thus characterised through a "pervasive negativity," according to Thomsen, and there are few opportunities to celebrate abortion as an essential part of healthcare and reproductive justice (2013, 150). Contributors to *Representing Abortion* engage with the subject of abortion in ways that demonstrate the limitations of choice and the individualisation of abortion, as well as the possibilities of broader reproductive justice frameworks; additionally, several of the representations examined in this book are actively engaged with reproductive justice and celebrating abortion.

Contemporary abortion studies

A discussion of the multiplicity and depth of feminist scholarship on abortion is outside the scope of this introduction. *Representing Abortion* comes into existence amidst a surge of feminist writing on abortion, for scholarly and popular audiences. Here I want to trace some key contours of this renewed interest in writing about abortion as it is embedded within more established lines of inquiry for two purposes. First, I wish to demonstrate how this book makes a unique contribution to this field and builds on the scholarship that precedes it; and second, I hope to provide readers with a starting point for further reading. I begin with a discussion of the recent eruption of abortion storytelling and narratives about accessing abortion as it is located within struggles for abortion access in the 1960s and 1970s, which was informed by the second-wave feminist maxim "the personal is political." The second theme I explore in abortion studies is the connection and disconnection between activists and lawmakers, which helps map out the dynamic and global scope of abortion debate and its effects on access, law, and health. Several books extend foundational feminist scholarship on anti-abortion ideology and activism, and the third theme focuses on the resurgence of the anti-abortion movement for the twenty-first century as well as how the polarisation of the abortion debate can be shifted through considering commonalities between pro-life and pro-choice positions. And finally, the past decade has seen an increase in writing that emerges from "scholar-providers" (Hann and Ludlow, this volume), who ground their analysis within their intimate knowledge of the abortion clinic as workers.

An invigorating development in abortion studies over the past five years has been an uncompromising turn towards telling stories about abortion across traditional and social media; Elizabeth Kissling calls such storytelling online a "vital mechanism of stigma-busting" (2018, 42). Scholars, journalists, and other writers have responded earnestly and passionately by publicly declaring their abortions and writing about abortion in order to spark political action. Reporter Kate McKenna's writing about the lack of access to abortion on Prince Edward Island centred the stories of PEI women as they navigated a hostile healthcare system and travelled long distances to access abortion, leading to the publication of a history of abortion access on the Island (2018). In India, *Youth Ki Awaaz* (Voice of Youth) uses abortion storytelling to challenge the common assumption that abortion is illegal and abortion stigma, as contributor Sucharita Sarkar analyses. *We Testify*, founded by Renee Bracey Sherman, emerged as an online space for intersectional abortion storytelling infused by reproductive justice and resisted the tendency for mainstream news sources to focus on white cisgender women's abortion stories (Sherman 2016). These are only three examples, but an intriguing thread throughout them is an unapologetic stance towards abortion that is reminiscent of an earlier feminist slogan for "free abortion on demand, without apology." In her conclusion to Jennifer Baumgardner's *Abortion & Life*, Rebecca Hyman characterises abortion storytelling as honouring and "resuscitating" second-wave consciousness-raising as a feminist method that resisted the silencing of women and aimed to build a political community (2008, 171). Recent collections of abortion narratives include *One Kind Word: Women Share Their Abortion Stories*, edited by Martha Solomon (2014); *Choose: Thirty American Abortions*, edited by Victoria Barrett and Meredith Counts (2019); and *Shout Your Abortion*, edited by Amelia Bonow and Emily Nokes (2018). Annie Finch's *Choice Words: Writers on Abortion*, the first collection of literary writings about abortion by several authors whose work bridges centuries and geography, was published in 2020.

The national context of accessing abortion frequently appears as a theme in abortion stories, and a distinct strand of recent scholarship focuses on the national and transnational contexts of abortion, particularly safe access and, relatedly, abortion legislation. Studies of national contexts are important because they offer insight into how political positions on abortion are symbols of national identity, or how laws about abortion – even those that are permissive – impact abortion access. Rachael Johnstone's *After Morgentaler: The Politics of Abortion in Canada* starts from the declaration that "abortion is not a stand-alone topic but a procedure inextricably tied to the status of women citizens" (2017, 15). In Canada, Johnstone argues, that status continues to be lesser than the status of men because of a gap between legality and accessibility; the uneven access to abortion will exist as long as abortion is not recognised as a positive right to healthcare (2017, 40). Lisa Smyth analyses parliamentary and popular discourse about abortion in Ireland in *Abortion and Nation: The Politics of Reproduction in Contemporary Ireland*, beginning from a high-profile case in 1992 (*Attorney General v. X*) where a High Court injunction was granted preventing a fourteen-year-old girl who had been raped from travelling with her family to access abortion. Smyth argues that this case had a destabilising effect on Irish national identity, because X and her family received great public sympathy that undermined the assumed patriarchal, conservative, and Catholic qualities of that identity and revealed support for limited access to abortion (2005, 2). A final example of national studies of abortion is Susanne M. Klausen's *Abortion Under Apartheid: Nationalism, Sexuality, and Women's Reproductive Rights in South Africa* (2015). This historical analysis is the first book-length study of abortion in any African country, and demonstrates how the subject of abortion was central to the preservation of apartheid. White women's sexuality and reproduction was legally and socially disciplined by the illegality of abortion as part of upholding white supremacist ideology, and illegal abortion was shaped by race and class so that Black and poor women were far more likely to undergo unsafe, illegal abortions. Abortion in South Africa is now legal, but Klausen's work is a salient reminder that unless abortion laws are interconnected with a broader struggle for social justice, including the struggle against racism and classism, such laws will continue to be discriminatory. Other scholars focus on comparative and transnational studies of abortion access, which facilitate learning and resource sharing between scholars, activists, and advocates; two recent examples include Colleen MacQuarrie, Claire Pierson, Shannon Stettner, and Fiona Bloomer's edited book *Crossing Troubled Waters: Abortion in Ireland, Northern Ireland, and Prince Edward Island* (2018) and Michelle Oberman's *Her Body, Our Laws: On the Front Lines of the Abortion War, from El Salvador to Oklahoma* (2018). Finally, Fiona Bloomer, Claire Pierson, and Sylvia Estrada Claudio's *Reimagining Global Abortion Politics: A Social Justice Perspective* (2019) is ambitious in its objective to identify global patterns in abortion politics; they assert that activism, international human rights norms, displacement, religion, nationalism, and culture are major themes that influence abortion legislation and safe access. Since the results of the 2016 US election, which emboldened anti-abortion activists and politicians, several book-length works on abortion legislation in the United States examine the impact of *Roe v. Wade* and consider the possibilities of challenges to the decision (Sanger 2017; Schoen 2017; Ziegler 2018).

Two smaller threads of recent abortion studies scholarship are important to mention in relation to this book: the contemporary anti-abortion movement and perspectives of scholar-providers. The anti-abortion movement is changing. The vision of a group of protesters (led by men) holding large placards and shouting at women entering an abortion clinic continues to accurately describe scenes in some parts of the world, but it has an outsized role in how anti-abortion activism is imagined. Through in-depth analysis of the public face of anti-abortion organisations in Canada and the United States, Paul Saurette and Kelly Gordon argue that the anti-abortion movement has evolved to be "pro-woman" in order to appeal to a wider base of supporters (2015). Contributions like Karissa Haugeberg's *Women Against Abortion: Inside the Largest Moral Reform Movement of the Twentieth Century* complicate the depiction of the anti-abortion movement as dominated by men by focusing on how anti-abortion activism has provided opportunities for women to resist narrowly defined gender roles (2017). Bertha Manninen's philosophical work on abortion maintains that both "pro-choice" and "pro-life" positions caricature and vilify one another, and she has been invested in considering commonalities and creating understanding between these positions (Manninen 2014; Manninen and Mulder 2018). Scholar-providers ground their scholarly analysis in the complex experience of working in abortion clinics, a position that has been surprisingly neglected in previous research on abortion. The valuable insights from this research can help guide arguments and activism for safe abortion access in a way that is grounded in the experiences of those who provide and have abortions, which often don't fit the politically expedient narrative of abortion as a choice to remove fetal or embryonic tissue. People accessing abortion ask to view fetal remains, refer to their fetus or embryo as a "baby," ask for support in actions like writing a letter explaining the abortion to the fetus, and experience grief following an abortion (Hurst 2020; Kimport *et al.* 2013; Ludlow 2008a, 2008b, 2012; Martin *et al.* 2017; Wiebe and Adams 2009). Acknowledging these realities does not threaten abortion access, nor does it diminish the experiences of those for whom abortion is an uncomplicated decision resulting in relief. Abortion providers offer a unique lens to champion abortion access in a way that holds the complexity of abortion experiences. Though it is tempting to understand these two areas of research as examining the "opposing sides" of abortion debates, what in-depth considerations of the anti-abortion movement and abortion clinic reveal are the limitations of a polarised conceptualisation of abortion.

Conclusion

Contemporary abortion studies is a growing and dynamic field that engages scholars across the social sciences, humanities, and health sciences, and captures the interest of the broader public. *Representing Abortion* is solidly within this field of study and popular interest, and is a collaborative effort to broadly respond to critical current discussions about abortion. What distinguishes this book from the excellent scholarship described above is its singular emphasis on representation, which provides a unifying thread to connect a diverse set of disciplinary and interdisciplinary approaches, geographical contexts, and cultural texts. Additionally, this book's international focus offers opportunities for considering how representations of abortion differ across national contexts, and potentially offers openings for transnational solidarity through cultural, clinical, and activist work. And finally, *Representing Abortion* is distinguished by its effort to bring together, in one book, scholarship that responds to over three decades of research on fetal imagery and abortion activism by engaging with the multifarious ways that artists, writers, clinicians, and performers have advocated for abortion.

This book is arranged into four parts. Each part begins with a short introduction to key themes as well as its chapters. "Seeing (and not seeing) abortion" explores the consequences of the anti-abortion movement's control over public discussions and images of abortion, which is often expressed as a fear of raising the topic. This fear results in silencing open acknowledgement of abortion, and chapters in Part I confront this silence. "Fetal materiality" grapples with the role of the fetal body in anti-abortion activism, the abortion clinic, and ritual and feminist art. The fetal body is significant as a formidable symbol in anti-abortion imagery, and it continues to be necessary to challenge the claim made by anti-abortion activism on this body, because the fetus is also significant in the lives of people who have abortions. "Abortion storytelling and memoir" delves into the multiple ways that people who have abortions narrate their experiences in order to widen understanding of how abortion is accessed worldwide. As abortion storytelling and memoir is perhaps the most visible way that arguments for abortion access are made publicly, chapters in this part of the book examine several examples to demonstrate how they exist within a legacy of storytelling for access and provide new ways of thinking about access. "Representations for new arguments" addresses the need to complicate and expand mainstream pro-choice discourse within the context of more sophisticated and modern anti-abortion activism. This includes the need to address the reality that people of all genders access abortion, that anti-abortion discourse increasingly bills itself as feminist and concerned about women, and that people experience their abortions complexly and not simply as a straightforward choice. The sections have been organised to facilitate connective reading; for example, readers will appreciate the storytelling work performed by some of the examples used in the first section, or they will recognise that some of the chapters that consider fetal materiality also put forward representations that support new ways to argue for abortion access. I have also arranged the sections so they can support use in the classroom when read alongside key readings on reproductive justice and provide tangible examples from which to begin analysis. When read this way, Part I introduces themes of abortion stigma and the power of anti-abortion ideology; Part II opens up conversations about the fetal image and body; Part III presents narratives of abortion that can generate discussion of abortion in various legal contexts and as connected to a broader vision for justice; and Part IV encourages readers to expand their understandings of abortion and envision new arguments for abortion access.

Note

1 People of all genders get pregnant and need access to abortion. Most feminist scholarship on abortion positions women as most affected by the regulation of abortion, and understandably so: women constitute the majority of people who have abortions. However, there is a growing awareness in activist and scholarly communities that transgender and non-binary people have abortions and face additional barriers to access, and that a reproductive justice approach to abortion

care considers gender inclusivity and gender affirmation as central to equitable abortion access (see Jones, Witwer, and Jerman 2020; Light, Wang, Zeymo, and Gomez-Lobo 2018; Strangio 2016; Sutton and Borland 2018). In this introduction, I use the more inclusive "person/people" generally, and refer to gender when it is appropriate; for example, I follow the use of "woman" if the scholar I cite does the same.

References

Barrett, Victoria and Meredith Counts, eds. 2019. *Choose: Thirty American Abortions*. Indianapolis, IN: Engine Books.

Baumgardner, Jennifer. 2008. *Abortion and Life*. New York: Akashic Books.

Bloomer, Fiona, Claire Pierson, and Sylvia Estrada Claudio. 2019. *Reimagining Global Abortion Politics: A Social Justice Perspective*. Bristol: Policy Press.

Bonow, Amelia and Emily Nokes, eds. 2018. *Shout Your Abortion*. Toronto: Between the Lines Press.

Buklijas, Tatiana and Nick Hopwood. 2014. "The Lonesome Space Traveller." *Making Visible Embryos*. www.sites.hps.cam.ac.uk/visibleembryos/s7_4.html.

Cornell, Drucilla. 1995. *The Imaginary Domain: Abortion, Pornography, and Sexual Harassment*. New York: Routledge.

Disch, Lisa. 2016. "Representation." In *The Oxford Handbook of Feminist Theory*, edited by Lisa Disch and Mary Hawkesworth, 781–802. Oxford: Oxford University Press.

Duden, Barbara. 1992. "Quick with Child: An Experience That Has Lost Its Status." *Technology in Society* 14, no. 3: 271–356.

——— 1993. *Disembodying Women: Perspectives on Pregnancy and the Unborn*. Cambridge, MA: Harvard University Press.

Egan, Carolyn and Linda Gardner. 2016. "Reproductive Freedom: The Ontario Coalition for Abortion Clinics and the Campaign to Overturn the Federal Abortion Law." In *Without Apology: Writings on Abortion in Canada*, edited by Shannon Stettner, 131–8. Edmonton: Athabasca University Press.

Finch, Annie, ed. 2020. *Choice Words: Writers on Abortion*. Chicago, IL: Haymarket Books.

Ginsburg, Faye. 1998. *Contested Lives: The Abortion Debate in an American Community, Updated Edition*. Berkeley, CA: University of California Press.

Hall, Stuart. 1990. "Cultural Identity and Diaspora." In *Identity: Community, Culture, Difference*, edited by Jonathan Rutherford, 222–37. London: Lawrence & Wishart.

Haugeberg, Karissa. 2017. *Women Against Abortion: Inside the Largest Moral Reform Movement of the Twentieth Century*. Urbana, IL: University of Illinois Press.

Hollows, Joanne. 2000. *Feminism, Femininity, and Popular Culture*. Manchester: Manchester University Press.

hooks, bell. 1992. *Black Looks: Race and Representation*. Boston, MA: South End Press.

Hurst, Rachel Alpha Johnston. 2020. "Abortion as a Feminist Pedagogy of Grief in Marianne Apostolides' *Deep Salt Water*." *Feminist Studies* 46, no. 1: 43–73.

Johnstone, Rachael. 2017. *After Morgentaler: The Politics of Abortion in Canada*. Vancouver: UBC Press.

Jones, Rachel K., Elizabeth Witwer, and Jenna Jerman. 2020. "Transgender Abortion Patients and the Provision of Transgender-Specific Care at Non-Hospital Facilities that Provide Abortions." *Contraception X* 2: 1–2.

Kimport, Katrina, Ushma D. Upadhyay, Diana G. Foster, Marry Gatter, and Tracy A. Weitz. 2013. "Patient Viewing of the Ultrasound Image Prior to Abortion." *Contraception* 88, no. 5: 666–70.

Kissling, Elizabeth. 2018. *From a Whisper to a Shout: Abortion Activism and Social Media*. London: Repeater Books.

Klausen, Susanne M. 2015. *Abortion Under Apartheid: Nationalism, Sexuality, and Women's Reproductive Rights in South Africa*. Oxford: Oxford University Press.

Light, Alexis, Lin-Fan Wang, Alexander Zeymo, and Veronica Gomez-Lobo. 2018. "Family Planning and Contraception Use in Transgender Men." *Contraception* 98, no. 4: 266–9.

Ludlow, Jeannie. 2008a. "Sometimes It's a Child *and* a Choice: Toward an Embodied Abortion Praxis." *Feminist Formations* 20, no. 1: 26–50.

——— 2008b. "The Things We Cannot Say: Witnessing the Trauma-tization of Abortion in the United States." *WSQ: Women's Studies Quarterly* 36, nos. 1/2: 28–41.

——— 2012. "Love and Goodness: Toward a New Abortion Politics." *Feminist Studies* 38, no. 2: 474–83.

MacQuarrie, Colleen, Claire Pierson, Shannon Stettner, and Fiona Bloomer, eds. 2018. *Crossing Troubled Waters: Abortion in Ireland, Northern Ireland, and Prince Edward Island*. Charlottetown: Island Studies Press at UPEI.

Manninen, Bertha Alvarez. 2014. *Pro-Life, Pro-Choice: Shared Values in the Abortion Debate*. Nashville, TN: Vanderbilt University Press.

Manninen, Bertha Alvarez and Jack Mulder, Jr. 2018. *Civil Dialogue on Abortion*. New York: Routledge.

Martin, Lisa A., Jane A. Hassinger, Michelle Debbink, and Lisa A. Harris. 2017. "Dangertalk: Voices of Abortion Providers." *Social Science and Medicine* 184: 75–83.

McKenna, Kate. 2018. *No Choice: The 3-Year Fight for Abortion on Prince Edward Island*. Winnipeg: Fernwood Press.

Mitchell, Lisa M. 2001. *Baby's First Picture: Ultrasound and the Politics of Fetal Subjects*. Toronto: University of Toronto Press.

Newman, Karen. 1997. *Fetal Positions: Individualism, Science, Visuality*. Stanford, CA: Stanford University Press.

Oberman, Michelle. 2018. *Her Body, Our Laws: On the Front Lines of the Abortion War, from El Salvador to Oklahoma*. Boston, MA: Beacon Press.

Palmer, Julie. 2009. "Seeing and Knowing: Ultrasound Images in the Contemporary Abortion Debate." *Feminist Theory* 10, no. 2: 173–89.

Petchesky, Rosalind Pollack. 1987. "Fetal Images: The Power of Visual Culture in the Politics of Abortion." *Feminist Studies* 13, no. 2: 263–92.

Phelan, Peggy. 1993. *Unmarked: The Politics of Performance*. London: Routledge.

Ross, Loretta and Rickie Solinger. 2017. *Reproductive Justice: An Introduction*. Berkeley, CA: University of California Press.

Sanger, Carol. 2017. *About Abortion: Terminating Pregnancy in Twenty-First Century America*. Cambridge, MA: Harvard University Press.

Saurette, Paul and Kelly Gordon. 2015. *The Changing Voice of the Anti-Abortion Movement: The Rise of "Pro-Woman" Rhetoric in Canada and the United States*. Toronto: University of Toronto Press.

Schoen, Johanna. 2017. *Abortion After Roe: Abortion After Legalization*. Chapel Hill, NC: University of North Carolina Press.

Sherman, Renee Bracey. 2016. "We Testify's Origin Story." *We Testify: Our Abortion Stories*. April 21, 2016. https://web.archive.org/web/20161009033742/http://wetestify.org/stories/we-testifys-origin-story.

Silverman, Kaja. 1996. *The Threshold of the Visible World*. New York: Routledge.

SisterSong. n.d. "Reproductive Justice." Accessed December 1, 2019. www.sistersong.net/reproductive-justice.

Smith, Andrea. 2005. "Beyond Pro-Choice versus Pro-Life: Women of Color and Reproductive Justice." *NWSA Journal* 17, no. 1: 119–40.

Smyth, Lisa. 2005. *Abortion and Nation: The Politics of Abortion in Contemporary Ireland*. Aldershot: Ashgate.

Solomon, Martha, ed. 2014. *One Kind Word: Women Share Their Abortion Stories*. Toronto: Three O'Clock Press.

Stabile, Carol. 1992. "Shooting the Mother: Fetal Photography and the Politics of Disappearance." *Camera Obscura* 10, no. 1: 178–205.

Stettner, Shannon. 2016. "The Unfinished Revolution." In *Without Apology: Writings on Abortion in Canada*, edited by Shannon Stettner, 333–47. Edmonton: Athabasca University Press.

Strangio, Chase. 2016. "Can Reproductive Trans Bodies Exist?" *CUNY Law Review* 19, no. 2: 223–45.

Sutton, Barbara and Elizabeth Borland. 2018. "Queering Abortion Rights: Notes from Argentina." *Culture, Health & Sexuality: An International Journal for Research, Intervention and Care* 20, no. 12: 1378–93.

Taylor, Janelle S. 1992. "The Public Fetus and the Family Car: From Abortion Politics to a Volvo Advertisement." *Public Culture* 4, no. 2: 67–80.

Thomsen, Carly. 2013. "From Refusing Stigmatization toward Celebration: New Directions for Reproductive Justice Activism." *Feminist Studies* 39, no. 1: 149–58.

Wiebe, Ellen R. and Lisa C. Adams. 2009. "Women's Experience of Viewing the Products of Conception after an Abortion." *Contraception* 80, no. 6: 575–7.

Ziegler, Mary. 2018. *Beyond Abortion: Roe v. Wade and the Battle for Privacy*. Cambridge, MA: Harvard University Press.

Part I

Seeing (and not seeing) abortion

Abortion is frequently labelled a polarising issue in popular culture, education, politics, and scholarship. As a result, abortion is a proscribed topic. The subject of abortion becomes invisible and silent, shrouded in fear of causing offence and misconceptions. There are good reasons for circumventing discussion of abortion in public. Avoidance shields those who are seeking or have had an abortion from exposure to violent anti-abortion rhetoric and abortion stigma, analysed by Gordon, Saurette, and Scuro in Chapters 6 and 15. However, the primary benefactors of this invisibility and silence are the proponents of anti-choice arguments, who obfuscate the realities of abortion with misinformation about the abortion procedure and its long-term effects, despite the reality that abortion is entirely safe where it is accessible and legal. And significantly, maintaining silence and invisibility to sidestep provoking those who are opposed to abortion in order to protect those who have had abortions inadvertently strengthens abortion stigma. In her foreword to *One Kind Word: Women Share Their Abortion Stories*, Judy Rebick discusses a student theatre group who wrote and performed a play celebrating the life of renowned Canadian feminist Doris Anderson, yet decided against including her pro-choice activism in the play because some members were anti-choice (2014). Rebick critiques this decision as misguided, and reminds her readers of the significance of testimonials from women who accessed abortion illegally or through labyrinthine restrictions (2014). Shannon Stettner concurs, arguing that it is only possible to "move beyond the polarizing rhetoric" about abortion through open and honest speech and writing that centres the everyday practice and experience of having an abortion (2016, 4). In Part I – Seeing (and not seeing) abortion, contributors engage with representations of abortion that model the openness and honesty that Stettner describes. Such engagement not only confronts abortion stigma, but also encourages thoughtful encounters with experiences and realities of abortion that can be difficult for both "pro-choice" and "pro-life" poles.

One of the most well-known acts of civil disobedience in France is "Le Manifeste des 343," a public declaration by a group of 343 women that they had had an abortion, a criminal act at the time of publication in 1971

(L'Obs 2007). Published in *Le Nouvel Observateur*, the petition argued that the criminalisation of abortion in France was a means to control women, leading to abortions performed in unnecessarily dangerous conditions because women were condemned to secrecy ("la clandestinité à laquelle elles sont condamnées"). Confronting the harm of secrecy, Rachel Marie-Crane Williams's "Secrets" is an analysis of her abortion through graphic memoir. Williams's abortion took place in 1988 when she was a sixteen-year-old girl living with her parents in the southeastern United States, and the narrator describes and analyses her abortion from the perspective of her adult self in the present. The story is singular, yet its themes resonate across time and place: the deliberate silencing of abortion in education and politics; the isolation experienced by people who become pregnant unintentionally, especially young people, due to inadequate or non-existent access to information about abortion; and the clandestine actions undertaken to obtain an abortion, even in contexts where abortion is legal. These themes create the conditions for abortion to be considered a "secret" – an experience that is "invariably tinged with a fear of discovery … leav[ing] people feeling muzzled, fearful, and ashamed" (Solomon 2016, 154). Keeping abortion experiences secret is an effective anti-abortion strategy, and Williams's chapter exists within a powerful legacy of making abortion visible through refusing secrecy.

Ordinary stories of abortion do not feature prominently in political responses to anti-abortion arguments and legislation, which instead focus on comparatively rare stories of rape, incest, fetal anomaly, and risk of death should the pregnancy continue. This happens because for many, it seems cruel and inhumane to force a person in those circumstances to carry a pregnancy to term. Protective silence about ordinary experiences of abortion and over-emphasis on rare experiences have corollary effects, and in her earlier work Jeannie Ludlow argues that abortion is consequently "trauma-tized" through the repetition of politically expedient narratives in pro-choice discourse (2008, 31). Elements of abortion become unspeakable, and Ludlow's chapter, "It's a boy!-borted: fetal bodies, graphic abortion, and the option to look," seeks abortion-positive representations of the fetal body, which is invisible in pro-choice discourse. As Lena Hann and Ludlow explore in Chapter 8, there is a curiosity and desire to view fetal remains by people who have abortions, and having the option to look can be an important component of patient-centred care. Through three seemingly disparate examples – an episode of the Netflix television show *BoJack Horseman*, the *Saga* comics series by Fiona Staples and Brian K. Vaughan, and Christian Mungiu's film, *4 Months, 3 Weeks, and 2 Days* – Ludlow argues that these representations of abortion offer abortion-positive representations of the fetus that present a wider range of responses to abortion than are currently accepted in mainstream pro-choice discourse.

Bringing the fetus to the forefront of abortion-positive narratives challenges the invisibility and silence that maintain abortion stigma, as well as the predominance of anti-abortion images of the fetus. Part II – Fetal materiality explores in depth the "social work of consensus building that these representations achieve" (Newman 1996, 5), and Manon S. Parry's chapter "Museums and the material culture of abortion" sets the stage for the following section through its consideration of the absent presence of abortion in medical museums. Parry's research on medical museums explores the paradox that although these museums are used as a source of information about human reproduction, and museum collections contain objects related to the history and procedure of abortion, curators are reticent to display these objects because of the organised power of the anti-abortion movement. Intriguingly, the refusal to incorporate displays and information on abortion in medical museums creates parallel responses by museum visitors to the avoidance of information on abortion and contraception in sex education that Williams references in her graphic narrative. In the absence of reliable information, visitors use their prior assumptions to fill in information, and anti-abortion activists flood the cultural landscape with inaccurate perceptions of the abortion procedure as violent, unethical, dire, and risky. Through analysis of its collection as well as interviews, Parry presents a project of "radically reimagining" the medical museum: the Museum of Contraception and Abortion in Vienna, Austria.

Michele Byers' chapter, "Who's late? *Degrassi*, abortion, history," brings Part I full circle by returning to narratives that capture the impact of silence and invisibility on ordinary abortion experiences through an analysis of abortion storylines in the *Degrassi* television franchise. In its multiple iterations – from the second series in the franchise, *Degrassi Junior High* (1987–1989) to the fifth and most recent series, *Degrassi: Next Class* (2016–2017), *Degrassi* is a cultural space where the national and transnational politics of abortion as well as unintentional pregnancy in Canada have been discussed, negotiated, and represented for a youth audience. The insistence of the show on providing representations of abortion for its viewers that counter the absence of information on abortion that its own characters face is rooted in the discourse of rights, and the characters analysed by Byers claim their right to have an abortion within a middle-class urban Canadian environment. The show's creators draw viewers' attention not only to how abortion is silenced in youth education but also to a tension between how abortion is understood and how it is enacted in Canada. Abortion is not recognised as a right in Canada, but instead as a "matter of health," which has led to unequal access across the country (Johnstone 2017, 156). Byers demonstrates how the geographical and social context of the show takes for granted the access to abortion as a part of healthcare, so abortion becomes an issue of a right to choose.

The chapters in Part I plant the seeds for the following sections in this collection, and resonances of the silencing of abortion echo throughout the book's chapters. The intellectual and political work of surfacing abortion in cultural representations introduced in this section lays the groundwork for considering fetal materiality, abortion storytelling, and memoir, and the chapters in this section point to the urgency of creating representations that broaden arguments for expanding and improving abortion access.

References

Johnstone, Rachael. 2017. *After Morgentaler: The Politics of Abortion in Canada.* Vancouver: UBC Press.

L'Obs. 2007. "Le 'Manifeste des 343 salopes' paru dans le *Nouvel Obs* en 1971." *L'Obs*, November 27, 2007. www.nouvelobs.com/societe/20071127.OBS7018/le-manifeste-des-343-salopes-paru-dans-le-nouvel-obs-en-1971.html.

Ludlow, Jeannie. 2008. "The Things We Cannot Say: Witnessing the Trauma-tization of Abortion in the United States." *WSQ: Women's Studies Quarterly* 36, nos. 1 and 2: 28–41.

Newman, Karen. 1996. *Fetal Positions: Individualism, Science, Visuality.* Stanford, CA: Stanford University Press.

Rebick, Judy. 2014. "Foreword." In *One Kind Word: Women Share Their Abortion Stories*, edited by Martha Solomon. Toronto: Three O'Clock Press.

Solomon, Martha. 2016. "Breaking the Silence Through Portrait and Story: Arts4Choice." In *Without Apology: Writings on Abortion in Canada*, edited by Shannon Stettner, 151–5. Edmonton: AU Press.

Stettner, Shannon. 2016. "Without Apology: An Introduction." In *Without Apology: Writings on Abortion in Canada*, edited by Shannon Stettner, 3–30. Edmonton: AU Press.

2 Secrets

Rachel Marie-Crane Williams

Secrets

By: Rachel Marie-Crane Williams

I have always known that my body can betray me.
These minor and major betrayals always remind
me that I am an animal at the mercy of nature.

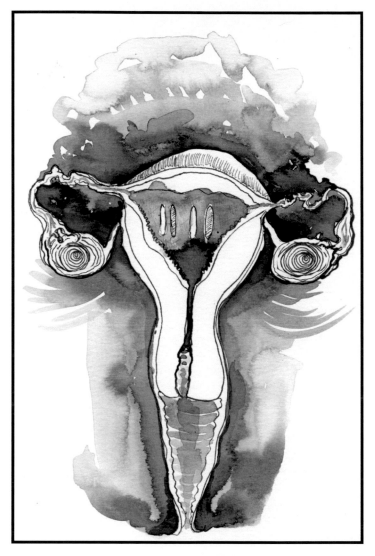

I will never be able to out-think the way my
body functions. I have been pregnant four
times. Once it was an accident, and the other
three times I worked like hell to make it
happen. In the end, I have birthed two healthy
children, had one miscarriage, and one abortion.

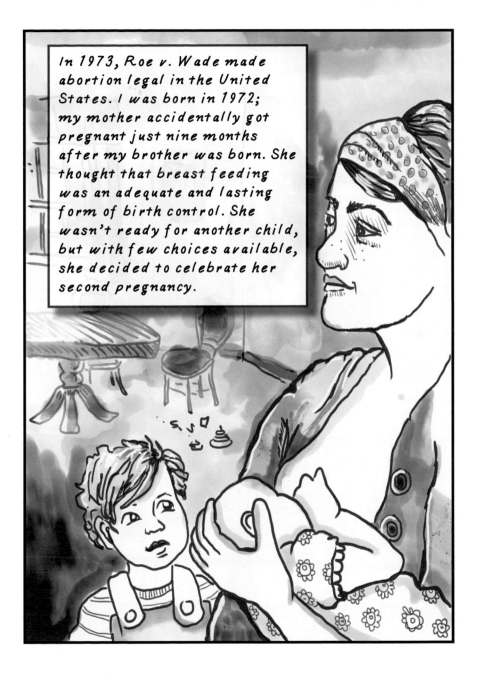

In 1973, Roe v. Wade made abortion legal in the United States. I was born in 1972; my mother accidentally got pregnant just nine months after my brother was born. She thought that breast feeding was an adequate and lasting form of birth control. She wasn't ready for another child, but with few choices available, she decided to celebrate her second pregnancy.

Sixteen years later, it was 1988. I started having sex in June, and by August I was pregnant. In 1988 1.6 million surgical abortions were performed in the United States.

In Canada, 1988 was the year that all legal restrictions related to abortion were lifted due to R. v. Morgentaler.

1988 was also the year that mifepristone was registered as a pill to use for medical abortions in France and China.

In the US, in 1988, 43.5 out of 1000 teen girls and women had abortions.

I lived in a very politically conservative area in the southeastern United States surrounded by swamps, pine trees, pigs, tobacco, and river water. Robert E. Lee, Jesus, and Ronald Reagan were idolized. My parents never said a word about sex, and I had no idea how to get a prescription for birth control. There was no sex education, no Internet, everyone was a Christian, and the unspoken expectation among "good people" was that "good girls" waited until they were married.

SEXIST, RACIST, HOMOPHOBIC, BIGOT, SEXIS

RACIST, HOMOPHO...   ST, RACIS

HOMOPHOBIC, B...   . HOM

SEXIST, RACIST,   EXIST

RACI...   ACIST

HO...   BIGOT

SE...   RACIST, H

A...   HOMOPHO

                                             EXIST, R

                                             HOB

I have tried to remember how I knew about abortion. I grew up in North Carolina, a state famous for electing Jesse Helms to the Senate. He was the architect of the Helms Amendment of 1973, which restricts US foreign aid from agencies who discuss or perform abortions. His sexist, racist, homophobic politics were inescapable. He believed abortion was a sin and that AIDS was a disease that struck "perverts" engaging in "unnatural acts."

I saw the famous movie, Dirty Dancing, in the fall of 1987. Without an abortion, there would have been no plot. This movie got many of us talking about what we would have done if we were "Baby" Houseman, Johnny Castle, or Penny Johnson.

It was filmed in Lake Lure in North Carolina so it was a popular film. One afternoon shortly after it was released, the teacher in our honors biology class naively asked the question, "When does life begin?" Little did he know that this question would spark a fierce debate. This argument would open up a permanent political rift between members of our class who believed life began at conception and abortion was wrong, and others who believed that women had a right to steer their reproductive journeys with access to safe and legal abortion. The teacher, red-faced, sat quietly horrified as we tore each other to bits. One girl left crying, many of the boys were silent, and a small number of those of us who were militantly pro-choice realized that we were in the minority.

*Little did I know, the following summer,
like Penny Johnson and "Baby," my life
would change forever...*

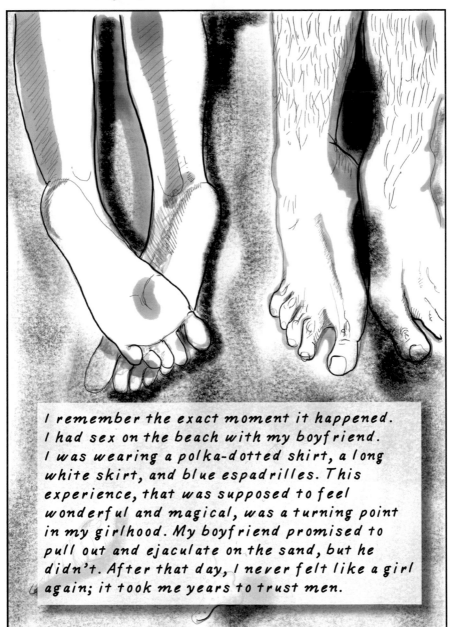

*I remember the exact moment it happened.
I had sex on the beach with my boyfriend.
I was wearing a polka-dotted shirt, a long
white skirt, and blue espadrilles. This
experience, that was supposed to feel
wonderful and magical, was a turning point
in my girlhood. My boyfriend promised to
pull out and ejaculate on the sand, but he
didn't. After that day, I never felt like a girl
again; it took me years to trust men.*

My period was two days late. It usually came as regular as the tide. I knew I was pregnant. Buying a pregnancy test was terrifying. I drove 45 miles away, so no one I knew would see me purchase it.

The closest Planned Parenthood was 130 miles away. I knew nothing about their feminist politics, or about reproductive justice. My mother was a nurse at the small hospital in our town. Everybody knew everybody. I was afraid that if I went to a doctor, or the public health clinic, to get tested or put "on the pill" she would hear about it and I would get in trouble.

After I peed on the long plastic stick, and
realized that indeed I was pregnant, I felt
trapped. I did not want to have a baby, I did
not want to get married and be stuck in my
tiny town forever. There were only a few girls
my age and pregnant, most were poor. Looking
back, I think many girls dropped out of our
public school as soon as they found out because
of shame and pressure. I had never known
a single person that admitted to having an
abortion. Abortion was taboo.

I hid the pregnancy test and grabbed our phone-book. I locked myself in my bedroom, took a deep breath and frantically searched the yellow pages for the word pregnancy and then abortion. The closest specialized health clinic, that advertised abortion services, was two hours away. In 1988, 64% of abortions in the United States were performed at clinics such as these.

I waited until my house was empty and made the phone call to set up an appointment. I was terrified they would tell me no. Looking back, I realize how privileged I was to be literate, have access to money, a support person, a telephone, and a car. I would only miss school, not work. There were plenty of women in my state who did not have these things. In spite of this, the whole thing seemed impossible, but I knew that I had to make it work. I vowed not to cry.

I told my best friend and swore her to secrecy. She agreed to take me to the clinic. I decided I did not want to ask my boyfriend for anything. If my parents found out I was pregnant, I feared there would be no choices except to have the child and get married.

Next, I asked my brother, who was only 18 months older, for the money. He gave me everything he had saved from working at a fast food restaurant on the weekends. He didn't ask a single question.

On most weekends, I worked at a store in the mall. The pay was terrible, and I knew that if I was frugal, I would be able to save some money with a bit left over to cover gas and our lunches for the day.

I counted every day until the abortion. Time seemed to crawl. I was fearful I might have a miscarriage. It was so isolating to have such a huge secret. Only four people in the world knew. I told my boyfriend not to talk to me until the whole thing was over. I did not expect him to support me emotionally, or know how to react to my stiff upper-lip routine. I bottled up all of my fears. I was sure I could handle my own problems.

I felt so afraid that I would go to hell, but I knew
that I _did not_ want to be pregnant. Even then, I
was not a religious person, but I struggled with
the decision. Having a child would impact my life,
my family's life, the life of my boyfriend, and his
family. I went to the library and looked at books
to create a realistic image I could hold in my mind
of the mass of cells multiplying in my uterus.
The embryo would be the size of a raspberry at 8
weeks.

The morning I was supposed to get an abortion looked like any other day outside my window, but I knew this day would change my life. I wore a black skirt and old underwear in case I bled. I desperately wanted to look respectable.

My friend and I drove in silence. We were supposed to be studying algebra, laughing with our friends, and reading Beowulf; instead we were driving to a huge city with a military base, tattoo parlors, and a women's clinic that provided abortions. Neither one of us had ever skipped school or driven that far. I had a small fortune, $400.00, in my purse. I had no idea how doctors would perform the abortion, or what the experience was going to be like. I anticipated pain. Later I learned that having an abortion is statistically much safer than having a baby and far less painful in most instances.

I remember the clinic as a nondescript single-level building. It seemed unremarkable. There were no raging protesters. When I checked in, I whispered to the receptionist. She asked my age, and I told her 16. I gave her a copy of my license. My friend watched television while I filled out paperwork. Within minutes, I was moved to a small room in the back of the clinic with five or six other women who were also waiting for abortions. I was relieved that I was not the only one. We sat on soft couches and the lights were low. We were shown a short video explaining the process. None of us were crying. I was surprised and ashamed that the women waiting with me were all older. Some wore wedding rings. While we waited awkwardly, we passed the time by talking softly about our situations.

I learned that a few were already mothers.

One older woman was starting to show.

She was very kind to me and could tell

I was frightened. She worked for the circus.

One by one we were called out of the room by a nurse. I confirmed I was pregnant and provided a urine sample. She took some blood and my blood pressure and I changed into a gown.
Finally, it was happening.

I felt hesitant when I walked into the procedure room. The doctor was a man. I had never had a pelvic exam. I felt so embarrassed to put my feet in the stirrups with my vagina in this older man's face. One of the nurses held my hand. The doctor explained the procedure step by step as he carried it out in a calm and kind voice. First, he positioned, washed, and numbed my cervix, which terrified me because I was so afraid of needles. Next, he dilated my uterus and placed a cannula into my cervix and uterus. I remember watching my stomach move up and down, the suction sound, and the cannister filling with tissue and blood. I was so thankful for the kindness of the staff at the clinic. I knew that they were courageous to provide abortions. When it was over, relief flooded my entire body. I thanked them over and over as I struggled to sit up. I felt faint and empty.

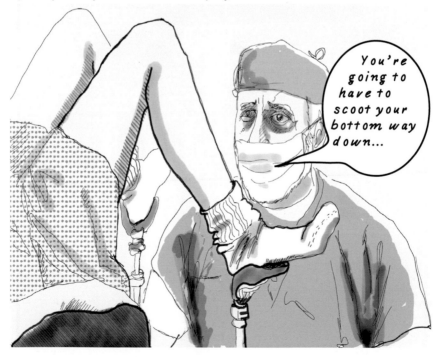

You're going to have to scoot your bottom way down...

When it was over, I walked to a small, quiet recovery area. The nurse brought me a soda; she said I had to wait for at least one hour to make sure that everything was going to be OK. I sat with a blanket and anxiously watched the clock. The other women in the room were quiet. As soon as the hour was up I asked to dress and leave. I was worried about my friend in the waiting room. I paid as I left with the wad of small bills that I had stashed in my purse. We drove home in silence. I was so grateful it was over. I slept curled up in the passenger seat on the way home.

The amount of bleeding after the abortion was alarming. My periods had always been extremely heavy, so I just assumed the bleeding in the weeks following the abortion might be as well. I decided not to tell anyone about the blood and hoped that it would stop eventually. The clinic nurse told me to call if I got a fever or passed a clot larger than a lemon. They sent me home with antibiotics, a prescription for triphasal birth control, and told me not to have sex for at least six weeks. They also gave me Tylenol for the cramping. I never had a follow- up appointment, but I did get the prescription for birth control filled. Despite this newfound protection, my fear of getting pregnant again loomed large like a dangerous storm cloud for many years.

The night of my abortion there was a football game. I
was bleeding profusely and felt shaky, numb, and tired,
but I went to the game. I did not want my parents to
suspect that anything was wrong. I also needed some
sense of closure. After the teams left the field, I found
my boyfriend and told him that the ordeal was over. We
broke up months later. We are still close friends, even
after 30 years. He never had children. I wonder if he has
any regrets about the abortion. I never felt like I needed
to ask his permission, or learn more about his opinion.
It was a decision that I felt was mine to make. He never
tried to talk me out of it.

My daughter is now 16. Today, if she faced an unwanted pregnancy in North Carolina, she would have to have an ultrasound, undergo counseling designed to dissuade her from getting an abortion, and wait 72 hours before having the procedure. She <u>would</u> have access to a medical abortion using mifepristone and misoprostol, instead of a surgical abortion, but she would need parental consent and it would cost approximately $1000. It is likely that getting health insurance to pay for it would be difficult.

She has two friends who are transgender. I wonder what getting an abortion would be like for them. Would they be misgendered? Would there be unnecessary questions or exams? Would it be easy to gain access?

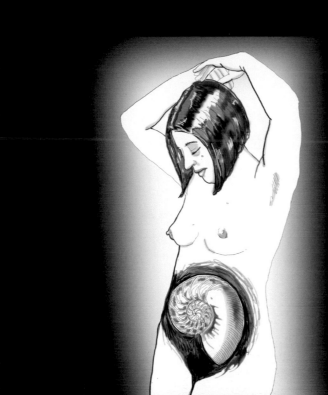

After the abortion, and before the birth of my daughter, my relationship with sex and my body was difficult. When I finally decided to get pregnant, it proved impossible. I underwent infertility treatments for nearly two years before I conceived. The infertility specialist assured me that there was no link between the abortion and my infertility. I knew this already, but infertility felt like karma. Until I got pregnant, I wondered if I had given up the one chance I might have had to have a child. In the end, I conceived both my children with the use of drugs, technology, and the help of very kind nurses at the hospital. It wasn't sexy but it was magical. I loved being pregnant.

Now that I am a grown woman approaching menopause, I no longer look at the world through the eyes of a scared 16-year-old girl. I know that if I had decided to have the child all those years ago, things would have been OK, but very different. I probably would have been a terrible and very unhappy mother. I might never have gone to a four-year college or graduate school. I would probably have been married to someone for a short time who was not ready for all of the responsibility a child entailed. I have never told my father about my experience. Even all these years later, I can't bring myself to break his heart. I once told my mother. She said softly, "I would have helped you." It took me years to overcome my shame and guilt. I had to forgive myself and recognize that it was not the abortion, but the secret and isolation that made things so difficult.

*Special thanks to Rylie, Michelle, Matthew, Don, Jack, and Gary

3   It's a ~~boy!~~ borted

Fetal bodies, graphic abortion, and the option to look

Jeannie Ludlow

Introduction: fetal materiality

About two-thirds into the abortion episode of Raphael Bob-Waksberg and Joanna Calo's animated Netflix series *BoJack Horseman*, Mr. Peanutbutter, whose wife is about to have an abortion, appears holding a blue Mylar balloon blazoned with "It's a Boy!" Mr. Peanutbutter has emended the balloon, scribbling out "Boy" and the exclamation mark and writing "borted" below, so the balloon reads "It's Aborted." This chapter demonstrates that Mr. Peanutbutter's balloon is more than a sight gag; it represents a major shift as an abortion-positive representation of the aborted fetus.[1] I became interested in representations of the aborted fetus while working as an abortion counselor in an independent clinic.[2] This clinic, like many independent clinics, provided patients with the "option to look" at their abortuses post-procedure, as a counter to anti-abortion misrepresentation and/or to provide a sense of closure to those who desire it (Hann 2016). Those of us who work in abortion care think about and interact with aborted fetuses on a regular basis.[3] Our work with the fetal body happens in a clinical space simultaneously separate from and overdetermined by cultural – and politicized – notions of abortion. In many regions of the U.S. and, increasingly, globally (as demonstrated by Side in this volume), these notions are circumscribed by the prolife/prochoice binary. Herein, I use "prolife" and "prochoice" to name political stances and ideas and images claimed by those stances. Both terms are contested and unstable, and I use them intentionally, invoking both that instability and the binary's cultural currency. I use the phrase "abortion-positive" to describe those representations that support abortion decisions and access without conforming to the narrow, politicized expectations of prochoice discourse.

According to this binary, the fetus belongs to anti-abortion discourse. In fact, the U.S. anti-abortion movement has created two subgenres of fetal representation: the dismembered fetal body, and the now-canonical unborn baby images, derivative of (if not derived from) Lennart Nilsson's fetal photographs, first made famous in *Life* magazine in 1965. These representations invoke the material fetal body in order to inspire pity for the

to-be-aborted fetus and have been in common use in anti-abortion propaganda since the 1970s. Feminist analyses have long critiqued these pro-
life representations for visually and conceptually disconnecting fetal body
from gestating body in a kind of symbolic abortion, yielding an effaced
woman and a floating (literally) signifier, unsupported by context or referent
(Dubow 2011; Duden 1993; Hartouni 1992; Mason 2002; Newman 1996;
Petchesky 1987; Stabile 1992). Anti-abortion claims on fetal representation have undergirded public support for many successful abortion bans, as
explained in Hann and Ludlow in this volume.

To counter anti-abortion images of fetal materiality, the prochoice
movement offers almost nothing beyond radical co-optation of anti-abortion
imagery, like the SisterSerpents collective, analyzed by Kovacs in this volume.
Abortion-positive discourse also has two subgenres of fetal representation,
but neither is graphical. In narratives of medically indicated abortion, the
fetus – remembered and grieved – remains unseen. Discussions of elective
abortion insist on legal and conceptual entwinement of the fetus with the
gestating body up to the moment of abortion (Little 1999; Arcana 1994).
As the procedure concludes, the fetus disappears, removed from the speech
act as from the uterus. Both narratives describe a move from entwinement
to severance to erasure. The aborted fetal body is an absent presence in pro-
choice discourses; bereft of symbols of fetal significance, our movement is
open to charges of being unsympathetic to those whose abortion experiences
are conflicted and of being out of touch with U.S. culture in general. This
chapter discusses four different representations of the aborted fetus from
three different graphic texts. These representations, neither stigmatizing
and apologetic nor tragic and simplistic, re-inscribe the materiality of the
aborted fetal body into abortion narratives, thereby offering abortion-
positive alternatives to erasure.

The abortion narratives analyzed herein – *BoJack Horseman*, "Brrap
Brrap Pew Pew" (season 3 episode 6, 2016); Fiona Staples and Brian
K. Vaughan's comic book narrative, *Saga* (2015–17); and Christian Mungiu's
Romanian film, *4 Months, 3 Weeks, and 2 Days* (Romania, 2007) –
illustrate the power of "hold[ing] the tension of opposites," holding in tension
two seemingly opposing principles without feeling compelled to resolve
them (Harris 2019). In this case the principles are the appropriateness of
a decision to abort a pregnancy and the potential material and emotional
significance of a fetus. These four representations honor the broad range of
responses among those seeking abortion care (indeed, among all pregnant
persons) to both fetal materiality and the understanding that abortion stops
a developing human from being born (Harris 2008, 2019). Other chapters in
this volume examine similar powerful tensions: Huerta's explanation of the
simultaneous contradictions embodied in Gloria Anzaldúa's *Coatlicue* State;
Latimer's reading of the importance of kinship to our conceptualizations
of the fetus in Marianne Apostolides's *Deep Salt Water*; and Yamagata-
Montoya's exploration of the spiritual significance of the fetus in the *mizuko*

kuyō ritual. In each case, holding the tension of opposites makes possible an abortion-positive engagement with fetal embodiment.

The four representations of the aborted fetus examined in this chapter are from sequential graphic narratives, broadly defined by Deborah Elizabeth Whaley to include "print titles" and "moving image[s] in television, film, animation, and video games" (2016, 11). They range from iconic to indexical; the analyses herein progress from the more symbolic to the more realistic or challenging, describing a narrative arc of increased ability to hold the tension of opposites and see aborted fetuses as consonant with abortion positivity. It is notable that all four of the abortions in these texts are experienced by characters embodying oft-subordinated cultural identities – racialized, young, financially insecure, and/or exiled. These texts, then, suggest a productive relationship between nuanced abortion discourses and reproductive justice. This makes sense, given that reproductive justice recognizes the inextricability of any person's life from their reproductive experience (Price 2010; Ross 2006). At the same time, the tension between fetal materiality and abortion positivity demands that audiences of these texts see differently.

In *The Imaginary Domain*, feminist legal philosopher Drucilla Cornell argues that our ability to see differently relies on the "imaginary domain": symbolic and representational systems that shape and grow from our imaginations. The arts, media messages, and public discourses provide a conceptual vocabulary which we use to imagine how we can matter within those systems (Cornell 1995, 33, 42). As Mallary Allen has found, conceptual vocabularies tend toward iterative reification; abortion narrators often shape their stories to the discursive mode of previously accepted abortion stories (2014). Cornell argues that, in order to break free from iterative reification, to imagine new ways to matter, we must be able to see differently, to re-shape our conceptual vocabularies through re-representation and re-symbolization (1995, 106). Re-symbolization involves, among other processes, a kind of re-speaking, using new signifiers to give different meanings to a sign (Cornell 1995, 33–4, 64); this tactic is enacted in both *Saga* and *BoJack Horseman*.

Re-symbolization of the aborted fetus

The power of iconicity: Mr. Peanutbutter's balloon

The Netflix adult cartoon, *BoJack Horseman*, stars Will Arnett as an anthropomorphized horse/washed-up former TV star struggling with addiction. His Vietnamese-American ghost writer Diane Nguyen, voiced by Allison Brie, has an abortion in the series' third season. Diane's abortion is presented unambiguously – neither she nor her husband Mr. Peanutbutter have qualms about it. They talk through their decision in almost stereotypical prochoice language, go to Planned Parrothood to speak with a doctor, and sit together in the waiting room prior to Diane's procedure. The episode disrupts this canonically prochoice narrative when Mr. Peanutbutter, a golden retriever, begins pulling his "It's a ~~boy!~~-borted" balloon through every scene.

Mr. Peanutbutter's unfailing support of Diane's decision, combined with his golden retriever personality, directs viewers to read the balloon literally, as a positive (albeit naïve) acknowledgment of this abortion's significance in their lives. At the same time, within a hegemonic cultural context that treats abortion as stigmatized or tragic, the emended message may be read as sobering, melancholic. The balloon's surprising, perhaps unsettling, potential derives from the unaltered part of the message. The pronoun in "It's a boy!" refers to a fetus at a gender-reveal party or a baby after childbirth; the joyful exclamation serves conceptually to connect unborn fetus to born baby. The "it" in "It's aborted," by contrast, directs viewers to imagine a presence usually erased or rendered absent in abortion-positive discourse: the material fetal body.

Mr. Peanutbutter's balloon enacts a re-symbolization of fetal materiality through an abortion-positive resignification of a widely recognizable symbol of the relationship between fetus and baby. This signifier – simultaneously benign and ambivalent – draws its power from the tension between cheerful image and unexpected text, in much the same way as graphic texts, according to feminist comics scholar Hillary Chute. Comics, she argues, work narratively via defamiliarization rather than mimesis; their narrative power is rooted in the "constant, active, uneasy back-and-forth" (Chute 2015, 198–9) between words and images (as is strikingly evident in Rachel Marie-Crane Williams's "Secrets," in this volume). The tension between the cheerful imagery and the sober text of Mr. Peanutbutter's balloon re-symbolizes the aborted fetus by inscribing "it" into an unapologetically abortion-positive message.

The fetus as present absence: Saga

Another example of re-symbolization of fetal materiality occurs in *Saga*, Fiona Staples and Brian K. Vaughan's critically acclaimed comic book series. Five years into the series the protagonists, Alana of Landfall and Marko of Wreath, find themselves in need of an abortion provider. Alana's unborn child has died in utero during a violent encounter with a space phenomenon called a Timesuck, which resembles a giant three-eyed fetus haloed by Saturnal rings, reminiscent of anti-abortion floating signifiers (Staples and Vaughan 2017a).[4] Fugitives from two warring cultures, the couple are exiled because of their interracial marriage and the hybrid identity of Hazel, their five-year-old daughter. As refugees, they cannot go home – anyone's home – for medical care. As the family grieves for "something that never even had a chance to be born," Petrichor, a Wreathian transwoman, kneels before Alana, saying, "Most Holy Mother" (Staples and Vaughan 2017b).[5] In a narrow panel drawn from Petrichor's perspective, readers look up on Alana's dolorous face and pregnant abdomen. "Petri," she explains, "he's **gone**. My baby is—"; Marko, down-panel and behind Alana, clarifies, "Some faiths on Wreath **revere** women who have suffered" and here he falters, unable or unwilling to name what has happened. He continues, "what **we** just have." In the next panel, Petri says, "Anyone carrying the remains of an unborn Wreath child is a **sacred vessel**." Alana angrily replies, "Bullshit." The following panel, tight and claustrophobic, shows her fragmented – upper lip to navel – hand over her swollen belly. "I'm a fucking coffin," she says. In the same conversation, Alana has her own discursive falter: "the child I'm carrying has … **had** horns …" (Staples and Vaughan 2017c). Alana's linguistic slip from "has" to "had" and her invocation of "the child," considered alongside Marko's inability to say "miscarriage," emphasize the failure of a nominally prochoice, technological society adequately to represent fetal anomaly and abortion. Her description of the child's horns invokes the denunciation of multiracial relationships that has exiled the family. This exchange simultaneously establishes the cultural contexts from which Alana and Marko come to their abortion experience and, in its multiple ruptures, reflects the need for the re-symbolization that the story enacts.

Seeking medical care for Alana, the family travels to Abortion Town on Pervious, the only planet permitting elective abortion. Declaring Alana "too far along," the legal abortion provider refers them to "the Badlands" where providers "are willing to do just about anything, no questions asked" (Staples and Vaughan 2017c). On their journey to "this planet's creepy back-alley option," Alana and Marko are awakened by a young child: Kurti, the deceased son, manifesting as a spectral boy of about Hazel's age. As the dead baby's decaying fetal tissue makes Alana ill, his Wreathian magic ability passes into her body. Channeling this magic inadvertently, she begins "forecasting" – projecting a simulated future for her son. Every spell has a cost, Marko tells her, and forecasting "hurts the heart" (Staples and Vaughan 2017d). Indeed, as they make their way across the Badlands, Hazel playing fart games with Kurti (whom she calls "imaginary brother"), Alana collapses of heart failure. She is saved by Hazel's magic and the extra-legal abortionist, who rushes out of her home (Staples and Vaughan 2017d). The abortionist is, as she admits, "a sight": a grey bipedal canine with lactating teats and blood-drenched hands (Staples and Vaughan 2017e). The wolf/abortionist, called an Endwife, turns out to be a careful and caring provider who safely and cleanly removes the dead fetus and tissue with Marko in attendance, while Hazel and Kurti wait upstairs. As the abortion is completed, the forecasted Kurti fades away, leaving Hazel alone.

Alana's ability to forecast for the short time that she is carrying the dead fetus reflects the dialogic relationship between reproduction and other aspects of lived experience that lies at the heart of reproductive justice. It also enacts a re-symbolization, in Cornell's terms, of the dead fetus/child, reclaiming it from politically overdetermined and materially effaced discourses of anomalous pregnancy. In this way, Staples and Vaughan give form to aspects of this particular abortion experience that remain invisible in most abortion-positive narratives. Like Mr. Peanutbutter's balloon, Staples's rendering of Kurti draws attention to the fetus as a significant presence in abortion narratives. Unlike the floating balloon, however, Kurti re-symbolizes the material fetal body as child. His twinned presence as spectral boy and dead fetus-to-be-aborted reinserts the fetus into the abortion narrative in a more substantive, albeit incorporeal, way. His death authorizes his visibility, simultaneously enacting and inverting the entwinement-severance-erasure trajectory of fetal anomaly abortion stories, disrupting the iterative reification of the familiar prochoice narrative.

Kurti's dramatic fade from the page during Alana's procedure makes legible the effects of abortion on the fetal form. *Saga*'s visual narrative defamiliarizes the aborted fetus, providing readers with an option to look at one of the most conflicted aspects of abortion experience. Artists, Cornell suggests, are uniquely positioned to deliver contingent representational vocabularies through processes of re-symbolization and re-representation (1995, 105); this suggestion is enacted in Fiona Staples's affective and abortion-positive re-symbolization of Kurti from absent presence to present absence. While re-symbolization involves using new signifiers to give different meanings to a sign, re-representation suggests an abstract reconceptualization or re-contextualization of culturally significant concepts – an ability to imagine meaning anew (Cornell 1995, 27, 43, 100); both *BoJack Horseman* and *4 Months, 3 Weeks, and 2 Days* use re-representation to imagine new meanings of the aborted fetus.

Re-representations of the aborted fetus

The reimagined fetus: Sextina's video

Re-representation of the aborted fetus in *BoJack Horseman* is crafted through irreverence. Early in the episode Diane, distracted by her pregnancy, accidentally tweets "I'm having an abortion" from the Twitter account of her client, teen pop star Sextina Aquafina. Sextina, like the other nonhuman animal characters in the series, is a human analog; it is relevant that she is a dolphin and coded Black. When Sextina learns about the tweet, she is outraged, then "her" tweet goes viral. Unwilling to give up her trending status, she goes public with a faux abortion story. Suddenly, the unpregnant, racially coded Sextina is the "face of the prochoice movement." Pregnant Diane, whose racial identity is primarily whitewashed in the series, moves discreetly through her abortion experience; meanwhile, Sextina's simulated abortion becomes the subject of headlines and male pundits. When Sextina finally gets to tell "her" story in a televised interview, she exclaims (as Diane has coached), "I wanted to destigmatize the procedure for all the women out there, so I'm … dropping a new single!" That single, "Brrap Brrap Pew Pew," provides an outrageous and irreverent foil for Diane's earnestly prochoice experience. The music video shows Sextina singing the song's hook – "Get dat fetus, kill dat fetus / Brrap brrap, pew pew" – while wielding a machine gun, and features ultrasound images of fetal dolphins with targets superimposed over them. At the end of the video, Sextina rides a weaponized wire hanger, shooting lasers at a floating signifier fetal dolphin as she sings, "I hope and pray to god my little fetus has a soul / Because I want it to feel pain when I eject it from my hole."

Diane is horrified by Sextina's direct deployment of anti-abortion discourse. But later, in the Planned Parrothood waiting room, she finds herself next to a sad-faced teenaged girl who loves Sextina. When Diane criticizes the video, the young white woman says, "It's a joke. You get that it's a joke, right? You don't really think she wants to shoot her fetus with a machine gun." Diane replies, "*I* get that it's a joke," suggesting by her emphasis that she does not trust others to get it. With this exchange, *BoJack Horseman* denounces the earnest, and sometimes condescending, prochoice political stance behind which we mask our evacuation of fetal bodies from abortion narratives. The teen girl calls Diane – and the movement – out for the ways our very narrow standards for appropriate discourse lead to erasure of an important element of some people's experiences and to a representational gap that affirms abortion stigmatization. "Getting an abortion is scary," the girl says, invoking protesters and medical tests, "and when you can joke about it, it makes it less scary, you know?" Bob-Waksberg and Calo's choice to pair Diane's earnest, elective abortion with Sextina Aquafina's satiric re-imagining of the anti-abortion fetus provides the episode's power. While Mr. Peanutbutter's Mylar balloon serves to re-symbolize the effaced fetal body in Diane's prochoice abortion narrative, Sextina realizes something completely different: a re-representation of an (admittedly fake) abortion of a materially present fetus, thereby providing the audience with an opportunity to imagine abortion anew.

Graphic narratives excel at representing the invisible, from thoughts and secrets to superpowers, through their "rich narrative texture: … flexible page architecture; … sometimes consonant, sometimes dissonant visual and verbal narratives; and … structural threading of absence and presence" (Chute 2008, 94; ellipses added). The tensions that give sequential graphic texts their power, tensions between equal-and-dissimilar narrative elements, mirror the power in these fetal narratives to exceed the prolife/prochoice binary, challenging audiences to hold the tension of opposites as we read or watch, to accept that abortion stops a developing human from being born and is an important facet of self-determination for the person in whose body the human develops. Thus do graphic texts simultaneously demarcate and expand the boundaries of the imaginary domain.

BoJack Horseman and *Saga* employ some of the most "conspicuously dialogic" elements of comics narratives in their representations of abortion (Chute 2015, 198–9), relying on the "technical hybridization of the realistic and the fantastic" that Donald Ault finds characteristic of the comics medium (2004). Comics texts challenge readers to discern meaning through processes of "rupture and suture" (Whaley 2016, 8–9). Whether hand- or digitally drawn, comics' illustrations provide a fertile foundation for new understandings, even of something as overdetermined as abortion experience.

The substantive fetal body: 4 Months, 3 Weeks, and 2 Days

If, however, we want these new vocabularies to matter on a broader cultural level, re-representation and re-symbolization cannot be limited to fantastical texts. Cristian Mungiu's 2007 Romanian film, *4 Months, 3 Weeks, and 2 Days*, utilizes a hyper-realistic depiction of the aborted fetus, demonstrating the wider applicability of re-representation and re-symbolization of abortion experience. A spare, claustrophobic film set in 1987, near the end of Ceauşescu's "Golden Age of Romania," *4 Months* follows Otilia and Gabriela (Găbița) as they procure an illegal abortion for Găbița. Slow transitions, long takes, enclosed spaces, and extended silences pull viewers laboriously through the night with Otilia, as she and Găbița borrow money, bribe officials, and secure a hotel room. They are hassled by hotel personnel and sexually assaulted by Mr. Bebe, the ironically named abortion provider. This harrowing narrative encapsulates a multi-layered critique of the crumbling socioeconomic infrastructure of late 1980s Communism intersected with sexist ideologies about women's social roles. A full analysis of the film's political critique lies outside the scope of this essay (Godeanu-Kenworthy and Popescu-Sandu 2014; Palmer-Mehta and Haliliuc 2011); this reading focuses, narrowly and reductively, on the film's single representation of the aborted fetal body.

After the abortion is complete, Otilia rushes into the hotel room to check on Găbița. When Otilia shakes her sleeping friend awake, Găbița turns partway and says, "I got rid of it. It's in the bathroom." In the scene that follows, Mungiu's use of long takes and background silence places the viewer uncomfortably close to Otilia, without tight shots or close-ups. From the foot of Găbița's bed, we watch Otilia walk hesitantly to the shining white bathroom. We see Otilia in profile on the threshold, touched with light. She remains unmoving for about twenty seconds, looking toward the bathroom floor. As she kneels there, our point of view shifts to face her, as if we were in the bright white bathroom, just beyond the object of her gaze. For about twenty-five seconds, she gazes at something we cannot see; her attention shifts briefly to her left as the telephone rings, then returns to the floor. She reaches forward with her right hand, pulling gently on something. At this moment, her face softens – jaw, eyes, and shoulders relax. The phone continues to ring, and Otilia leaves the frame to answer it. The camera pans down, and we see what she saw: a small, fully formed fetal body covered in a clear red gelatinous substance, partially wrapped in a white bath towel. The fetus lies on its right side, and we can see its face and left arm. The camera holds steady on the fetal body for almost twenty-five seconds, and viewers gaze as Otilia has gazed, while she speaks off screen to Găbița about finding a bag to wrap it in.

Mungiu's decision to have Otilia, with whom the audience has had the opportunity to develop sympathy, gaze at the fetal body slowly, with consideration, is possibly pedagogical; it models for viewers a way to consider the materiality of the fetus in the film and, by extension, after abortion. Otilia's initial reluctance to look shifts to a kind of gentle awe, a progression which the film records and then provides viewers time to replicate. As we gaze, we hear the two women trying to find something in which to smuggle the fetal body from the hotel. Their conversation layers onto our gazing, a reminder that facing the fetus with unmitigated discomfort/awe is ultimately a privilege; like those who opt for abortion, we must confront the messy fact of fetal materiality. Otilia returns to the bathroom doorway, trying unsuccessfully to fit the fetal body into the plastic bag Găbița has brought. As Găbița begs her friend to bury the fetus, not just dispose of it, Otilia dumps her shoulder bag on the floor, scoops the fetus into the white towel, and stuffs both into her purse. Viewers follow Otilia out into the night, where she hunts for an appropriate place to dispose of the fetal body. Finally, she runs into a building, up several flights of stairs, and drops her purse into a trash chute. With its hyperreal image of the aborted fetal body, and the simultaneity of respect and exigency concerning it, Mungiu's film enacts a re-representation of the fetus as a body that matters in abortion-positive contexts. At the same time, because the film is ultimately less about abortion than about the failure of several socioeconomic systems – communist, capitalist, and unauthorized – adequately to address the needs of women's real lives, the fetal body is metaphor rather than metaphorized, and thereby re-symbolized.

Conclusion: the generative fetal body

BoJack Horseman, *Saga*, and *4 Months, 3 Weeks, and 2 Days* present abortion narratives that exceed standard prochoice discourses and resonate with the discourses of reproductive justice. They do not demand of their audiences unconflicted consideration of abortion; they elevate discomfort in service of destabilization, thereby creating a more inclusive and representative understanding of abortion experiences. They suggest that conflict is normal, healthy – even people who seek abortion care have conflicted feelings. Uninterested in normalizing abortion through oversimplification, they invite audiences into the tensions, the ambivalences that characterize abortion experiences.

As these texts demonstrate, abortion narratives that envision the fetus are not necessarily oppositional to abortion rights. In fact, the "uneasy back-and-forth" (Chute 2015, 199) between fetal materiality and abortion positivity explored in this chapter exemplifies holding the tension of opposites

(Harris 2019), enabling readers to recognize, simultaneously, the emotional significance of the material fetal form and the appropriateness of an abortion decision. Read together, comparatively and cross-contextually, a diversity of graphic abortion representations can model the re-representation and re-symbolization Cornell calls for, providing audiences with an option to look at even the most conflicted aspects of abortion experience. In the end, even an overdetermined and politically fraught figure like the aborted fetus can be re-imagined within a generative and generous abortion-positive discourse that honors the widely varied experiences of pregnant/aborting persons and their loved ones.

Notes

1 "Fetus," herein, is used vernacularly to signify a developing human at any gestational age from implantation to birth or post-abortion.
2 A clinic not affiliated with the Planned Parenthood system.
3 See Lena Hann, "Providing the Option to Look"; Lisa Harris, "Second Trimester Abortion Provision"; Jeannie Ludlow, "Sometimes It's a Child *and* a Choice"; Wendy Simonds, *Abortion at Work*.
4 *Saga*, like many comic books, is unpaginated.
5 Quoting comics texts in a word-processed document is imperfect; the printing style of this book cannot adequately capture the artisanship and nuance of graphic lettering. In this chapter, all emphases and ellipses in quotes are from the original, unless otherwise noted.

References

Allen, Mallary. 2014. "Narrative Diversity and Sympathetic Abortion: What Online Storytelling Reveals about the Prescribed Norms of the Mainstream Movements." *Symbolic Interaction* 38, no. 1: 42–63.

Arcana, Judith. 1994. "Abortion Is a Motherhood Issue." In *Mother Journeys: Feminists Write about Mothering*, edited by Maureen T. Reddy, Martha Roth, and Amy Sheldon, 159–65. Minneapolis, MN: Spinsters Ink.

Ault, Donald. 2004. "Preludium: Crumb, Barks, and Noomin: Re-Considering the Aesthetics of Underground Comics." *ImageTexT: Interdisciplinary Comics Studies* 1, no. 2. www.english.ufl.edu/imagetext/archives/v1_2/intro.shtml.

Bob-Waksberg, Raphael, and Joanna Calo. 2016. *BoJack Horseman*. Season 3, episode 6, "Brrap Brrap Pew Pew." Aired July 22, 2016, Netflix. www.netflix.com/watch/80073222?source=35.

Chute, Hillary. 2008. "The Texture of Retracing in Marjane Satrapi's *Persepolis*." *Women's Studies Quarterly* 36, no. 1/2 (Spring): 92–110. https://doi.org/10.1353/wsq.0.0023.

——— 2015. "The Space of Graphic Narrative: Mapping Bodies, Feminism, and Form." In *Narrative Theory Unbound: Queer and Feminist Interventions*, edited by Robyn Warhol and Susan S. Lanser, 194–209. Columbus, OH: The Ohio State University Press.

Cornell, Drucilla. 1995. *The Imaginary Domain: Abortion, Pornography and Sexual Harassment*. New York: Routledge.

Dubow, Sara. 2011. *Ourselves Unborn: A History of the Fetus in Modern America*. Oxford: Oxford University Press.

Duden, Barbara. 1993. *Disembodying Women: Perspectives on Pregnancy and the Unborn*. 1991. Translated by Lee Hoinacki. Cambridge, MA: Harvard University Press.

Godeanu-Kenworthy, Oana, and Oana Popescu-Sandu. 2014. "From Minimalist Representation to Excessive Interpretation: Contextualizing *4 Months, 3 Weeks, and 2 Days*." *Journal of European Studies* 44, no. 3: 225–48. https://doi.org/10.1177/0047244114524148.

Hann, Lena. 2016. "Providing the Option to Look: Independent Clinic Workers' Approaches to Fetal Viewing Practices." Unpublished dissertation, Community Health. Champaign, IL: University of Illinois. http://hdl.handle.net/2142/93055.

Harris, Lisa. 2008. "Second Trimester Abortion Provision: Breaking the Silence and Changing the Discourse." *Reproductive Health Matters* 16, no. 31 (Supplement): 74–81.

———2019. "The Moral Agency of Abortion Providers: Conscientious Provision, Dangertalk, and the Lived Experience of Doing Stigmatized Work." In *Ethical Issues in Women's Healthcare: Practice and Policy*, edited by Lori d'Agincourt-Canning and Carolyn Ells, 189–208. New York: Oxford University Press.

Hartouni, Valerie. 1992. "Fetal Exposures: Abortion Politics and the Optics of Allusion." *Camera Obscura* 29: 130–49.

Little, Margaret Olivia. 1999. "Abortion, Intimacy, and the Duty to Gestate." *Ethical Theory and Moral Practice* 2, no. 3 (September 1999): 295–312.

Ludlow, Jeannie. 2008. "Sometimes It's a Child *and* a Choice: Toward an Embodied Abortion Praxis." *Feminist Formations* 20, no. 1 (Spring): 26–50.

Mason, Carol. 2002. *Killing for Life: The Apocalyptic Narrative of Pro-Life Politics*. Ithaca, NY: Cornell University Press.

Mungiu, Cristian, dir., prod., and screenwriter. 2007. *4 Months, 3 Weeks, and 2 Days*. Bucharest, Romania: Mobra Films. DVD.

Newman, Karen. 1996. *Fetal Positions: Individualism, Science, Visuality*. Writing Science series, edited by Timothy Lenoir and Hans Ulrich Gumbrecht. Palo Alto, CA: Stanford University Press.

Palmer-Mehta, Valerie, and Alina Haliliuc. 2011. "The Performance of Silence in Cristian Mungiu's *4 Months, 3 Weeks, and 2 Days*." *Text and Performance Quarterly* 31, no. 2 (April): 111–29. https://doi.org/10.1080/10462937.2010.531282.

Petchesky, Rosalind Pollack. 1987. "Fetal Images: The Power of Visual Culture in the Politics of Reproduction." *Feminist Studies* 13, no. 2: 263–92.

Price, Kimala. 2010. "What Is Reproductive Justice? How Women of Color Activists Are Redefining the Pro-Choice Paradigm." *Meridians: Feminism, Race, Transnationalism* 10 (Spring): 42–65.

Ross, Loretta. 2006. "Understanding Reproductive Justice: Transforming the Pro-Choice Movement." *Off Our Backs* 36, no. 4: 14–19.

Simonds, Wendy. 1996. *Abortion at Work: Ideology and Practice in a Feminist Clinic*. New Brunswick, NJ: Rutgers University Press.

Stabile, Carol. A. 1992. "Shooting the Mother: Fetal Photography and the Politics of Disappearance." *Camera Obscura* 28: 179–205.

Staples, Fiona, artist, and Brian K. Vaughan, writer. 2017a. *Saga*. Vol. 7 no. 40. Portland, OR: Image Comics.

———2017b. *Saga*. Vol. 7 no. 42. Portland, OR: Image Comics.

———2017c. *Saga*. Vol. 8 no. 43. Portland, OR: Image Comics.

———2017d. *Saga*. Vol. 8 no. 45. Portland, OR: Image Comics.

———2017e. *Saga*. Vol. 8 no. 46. Portland, OR: Image Comics.

Whaley, Deborah Elizabeth. 2016. *Black Women in Sequence: Re-inking Comics, Graphic Novels, and Anime*. Seattle, WA: University of Washington Press.

4 Museums and the material culture of abortion

Manon S. Parry

Museums have a potentially significant role in the representational landscape of abortion, as they continue to be rated highly as a source of reliable information in surveys of public trust (Schneider 2017). In the United States, high-profile museums tend to stay away from the topic of abortion, however, as they face intense scrutiny from lobby groups. The National Women's History Museum project, for example, has encountered repeated attacks from Republican politicians and anti-abortion groups trying to block their $400 million proposal for a new museum on the National Mall. Opponents claim the museum will represent a feminist agenda and become "an ideological shrine to abortion" (Bassett 2014). In response, museum president Joan Bradley Wages has declared that the subject will never be a featured topic of their exhibitions, given their reliance on fundraising and the political will needed to establish a new museum, saying, "we cannot afford, literally, to focus on issues that are divisive" (Stone 2011).

In Europe, although debate is seemingly less polarized, mainstream museums are similarly silent, reflecting the underrepresentation of women in exhibitions in general, and the marginalization of reproductive health topics specifically. This is particularly ironic, given the long history and ongoing tradition, as Jennifer Tyburczy notes in her article "All Museums Are Sex Museums," of displaying the female body, "dead or alive, as an acceptable form of public sexual consumption" (2012, 202). In fact, when sex is an element of exhibitions, the related topics of contraception and abortion are largely ignored, replicating the same imbalance in representation common in film and television (Parry 2013, 129–33).

At moments where abortion rights erupt in public discourse, as in Ireland's 2018 referendum on abortion legalization, "cultural activism" also spikes, with the production of art supporting or opposing reform as well as a rush to collect it in museums and archives (Pes 2018; Malone 2020; Side, this volume). In general, however, these activities are noteworthy because of the more typical silence of these cultural institutions. This is insufficient in the context of rising attempts to restrict reproductive rights, especially given the instrumental role of representation in media and culture in this political project.

Even in medical museums, which contain a wealth of material culture related to abortion, from folk recipes for abortifacients, to tools and illustrations of techniques, the subject does not usually feature as a prominent part of permanent displays. Where they do appear, both abortion and contraception are similarly depicted – in narratives of progress presenting a steady improvement from the "bad old days" of ignorance and danger, through medical discoveries that made contraception more reliable and abortion safer. The objects displayed are likely to juxtapose the herbs and techniques of folk wisdom with genealogies of improving medical technologies (from the first pills to injectable contraceptives, for example). Regardless of their lack of direct engagement with these topics, as I discuss here, medical museums are already implicated in contemporary abortion politics.

Anti-abortion groups fill the gap with their own, privately funded projects, misrepresenting the history of the women's movement and the realities of abortion practices in the process (Parry 2015). This is particularly evident in the United States, where opponents promote exhibitions as important tools for influencing voters and policymakers (Pecorin 2017; Christian Patriots for Life 2014). Abortion is also a regular feature of "Hell Houses" created for Halloween by Evangelical Christian groups, which combine exhibitions and performance to create haunted-house-type scenes of the consequences of "sinful" behaviour (Lum 2014).

Advocates for abortion access are also beginning to take on independent exhibition projects, such as the "AR-TI-FACTS Exhibit," a travelling exhibition curated by Melissa Madera, founder of "The Abortion Diary," and touring America since 2015 (2013), or the newly launched Vagina Museum in London, which director Florence Schechter hopes will lead to spin-off projects in places where abortion rights are especially fragile, including Northern Ireland and the United States (Haynes 2019). Although such activities are far different to the traditional museum model based in historical collections, there are also occasional examples of successful projects in more established institutions, such as the "Who Chooses" programme of facilitated discussions in a historic house run by the Matilda Joslyn Gage Center in Fayetteville, New York (Pharaon *et al.* 2015, 65).

Although the American context appears to be the most prominent place in which museums have been mobilized for abortion politics, the struggle over representation is becoming increasingly significant in Europe as well, where American anti-abortion groups fund campaigns and women's rights are increasingly under attack in the rising tide of right-wing populism across the continent (Wheaton 2014; Juhász and Pap 2018; Heck 2019). In this chapter, I draw primarily on my current research on the social relevance of European medical museums, to analyse the deliberate and inadvertent, explicit and implicit narratives constructed in the interactions there between objects, staff, and visitors.[1] Often lacking interpretive texts, items on display spark intense curiosity and stimulate remarkable conversations between staff and visitors. I then focus on a radical reimagining of the modern medical museum, in the form of the Museum of Contraception and Abortion in Vienna, Austria. This project offers an important and in fact unique resource for engaging with diverse audiences on these subjects. I conclude by considering the potential museums offer for engaging diverse audiences in productive reflection on experiences of abortion, from historical and contemporary perspectives.

Medical museums and the representation of abortion

Medical museums first flourished in the eighteenth century, intended primarily for the education of doctors and situated within universities with access limited to staff and students, or open to the public in "popular" anatomical shows for commercial profit for general audiences, couched as scientifically informative (Sappol 2002). While there are few remaining traces of the original public exhibitions, many historical collections survive across Europe, mostly housed in university museums or as donations to larger public institutions for the history of science and medicine. These collections are increasingly opened up to broad audiences, who are also flocking to the more recent phenomenon of plastinated anatomical exhibitions such as *Body Worlds*, which has attracted more than 44 million visitors since its debut in 1995 (von Hagens 2017).

Both the modern plastinated projects and the historical museum collections typically include an array of visually arresting objects related to human reproduction, such as human specimens including embryos and fetuses depicting stages of development. In fact, while the male body has for centuries served as the standard for representing human anatomy, in anatomical illustrations, models, textbooks, museums, and theories, women were featured *only* in reference to their sexual organs and reproductive functions (Schiebinger 1986; Giacomini *et al.* 1986). The creator of the plastinated anatomy process, Gunther von Hagens, has been criticized for perpetuating this imbalance in his contemporary exhibitions. His representational strategies suggest his approach is heavily influenced by the traditions of his predecessors. One of the most striking figures in the *Body Worlds* series, for example, is a reclining pregnant woman, naked even of skin, with her fetus still in situ in her womb. The exhibit recalls the classic anatomical model known as the Anatomical Venus, a full-size naked female figure made of wax, with real human hair, shown reclining on a silk or velvet bed, with dissected internal organs and a fetus in the womb. Such Venuses were a central attraction of popular anatomical museums, and those that have survived continue to draw fascinated visitors. Although traditional medical museums are reluctant to be associated with the commercial activities of Von Hagens and his contemporary competitors, both types of collections commonly exemplify the intersection of sex, science, and spectacle that has characterized medical exhibitions from their earliest years through to the present day (Ebenstein 2016).

The most common materialization of pregnancy in these venues, however, is not the pregnant woman, but the lone fetus. This echoes, in Rebecca Whiteley's words, the "maternal erasure" common to the ubiquitous portrayals of the "floating fetus" first identified by Rosalind Pollack Petchesky (Whiteley 2019; Petchesky 1987). Women's bodies tend to be cut out of the picture, quite literally, in anatomical illustrations, medical models, and human specimen preparations, which focus on the reproductive organs or the fetus displayed inside, or apart from, a uterus. In fact, in the specimen jars of the medical museum, the floating fetus actually appears – and not as a flat image, but in three dimensions; not as a representation of the real, but as the real thing itself (Figure 4.1).

Figure 4.1 Example of a "floating fetus" as commonly found in medical museums. This one is around three months and shown with membranes and placenta. Originally from the Histological Laboratory Amsterdam, c.1920. Now housed in the collection of Museum Vrolik, Amsterdam.

Source: Courtesy of Museum Vrolik, Amsterdam University Medical Centre.

The *Body Worlds* series includes sections on the development of the fetus as well as a special exhibition devoted to the topic. Both have been reviewed for anti-abortion publications, with some declaring them even more effective than the 1965 *Life* magazine series widely credited for its powerful role as "visual rhetoric" in the argument for fetal personhood. As a reviewer who visited the fetal development exhibition at the Oregon Museum of Science and Industry reported on the anti-abortion website LifeNews.com in 2015,

> [t]his exhibit humanized the unborn more than Lennart Nilsson's fetal development images or the graphic abortion images do, both of which we use in our outreach brochure ...Why? Because in this exhibit *you're in the personal, physical presence of unborn children.*
>
> (Brahm 2015; emphasis in original)

"Babies in bottles," as they are commonly known among museum staff and visitors, are some of the most controversial objects displayed in medical museums, but they are also some of the most popular. Part of the controversy surrounding them comes from the manner in which they were collected, often without the permission of the person whose body they were originally growing within. Although we know very little about the origins of most specimens, historians have found evidence both of doctors secretly keeping remains for their research use and of parents donating the dead embryo or fetus to their doctor for preservation in museum collections (Ray 2018; Withycombe 2018).

An additional complication with their display arises from the very pronounced bodily deformities evident in some fetuses that were collected as examples of "monstrous births" during childbirth, after their death *in utero*, or shortly after delivery (Guerrini 2005). Discussions about whether these are suitable for general audiences, as opposed to medical specialists, focus on the possible responses generated – whether viewers will react "appropriately" or with fear or revulsion; the potential distress they could cause, especially to pregnant women; and more recently, whether people with disabilities and other critics will see such exhibitions as a modern-day "freak show," cloaking spurious entertainment in the guise of education (Delin 2002).

The important role these collections play in generating conversations and reflection around reproduction and abortion is underestimated by stakeholders who argue against their display. Often citing concerns for younger visitors, some staff (usually from marketing or education teams rather than the curatorial department) frequently assert that these items are too upsetting, despite the obvious interest of visitors. Their assumptions, however, appear to be based on an adult sense of the diseases and decisions the exhibits may represent. In fact, young visitors are less likely to be distressed and more likely to be intrigued, as curatorial staff often report. Some curators have expressed concern, however, that for adolescent girls especially, if these are the first fetal specimens they have ever seen, this may negatively impact their views on having children by creating an exaggerated sense of the risks of pregnancy. This potential problem is of course exacerbated by the medicalized representation of pregnancy and childbirth in medical museums in general and by the broader cultural silence on the range of issues that accompany conception, pregnancy, and childbirth.

While the LifeNews.com quote above claims that these collections have an unequivocal power to communicate an anti-abortion message, staff report a wider array of responses from museum audiences. Although there is little systematic or published research on these reactions, curators and tour guides tell me that displays of embryos and fetuses generate affecting responses from visitors, especially women, who may then share their personal experiences with prenatal testing, pregnancy loss, or raising a child with a disability.

Sara Ray, a historian of medicine who has volunteered as a tour guide at the Mütter Museum (part of the College of Physicians of Philadelphia), notes that almost every time she takes people around the collection of fetuses with visible abnormalities, visitors say something that touches on issues of disability, abortion, and pregnancy loss. In response to a group of boys from a Catholic High School, who complained that the museum should not be "celebrating abortion," she explained the context of the collections – how they came from a time before fetal imagery (in the nineteenth century), and were most likely the result of late-term miscarriages or stillbirths. On another occasion, a woman who provided late-term abortion care noted that she had seen many bodies similar to those shown in the museum. As Ray later reflected when we discussed these kinds of encounters,

> [t]hat tour really helped me grapple with these collections as spaces of pregnancy loss; it helped me realize how important it is to not shy away from the emotional complexities of miscarriage, stillbirths, and abortion but embrace them as really central pillars of these collections.[2]

While the social stigma surrounding abortion may discourage some women from disclosing their own, in numerous medical museums I have visited curators report that attendees discuss the broader history or comment on the legal situation today. Women who have terminated a pregnancy or experienced a miscarriage due to fetal abnormalities are also known to visit medical museums to learn more about a particular condition, or as part of their grieving process. In one museum, where there is an ongoing collaboration with genetics researchers, one doctor even advises pregnant women to view the fetal specimens while they wait for their results from prenatal testing.

Other objects relevant to abortion typically found in medical museum collections include surgical instruments for performing the termination, although these appear to be much less frequently shown than the obstetrical forceps often on display as part of any reference to pregnancy and childbirth.

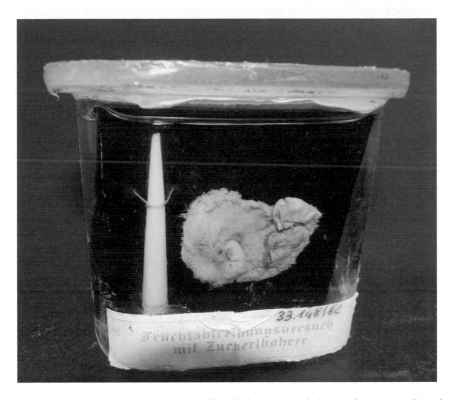

Figure 4.2 Uterus perforated in an illegal abortion and the implement used in the procedure. Originally from the collection of the Semmelweis clinic, c.1950.

Source: Photograph by Eduard Winter. Courtesy of the Narrenturm-Natural History Museum, Vienna.

Some human remains collections also contain examples of ectopic pregnancies, and perforated uteri damaged by attempted abortions (Figure 4.2). I have only ever seen these exhibited as examples used to teach medical students about potential "cases" they might encounter, usually shown without any explanatory text, rather than addressed in terms of reproductive politics. Overall, in medical museums in general the experiences of women are sublimated to those of their doctors or their fetuses.

While the museum collections discussed here raise difficult questions regarding the use of diagnostic technologies, disability rights, and eugenic ideology, as well as the painful issues of fertility problems, infant death, and parental grief, all are part and parcel of the process of trying to conceive or becoming a parent. Even so, these topics remain relatively private, and marginalized in culture and public debate. The silence surrounding miscarriage is particularly problematic, given that around 20% of known pregnancies end in loss (the rates of pregnancies lost before implantation or before pregnancy is detected are thought to be much higher – 70% (Danielsson 2019)).

Given the success with which the anti-abortion movement has mobilized fetal imagery for their cause, some visitors may mistake collections as evidence of abortion rather than the result of complications in fetal development or pregnancy. Yet restricting the display or discussion of these materials extends the cultural silence around abortion and pregnancy loss that contributes to the shame and stigma associated with both. This would also suppress the valuable opportunities that regularly emerge when diverse visitors encounter such collections, on individual visits or as part of group tours. As Ludlow argues in her essay in this book, both anti-abortion and pro-choice narratives restrict the range of stories people share and engage with on the topic, erasing complexities such as doubt, grief, joy, or disinterest. In a museum setting, where visitors and staff begin to talk, inspired by the objects on display and opened up to the longer historical view of attempts to control fertility, a more nuanced and less polarized debate might be possible than in the broader public sphere. New exhibition strategies are required, however, to shift the representation out of the context of fetal development, and to consider more broadly the realities of women's health, prenatal testing, and the political, legal, and economic frameworks that influence reproductive rights.

The Museum of Contraception and Abortion

The Museum of Contraception and Abortion offers just such an opportunity. Founded by a gynaecologist and housed in the same building as his medical office in Vienna, the museum is claimed to be the first of its kind in the world.[3] Dr Christian Fiala opened the clinic in 2003, and the museum in 2007, paid for with an inheritance from his father. Young people, Fiala claims, are increasingly removed from the history of the long struggle for effective contraception and have little idea of the difficulties limiting pregnancies prior to the development of the pill. As a result, they significantly underestimate natural fertility rates and the risk of unintended pregnancy. His goal with the museum, then, is not just to teach *how* to use contraception but *why*.

The project has faced considerable opposition, although the museum attracts growing numbers of visitors as well as positive media coverage. Austria is a predominantly Catholic country, and while rapidly changing, there remains a considerable difference in attitudes between the city and the countryside. Throughout the country, abortion is legal, but only up to sixteen weeks, meaning that approximately 300 women per year travel to the Netherlands to terminate pregnancies after this cut-off date (Gynmed n.d.; Fiala, interview, 21 October 2018). Contraception and abortion are not covered by the welfare system, so both must be privately paid for, and there are few abortion providers – even in Vienna there are only three dedicated private clinics. However, many abortions are performed in private practice, which is also legal (Fiala, personal communication, 14 January 2020).

In the beginning, the museum struggled to locate objects for its collection, as both abortion and contraception are relatively private topics, and relevant artefacts are awkward to preserve. As Fiala notes, when someone's grandmother dies, "everyone wants her jewellery but the diaphragm was probably more important to her," although family members may not think to save it. It took four years to develop the collections and create the permanent exhibition before opening the museum to visitors, and now news of the project has spread internationally, and people around the world contact them to offer objects for donation. They currently house around 3,000 items, as well as scanned books (which can be downloaded free of charge from their website).

The permanent exhibition begins with a statement by Freud calling for a safe option for women. Spread over two main rooms, the narrative details the development of scientific knowledge of reproduction and contraception, highlighting crucial milestones such as the discovery of the most fertile days in the menstrual cycle in the 1930s, as well as the various methods used to intervene in conception. This includes traditional methods such as withdrawal, various designs of intrauterine devices, and eventually the contraceptive pill, as well as myths such as vaginal douching with Coca Cola. Describing desperate methods for abortion, one section focuses in detail on the harsh penalties for abortionists who were convicted. There are references to campaigns to legalize abortion, and profiles of important figures internationally who worked to increase abortion access. The kitchen table of the illegal abortionist is contrasted in one corner of the last room with an image of the modern clinic across the hall from the museum, which is displayed on the opposite side of the room (Figure 4.3).

This presentation echoes the standard narrative of progress common in more traditional medical museums, by juxtaposing symbols of past and present. A recent documentary photography book drawing on the museum's collection takes a similar approach, highlighting the tools and scenes of illegal or unscrupulous abortionists to illustrate the importance of high-quality legal, medical services (Abril 2018). It is a compelling approach, which emphasizes the long history of people trying to control their fertility, and the hardships caused by a lack of legal and effective methods. Yet this linear narrative of progress is misleading and does not address the relatively recent criminalization of abortion that attempted to end a much longer tradition of widely used non-medical strategies for ending pregnancies (Riddle 1999).

Historians have shown that although fertility control was very difficult in previous centuries, there were accepted methods before the practice was suppressed and criminalized in the nineteenth century (McLaren 1990; Riddle 1994). This clampdown contributed to the rise of unsafe practices, which

Figure 4.3 Image representing the kitchen table as the operating space of an illegal abortion.

Source: Photograph by Manon Parry. Courtesy of the Museum of Contraception and Abortion, Vienna.

could be lethal. However, the dangers of all abortions have been exaggerated to justify restricting its provision to medical gatekeepers (Reagan 1998). As the women's health movement of the 1960s demonstrated, with access to the appropriate tools and techniques, people without medical training could safely perform vacuum aspiration abortions, for example (Schoen 2013).

Yet this standard narrative is also a core element of campaigns to "keep abortion (safe and) legal" by feminist groups. Their concession to medical expertise in this regard replicates the compromises of the earlier birth control movement, in which feminists made alliances with medical professionals to overcome their opposition, and to build credibility for contraceptive services (Gordon 1976). The availability of medical abortion (the so-called abortion pill, using mifepristone and misoprostol) has opened up this issue once again, now that individuals can research and purchase the drugs online and use them with or without a consulting medical professional's advice, at least in the first ten weeks of pregnancy. The museum founder, Fiala, is quite critical of medical control of access to abortion, such as the need for doctors' signatures to access services, as well as waiting-period restrictions, and limited abortion provision. In Austria, he concluded, doctors were happy to diagnose problems in a developing fetus but then "leave women alone" if they decided to terminate the pregnancy as a result. His critique is not yet part of the museum's exhibition narrative, however.

Reactions to the museum have shifted in recent years. Religious organizations were previously very negative, and demonstrators calling it the "death museum" attempted to prevent school groups from going inside. A Catholic group tried unsuccessfully to force the firing of a school director for sending students. For the first ten years the project was denied any public funding, and a former finance minister illegally intervened to prevent tax reduction being applied to the project. The museum was also subject to two parliamentary inquiries but has survived. Some protests continue but have "diminished in intensity" in recent years, and Fiala reports that it is rather rare to attract negative reactions now, although they are still told when they apply for funding that it would be easier if they dropped the word abortion from the museum title.

Staff have encountered strong emotional reactions from visitors, especially from older women, who sometimes cry, and often tell their own stories (some of which the museum is collecting to include in a film and an archive). Every month school groups attend, and their accompanying teachers often also tell their personal stories about contraception (but not abortion) in front of the students. A staff member on the ticket desk told me that after she started working there, her friends and acquaintances began revealing their own abortion experiences, illustrating how hidden the subject was in her own circle, as well as the power of this project to break that silence.

The museum is positively described in travel guides and attracts rising numbers of individual visitors from other countries, as well as healthcare professionals including midwives and gynaecologists. There are increasing inquiries from researchers, and more media requests, suggesting that their goal to bring the topic back into public debate is being met, and with a mostly positive response (Zorn 2014; Fiala, interview, 21 October 2018).

Conclusion

Hann and Ludlow argue in Chapter 8 that attempts to counter powerful anti-abortion imagery with photographs of dead women (killed by illegal abortion), or with scientific rhetoric, are inadequate. They suggest the suppression of images and discussion of the fetal tissue that results from abortion – for fear that it could be used by abortion opponents – has created a problematic culture of silence around the realities of abortion

care. I agree and argue here that this intersects with the exclusion of pregnant women's perspectives, even or especially in the medical museum. As
in mass culture more broadly, in museums the sexualized woman's body
is everywhere to be seen, while in stark contrast, her *reproducing* body
is barely visible. While the medical museum cannot solve all of these
issues alone, it seems like a relevant place to begin. As I have argued here,
women's reproductive health should become a more central topic, given
that these collections include a range of relevant materials. These museums
also need to reconsider their interpretive strategies, which usually privilege
the perspectives of medical practitioners, to address the wider range of
people and practices involved in the management of reproduction in the
past and the present.

Given the instrumentalization of museums by anti-abortion groups, and
the resonances of some of the most classic objects in these collections with
their visual and rhetorical strategies, these museums already participate
indirectly in abortion politics. Making the informal discussions between
visitors and curators a more explicit part of their interpretive frameworks
would provide a platform for the wider experiences of abortion that these
polarized discourses ignore. Instead, avoiding the issue allows a vocal
minority to set the terms of debate and dominate the discussion.

Notes

1 These findings and the case studies I discuss here draw on the research for my
current book project, "Human Curiosities: The Social Relevance of Medical
Museums." www.manonparry.com/books/human-curiosities. Accessed 14 June
2019.
2 All details from this section come from a personal communication with Sara Ray,
email 3 December 2019.
3 All details from this section, unless otherwise noted, come from an interview with
Christian Fiala, Vienna, Austria, 21 October 2018. For more information on the
museum, see their website at http://en.muvs.org.

References

Abril, Laia. 2018. *On Abortion*. Stockport, UK: Dewi Lewis.
Bassett, Laura. 2014. "Michele Bachmann Rails Against Proposed National Women's
History Museum." *Huffington Post*, 7 May 2014. www.huffingtonpost.com/
2014/05/07/michele-bachmann-womenshistorymuseum_n_5283194.html?utm_
hp_ref=fb.
Brahm, Josh. 2015. "Incredible Display with the Bodies of Miscarried Babies
Reveals the Humanity of Unborn Children." *LifeNews.com*, 22 May 2015. www.
lifenews.com/2015/05/22/incredible-display-with-the-bodies-of-miscarried-
babies-reveals-the-humanity-of-unborn-children.
Christian Patriots for Life. 2014. "National American Holocaust Memorial."
Accessed 10 June 2019. www.cpforlife.org/tour.

Danielsson, Krissi. 2019. "Making Sense of Miscarriage Statistics: What the Conflicting Research Really Means." *Verywell Family*, 15 March 2019. www.verywellfamily.com/making-sense-of-miscarriage-statistics-2371721.

Delin, Annie. 2002. "Buried in the Footnotes: The Absence of Disabled People in the Collective Imagery of Our Past." In *Museums, Society, and Inequality*, edited by Richard Sandell, 84–97. New York: Routledge.

Ebenstein, Joanna. 2016. *The Anatomical Venus: Wax, God, Death and the Ecstatic*. London, UK: Thames and Hudson and Artbook/D.A.P.

Giacomini, M., P. Rozée-Koker, and F. Pepitone-Arreola-Rockwell. 1986. "Gender Bias in Human Anatomy Textbook Illustrations." *Psychology of Women Quarterly* 10, no. 4 (December): 413–20.

Gordon, Linda. 1976. *Woman's Body, Woman's Right: A Social History of Birth Control in America*. New York: Penguin Books.

Guerrini, Anita. 2005. "The Creativity of God and the Order of Nature: Anatomizing Monsters in the Early Eighteenth Century." In *Monsters & Philosophy*, edited by Charles T. Wolfe, 153–68. London: College Publications.

Gynmed n.d. "Legal Regulation of Abortion in Austria." www.gynmed.at/en/abortion/austrian-law. Accessed 14 June 2019.

Haynes, Suyin. 2019. "'We Want to Tackle That Stigma.' Inside the World's First Museum Dedicated to the Vagina." *Time*, 15 November 2019. https://time.com/5728259/vagina-museum-london.

Heck, Wilmer. 2019. "Anti-Abortus Lobby Voelt Wind in de Rug." *NRC.nl*, 12 June 2019. www.nrc.nl/nieuws/2019/06/12/anti-abortuslobby-voelt-wind-in-de-rug-a3963341.

Juhász, Borbála and Enikő Pap. 2018. "Backlash in Gender Equality and Women's and Girls' Rights." Brussels: European Parliament's Policy Department for Citizen's Rights and Constitutional Affairs.

Lum, Kathryn Gin. 2014. "These Evangelical Haunted Houses Are Designed to Show Sinners That They're Going to Hell." *The Washington Post*, 30 October 2014. www.washingtonpost.com/posteverything/wp/2014/10/30/these-evangelical-haunted-houses-are-designed-to-show-sinners-that-theyre-going-to-hell/?utm_term=.842d62e2190c.

Madera, Melissa. 2013. "'AR-TI-FACTS' Exhibit." http://theabortiondiarist.com/abortion- ar%c2%b7ti%c2%b7facts-exhibit. Accessed 10 June 2019.

Malone, Brenda. 2020. "Recording Change: Collecting the Irish Abortion Rights Referendum." In *Museums, Sexuality, and Gender Activism*, edited by Joshua G. Adair and Amy K. Levin. Oxford and New York: Routledge.

McLaren, Angus. 1990. A History of Contraception from Antiquity to the Present Day. Oxford: Basil Blackwell.

Parry, Manon S. 2013. *Broadcasting Birth Control: Mass Media and Family Planning*. Rutgers, NJ: Rutgers University Press.

Parry, Manon S. 2015. "Feminist Opposition to Abortion: Reframing Histories to Limit Reproductive Rights." *Yearbook of Women's History* 35. Verloren Publishers: Amsterdam NL. December: 107–18.

Pecorin, Allison. 2017. "Abortion Exhibit – That's What Missouri Capitol Museum Needs, Lawmaker Says." *The Kansas City Star*, 25 February 2017. www.kansascity.com/news/politics-government/article134962754.html. Accessed 10 June 2019.

Pes, Javier. 2018. "Ireland's National Museum Is Collecting Protest Art Made During the Historic Abortion Referendum." *artnet news*, 14 June 2018. https://news.artnet.com/art-world/wanted-irelands-national-museum-seeks-protest-banners-created-countrys-historic-vote-abortion-1302443.

Petchesky, Rosalind Pollack. 1987. "Fetal Images: The Power of Visual Culture in the Politics of Abortion." *Feminist Studies* 13, no. 2: 263–92.

Pharaon, Sarah, Sally Roesch Wagner, Barbara Lau, and María José Bolaña Caballero. 2015. "Safe Containers for Dangerous Memories." *The Public Historian* 37, no. 2: 61–72.

Ray, Sara. 2018. "On Mothers and Monsters: Maternal Testimony, Monstrous Births, and Embryology, 1700–1849." Paper presented at the seminar series in body history, Utrecht University, 7 November 2018.

Reagan, Leslie J. 1998. *When Abortion Was a Crime: Women, Medicine, and Law in the United States, 1867–1973*. Berkeley, CA: University of California Press.

Riddle, John M. 1994. Contraception and Abortion from the Ancient World to the Renaissance. Cambridge, MA: Harvard University Press.

Riddle, John M. 1999. Eve's Herbs: A History of Contraception and Abortion in the West. Cambridge, MA: Harvard University Press.

Sappol, Michael. 2002. *A Traffic of Dead Bodies: Anatomy and Embodied Social Identity in Nineteenth Century America*. Princeton, NJ: Princeton University Press.

Schiebinger, Londa. 1986. "Skeletons in the Closet: The First Illustrations of the Female Skeleton in Eighteenth-Century Anatomy." *Representations* 14, Spring: 42–82.

Schneider, Colleen Dilen. 2017. "People Trust Museums More Than Newspapers. Here Is Why That Matters Right Now (DATA)." 26 April 2017. www.colleendilen.com/2017/04/26/people-trust-museums-more-than-newspapers-here-is-why-that-matters-right-now-data.

Schoen, Johanna. 2013. "Living Through Some Giant Change: The Establishment of Abortion Services." *American Journal of Public Health* 103, no. 3: 416–25.

Stone, Andrea. 2011. "National Women's History Museum Placates Conservatives to Get Bill Passed in Congress." *Huffington Post*, 8 August 2011 (updated 10 August 2011). www.huffingtonpost.com/2011/08/08/national-womens-history-museum_n_919916.html.

Tyburczy, Jennifer. 2012. "All Museums Are Sex Museums." *Radical History Review* 1, May: 199–211.

Von Hagens, Gunter. 2017. "Gunter von Hagens' Body Worlds, Facts and Figures." https://bodyworlds.com/wp-content/uploads/2017/09/1498134149_bw_factsnumbers_chjun171.pdf. Accessed 14 June 2019.

Wheaton, Sarah. 2014. "Anti-Abortion Groups Inspire Abroad." *Politico.com*, 2 May 2014. www.politico.com/story/2014/05/europe-anti-abortion-advocates-106285.

Whiteley, Rebecca. 2019. "Figuring Pictures and Picturing Figures: Images of the Pregnant Body and the Unborn Child in England, 1540–c.1680." *Social History of Medicine* 32, no. 2 (May): 241–66.

Withycombe, Shannon. 2018. *Lost: Miscarriage in Nineteenth-Century America*. Rutgers, NJ: Rutgers University Press.

Zorn, Josef. 2014. "Everything You Didn't Know You Wanted to Know About Abortion." *Vice*, 27 February 2014. www.vice.com/en_us/article/4w7x8d/museum-for-contraception-and-abortion-vienna-austria-christian-fiala-exhibits.

5 Who's late?

Degrassi, abortion, history

Michele Byers

Introduction

Since the first season of *Degrassi High* (1989), when twins Erica and Heather Farrell pushed through angry protesters to enter an abortion clinic, the Canadian TV franchise has offered a number of story arcs in which a character chooses to have an abortion. This chapter looks at these narratives – Erica on *Degrassi High* (1989), Tessa on *School's Out* (1992), Manny on *Degrassi: The Next Generation* (2004), and Lola on *Degrassi: Next Class* (2017) – and considers what we might learn from them.[1] While journalists have discussed *Degrassi*'s representations of abortion in detail, relatively little academic work has done the same. It's hard for me to speculate as to why this is the case – perhaps it is simply that Canadian television remains somewhat under-studied, even today.

Canadians have always watched American TV; Canadian writers and producers have grown up with, and admire, their American counterparts. Still, the particular context of production of Canadian television *is* different and needs to be accounted for. Two articles about *Degrassi* are instructive in relation to this complexity. Elana Levine, an American scholar, describes travelling to the *Degrassi* lot, hoping to address "the role of Canadian identity in the program's creation" (2009, 155). She finds her interviewees "vague" and "ambivalent," which she links to the tension of producing something local with universal (that is, global/American) appeal (Levine 2009, 158–9). In her response to Levine, Serra Tinic draws on her own work, where she found industry people in Canada quite able to articulate a "Canadian sensibility in storytelling" rather than an identity, noting that one would not assume a clear relationship between Hollywood and a unified version of Americanness (2009).[2] Even more compelling is her rejoinder that Levine's choice to begin with the *TNG* rather than the earlier series elides something central to the question being asked (Tinic 2009, 168). She writes, "*Degrassi* was publicly funded as an experimental, educational television series that could perhaps be viewed as a kind of community intervention. … Produced within a public broadcasting system and thus relatively buffered from risk averse advertisers" (Tinic 2009, 169). She also mentions that the original series, co-produced with PBS, was heavily edited for American distribution, pointing to long-standing national differences in what is "sayable" on television. This is important to my own reading of abortion on *Degrassi*, and to my sense of how this context plays a role in practices of "sayability" or what might be thought of as a kind of discursive solvency in the face of various pressures to tell a story in a certain way. In what follows, I consider *Degrassi* as a cultural space where abortion is negotiated. I suggest that while the context of production is important, what is "sayable" at the national level is always in tension with what is "sayable" within the highly desirable, transnational circuits of distribution through which television (and capital) circulates.

Studies of abortion on television

In a 1959 issue of the *British Medical Journal*, I found an article that describes an episode of *Lifeline* as "preventative medicine" taking aim at a "major social evil" (criminal abortion), whose incidence in Great Britain at the time is described as "appallingly high … and shockingly squalid" ("Abortion on TV" 1959, 638). I mention this to point out the long-standing practice of representing abortion on TV: 60 years! Rosalind Petchesky's (1987) "Fetal Images," which argues for a vigorous engagement with the contested terrain of visual culture, and Kathryn C. Montgomery's (1990) analysis of the context in which *Maude* became the first American network series to feature abortion, underscore that televisual representations have always been used to advance political arguments. Montgomery's work also outlines how the *Maude* episode cemented network fears about the potential for audience and advertiser backlash that shaped the representations of abortion that followed in the United States.

While little academic research on representations of abortion was published after the mid-1990s, 2014 saw sociologists working in reproductive health begin publishing empirical work in this area. Gretchen Sisson and Katrina Kimport found "abortion stories are more common," but also less accurate, "than popular discourse suggests" (2014, 417). In particular, they found death was a prevalent outcome related to the decision to seek an abortion, demonstrating abortion's ongoing "stigma" (Sisson and Kimport 2014, 417). Focusing on the decade between 2005 and 2015, the authors found that characters who had abortions on TV were "whiter, wealthier, and younger," and far less likely to be parents, than those seeking abortion in real life; "self-focused reasons" for seeking abortion were overrepresented compared to "other-focused" or structural reasons; abortion tended to happen to peripheral, rather than central, recurring characters, and characters rarely faced barriers to abortion, or, if they did, the barriers "rarely prevent[ed] characters from obtaining abortion" (Sisson and Kimport 2016, 449–50; 2017, 65).

Critical press accounts of abortion on TV are more extensive than academic ones. In 2000, Audrey Fisch noted how impressed she was that WB series *Felicity* actually used the word abortion. In 2004, Kate Aurthur reported *The O.C.* creator Josh Schwartz's decision to avoid the word abortion on his show because "the show would sink under the weight of it." By 2014, many feminist journalists regularly took note of the dissonance between representation and "real life" (Rosenberg 2015; McNamara 2017; O'Keeffe 2017; Rankin, 2017), while others took up the emergence of new, more nuanced narratives that made inroads into some representational gaps (Jones 2017; Betancourt 2018; Dionne 2019). In an interview with Nivea Serrao, long-term *Degrassi* executive producer Steven Stohn describes the shift from a desire for "balanced storytelling" in the 1980s to a more supportive environment in the early 2000s, and, finally, the representation of abortion as "commonplace" in 2017 (Serrao 2017).

"Maybe it's wrong, but I don't care" (Erica, 1989)

In 1989, Erica becomes pregnant after a summer romance at camp. Abortion is hotly debated at school; everyone has a strong opinion, including Erica's twin sister, Heather, who is very much opposed. In *SO*, the finale to the classic *Degrassi* series, Tessa Campinelli becomes pregnant after becoming involved with Joey Jeremiah (a main character), who already has a girlfriend. In 2004, on *TNG*, Manny Santos becomes pregnant after she sleeps with Craig, who she is hoping to "steal" away from his girlfriend, Ashley. Finally, in 2017, Lola becomes pregnant after having sex with a boy, Miles, at a party, while Miles is grieving his boyfriend, Tristan, who is in a coma. If we agree that what is sayable, and unsayable, on television is at least partly tethered to national politics, then the timing of these episodes is important. Though the first abortion on *Degrassi* took place in 1989, the first pregnancy occurred two years earlier when another central character, Spike, became pregnant and gave birth to Emma. 1987 was just a year shy of the *Morgentaler* decision. 1989 was the year *Tremblay v. Daigle* found that a fetus does not have legal status as a person in Canada; the year Bill-C43, which criminalized abortion, passed in the House of Commons, only to be defeated in the Senate (Johnstone 2017). Series creator Linda Schuyler points out:

> I never could have done a scene where Lola's got her feet on the stirrups and the doctor is talking to her in the 80s … It was a time of political unrest, so we had our girls have to fight through demonstrators outside abortion clinics.
>
> (Alter 2018)

Demographically, the characters who have abortions on *Degrassi* are quite similar. Three are white and 16; all four are middle-class and urban;

they attend public school, live at home, and appear to be cis-gendered and straight. None was sexually active prior to the boy with whom she became pregnant, though only one was in a relationship. All of the characters had murky ideas about, but used, birth control. All of the characters explain their choice to abort as linked to being too young and having other things they want to do with their lives. In this, the characters and stories on *Degrassi* fit well within the parameters found by Sisson and Kimport (2016). What is different is that none of these is a peripheral character and none of these arcs combine rape or incest with abortion narratives – although several of the stories feature infidelity.

Unlike the characters examined by Sisson and Kimport, none of these young women experience injury or death because of or after considering/ having an abortion (2014, 2016). Though they were represented as emotionally grappling with their decision, most explicitly expressed relief. Similarly, the *Degrassi* characters largely faced social rather than legal or logistical challenges to access (Sisson and Kimport 2017). The only physical access issue represented was the protest outside the clinic on *DH*. Once inside, however, all the clinics were represented as clean, bright, and professional, and the staff as kind, helpful, and offering succinct answers to questions without any judgement.

Despite the ease in accessing abortion, there were other obstacles. The characters faced some consequences from being outed in public: Erica faced verbal abuse, graffiti on her locker, and a physical altercation with an angry classmate; Manny and Lola were publicly embarrassed. All were afraid of their parents' reactions. While support is not examined in Sisson and Kimport's work, this was an important aspect of the way I read access being represented on *Degrassi*. Heather ultimately accompanies her sister, helping her through the protesters. Manny eventually gets the support of her mother and her best friend, Emma. Lola's classmate, Yael, insists on going to the clinic with her; later, her friends offer support and affirmation. Tessa is the only character who is not shown getting any support.

While Sisson did look at genre, her work does not address tone, which is, in my reading, very important (2017). The *DH* arc is quite sombre; even a bit frightening. While Erica's rights are validated, she encounters multiple obstacles including threats and violence. Although abortion offers Erica relief, her twin sister experiences the abortion as traumatic, and has nightmares for several episodes. Tessa's abortion is the most neutrally represented: no one finds out that she is pregnant. Manny's story includes multiple public blow-ups and passionate speeches articulating both pro-choice and anti-abortion positions.[3] Ultimately, the tone of these episodes affirms "legal choice as a pragmatic necessity but defin[es] abortion as a morally undesirable act" (Condit 1990, 133). Lola's arc is the most significantly different in tone, using humour and showing Lola experiencing no obstacles or negative consequences.

If I use Sisson and Kimport's framework to consider abortion on *Degrassi*, a couple of interesting things emerge. First, Tessa is an outlier. We know least about her story, and her presence on the series ends after her abortion. Although she is a recurring character, she functions more like a peripheral character, which affirms that abortion narratives have the most complexity and nuance when they are written into the stories of core characters who are known to viewers long before they become pregnant and continue to be known to them long after. Second, Manny's story is also an outlier. The importance of this arc (and a lot has been written about it) emerged because of the controversy that was generated when its specialty child- and youth-focused US network (The N) refused to air it. In Canada, at the time, there was little interest in revisiting the abortion debate and the episode raised virtually no controversy. However, the series' move to CTV in Canada, and The N in the US, created different conditions of "sayability" in relation to abortion in 2004 than had been true in 1989 and 1991 (Mohabeer 2005). By the time *NC* was being produced, *Degrassi*'s executives had publicly articulated their desire to return to their public education roots (Ahearn 2016; Dickson 2017). Though abortion politics was more fraught in the US in 2017, the series' move to Netflix (and Family Channel in Canada), and growing social media activism about abortion, created space for another discursive shift. It is to these discernible shifts in "sayability," in relation to the earliest and most recent abortion arcs on *Degrassi*, that I now turn.

"My name is Lola Pacini. Yesterday I was pregnant, and now I'm not." (Lola, 2017)

Celeste Condit argues that post-*Wade*, television narratives sought balance in order to avoid the pitfalls encountered by *Maude*'s producers and network upon its pre-*Wade* release (1990). This led to the homogenization of abortion narratives, and "encouraged a particular, circumscribed cultural meaning for the practice of abortion, supporting legal choice as a pragmatic necessity but defining abortion as a morally undesirable act" (Condit 1990, 133). After considering three decades of *Degrassi*, I think Condit's reading remains persuasive, at least until 2017. Mirroring Saurette and Gordon's findings on changes in pro-life lobbying in Canada, over time we can see the series move away from fetal-centric, pro-life arguments (2016). While Stettner, Burnett, and Hay argue that choice as a rhetorical strategy is inadequate for addressing abortion today, choice, and thus a liberal notion of rights, remains the central discursive structure through which the logics of abortion operate, narratively, on *Degrassi* (2017).

One of the biggest fields of change between the 1989 and 2017 *Degrassi* abortion episodes is technological. While the language for talking about the actual practice of abortion, and the clinics where abortions are performed, don't change a lot, other technologies of reproductive health are different.

The one that caught my attention was the pregnancy test. Erica has to take the test twice. It comes in a large box, involves two test tubes, and takes two hours to give a result. She has to do the test at home, at night. Lola, by contrast, takes her pregnancy test in the school bathroom. It's the now familiar small stick, with the result given in block letters (YES/NO) in about two minutes. While this may seem beyond the specific question of abortion, the test is symbolic of the broader changes in reproductive health that happened between 1989 and 2017. The other major technological change involves the development of online culture. Erica's knowledge of abortion comes from home, peer culture, and her church community. By contrast, access to technology gives Lola space to explore questions about abortion before she is ready to talk to others in person. Further, technology links Lola to other young women who share her experience: "Nikki Minaj had an abortion during high school," her friend Yael tells her. Taking this to heart, Lola uses her vlog as an online platform to share her story, connecting with the participants in, and viewers of, the #ShoutYourAbortion and #YouKnowMe campaigns.

Secrecy and shame shape the discursive practices of abortion representation. On *DH*, the abortion debate happens on two levels, which are presented as discrete: public (political) / private (relational). The private discussions occur between Erica and her twin, often in their shared bedroom, while the public discussions happen most significantly in the classroom. Conversely, in Lola's arc there is no bedroom story: most of the narrative unfolds in public space. This reinscribes the way shame and secrecy shape these stories. Erica's choice remains private; it is something she shares with her sister only. In the end, her abortion remains a secret, while Lola's choice transcends the private sphere, becoming part of the public discourse of abortion. In 2017 the narrative explicitly challenges the issues of secrecy and shame in ways that are beyond what was "sayable" in 1989. Frankie tells Lola: "Making that difficult choice and standing up for it. You're courageous. We should go out and celebrate." And Yael tells her: "The point is, a lot of women have abortions and don't feel any shame."

How to read the relationship between these two stories is complicated, however, and should not be thought of as simply a progress narrative, but also as a question of how neoliberal notions of subjecthood increasingly organize our understanding of individual public acts. To underscore this, let me turn to a key scene from "A New Start, Part II" (*DH* 1002), which demonstrates a commitment to balance, but also to a particular educational process, very much rooted in the context of the series' production.

HEATHER: Abortion's wrong, it's like murder.
LUCY: It's not! … It's a fetus. I mean, it's no more a baby than an acorn is an oak tree.
…
HEATHER: Well in our church abortion's wrong.

LD: Excuse me, but what right does any church have to say what a woman can and can't do with her own body? What about the rights of the woman?

TIM: What about the people who want to have children, but can't? I mean, wouldn't it be better if the babies were allowed to live so that they could be adopted?

LUCY: So now women are just baby factories? Incubators without rights? What if the woman doesn't want to have the baby? Maybe she was raped, or maybe she got pregnant by accident. Is it right to force her to keep the fetus? You're denying her choice.

LIZ [to Spike]: You had a baby, tell them.

SPIKE: Just because I had Emma doesn't mean I know what's right.

…

BLT: Isn't abortion dangerous?

HEATHER: Yeah. We know a woman who had an abortion. And now she can't have kids.

LD: If it's done properly, an abortion is safer than having a baby.

…

MICHELLE: Some people believe that human life starts when the child is conceived. They say it produces blood at about 20 days, and there's a heartbeat around 24 days. Blood and a heartbeat, that's at least partly human. I don't think it's right to kill it.

This scene is lodged in the memory of many people I've spoken to over the years. It articulates the multiple discourses on abortion that were circulating at the time, linking them to broader questions outside of individual choice – even though this is one of the strands. Like much of the original *Degrassi*, it is framed as a teachable moment.

By the time we get to *NC*, many things have changed, and *NC* can be read as part of the grassroots response to these changes. When Yael asks what could be more important than working on their class presentation, Lola simply answers: "I'm getting an abortion." When she finally tells her best friends the truth:

FRANKIE: I would have supported you. Even if it wasn't the right decision for me.

SHAY: Yeah. Truthfully, I don't know what I would do if I was actually pregnant.

FRANKIE: Me neither. Making that difficult choice, and standing up for it … you're courageous.

While the tone is much clearer in 2017, the broader discourses that tie abortion to other questions – whether about rights or social justice – are less visible.

One of the interesting things about the 1989 episode is that all the characters (except maybe Erica) appear to know and be able to articulate clear opinions on abortion. Balance is achieved by giving polarized or binary-framed positions to different characters, including female and male students, and by centring the episode in public space and within the context of formal debate. In 2017, there is less concern for this kind of balance; the frame centres Lola and highlights the female-identified voices of those who support/echo rather than challenge her position. The centring of online culture, rather than the classroom, also changes the tone of the episode. While itself not unproblematic, online culture is presented as an agentic space where multiple perspectives, including first-person perspectives on abortion, can be shared. This re-centres the importance of the voices of young women who have had abortions as they speak about their experiences, eschewing the question of finding balance in the opinions of everyone in the classroom.

Between 1989 and 2017, the language used to discuss abortion on *Degrassi* changed, with fewer references to religion, "killing," and "murder." The fetal-centrism of the earlier period becomes less evident; there is less talk of "babies," and while "fathers" make an appearance, it is brief. This is in keeping with the finding that, in Canada, pro-abortion discourses have shifted away from these things. The one fetal-centric issue that is not noted in any of the literature, but is significant in this text, is the rooting of anti-abortion rhetoric in characters who tell stories about how they could have been aborted. On *DH*, Liz explains that her father beat her mother when she wouldn't have an abortion. And while it isn't the focus here, it is worth noting that this discourse is central to the abortion narrative in *TNG*. Emma sees her mother's teenage pregnancy as a mirror of Manny's, and Manny's fetus as a mirror of herself. As Emma and Liz are central characters, they demonstrate how, in the name of balance, anti-abortion rhetoric seeps into liberal discourses of choice. This type of rhetoric is not offered in 2017.

Access is taken for granted across the board on *Degrassi*, in keeping with Doull *et al.*'s (2017) findings, as well as the series' Toronto setting. Though, as noted, none of the characters face challenges to accessing abortion services, there are still two observable changes. First, *DH* showed aggressive protesters outside the abortion clinic. Second, the 2017 story actually follows Lola into the procedure room, showing Lola with her doctor as he explains the procedure in detail. The most significant moment comes when Lola asks: "Am I the first 16-year-old you've ever done this to?" To which he answers, kindly: "You're not the first today." Again, this speaks to tone and the significant shifts that occurred between 1989 and 2017. While both episodes offer medical details about abortion, only *NC* takes the viewer into the procedure room, and shows them the doctor as a person who engages in this type of medical work regularly.

In the 1989 episode, despite a very public articulation of pro-choice positions from Lucy and LD, Erica seems unable to reach out to them for support. Even though Spike tells Heather that she respects Erica's choice, Spike doesn't reach out to offer Erica her support. The dominant voices

Erica hears are unsupportive, and the framing of abortion as a "morally undesirable act" persists as Heather insists that even if she is coming with Erica, she thinks what she is doing is "wrong." In the *DH* episode, choice is less discursively invested *in* Erica than *about* her abortion. In the two central moments where choice is highlighted, she is a passive presence. In the classroom scene, Erica initiates the debate but does not express an opinion. In the second, Heather talks to Spike about Erica, but Spike never talks to her. Lola, however, is able to reach out to a variety of people in 2017, and they all articulate support for her decision, regardless of the choices they might make. Throughout the episode people affirm her choice, tell her she is "courageous," and take her out to celebrate.

Conclusion

Why think about abortion on *Degrassi*? Most simply, *Degrassi* is one of the longest-running and widest-circulating TV series in Canadian history, and its longevity allows us to track how changes in televisual culture, representations of abortion, social policies, and movement languages have changed (or not) over time. This study demonstrates that there is remarkable stability in *Degrassi*'s representations of abortion over time. That is, the stories are pro-choice, but pro-choice discourse is moderated by a desire to offer discursive balance. This series does this by making characters seeking abortion share centre stage with characters who morally oppose it. This study also shows that while national context influences content, many other things, such as global distribution networks, mediate national context. In Canada, abortion does not occupy the same politically fraught space that it does in, for example, the US. However, because American markets represent the "holy grail" of Canadian television distribution, there may be a strong incentive to produce content that "fits" through the gates American distributors keep.

It is worth reiterating the finding that the more central a character is, the more significant and complex their abortion arc will be. Tessa's story never comes into focus the way the other stories studied here do. As a secondary character for many years, we *know* Tessa, but this is the most significant thing that happens to her, and it's the last. We know Erica, Manny, and Lola before their abortions, and after. These events are significant, but do not define them. The problem of telling abortion stories with peripheral characters raises other issues related to representation, including regional representation – because questions of access are regional questions (Johnstone 2017).[4] What would a *Degrassi* story about someone's cousin from Prince Edward Island who couldn't get an abortion at home look like? What does *Degrassi*, and what do these questions, look like if we move the series from downtown Toronto to Moncton, Summerside, Fort Hope, Fogo Island, or Eskasoni, or if we move it to an urban community where there are more immigrants and refugees, more poverty, and so on?

There are a few things missing from existing studies of television and abortion that I think are worth more scrutiny. First, how structures of support, as well as obstacles, are narratively articulated should be examined. Second, we need work that focuses on teen TV on its own, because teen TV allows for a particular heuristic that is less available on adult TV, and we see this at work, albeit in different ways, in both the 1989 and 2017 *Degrassi* arcs.[5] While young people may be overrepresented in televised stories about abortion, the experience of sex, pregnancy, and abortion is mediated by age. Young people's relationship to the law, citizenship, and the Charter is complicated, and, as such, is a worthy space for specific analysis. There are also clearly things missing from these texts. Most significantly, we need a more inclusive picture of young women having abortions and more narratives that engage questions of access. Both omissions point to the need for diverse storytellers, who will bring their own intersectional inflections to the story of abortion. This is key to moving from a politics of choice to one of reproductive justice (Thompson-Spires 2007).

There are still lots of projects to do on *Degrassi*.

That's an invitation.

Notes

1 Hereafter *DH* (*Degrassi High*), *SO* (*School's Out*), *TNG* (*Degrassi: The Next Generation*), and *NC* (*Degrassi: Next Class*). Note that *Degrassi Junior High* ran from 1987–1989; *Degrassi High* ran from 1989–1991; *Degrassi: TNG* ran from 2001–2015; *Degrassi: Next Class* ran from 2016–2017.
2 My own *Degrassi* interviews from that period are full of references to Canadianness.
3 Because Manny is Emma's best friend, this arc also links us intertextually to the earlier arcs about Spike's pregnancy and Erica's abortion. The intertextual implications of the relations of characters who traverse the *Degrassi* multiverse are beyond the scope of this essay, but definitely worth exploring further. See Lefebvre, "Adolescence through the looking-glass."
4 Which is also a question about television production.
5 Although certain legal, medical, and political dramas may show evidence of it.

References

"Abortion on TV." 1959. *The British Medical Journal* 1, no. 5122: 638.
Ahearn, Victoria. 2016. "'Degrassi' back to roots with 'Next Class.'" *HuffPost*. January 1, 2016. www.huffingtonpost.ca/2016/01/01/degrassi-netflix-sensational_n_8903018.html.
Alter, E. 2018. "Show creator looks back at 4 decades of 'Degrassi,' from abortion to Drake." *Yahoo! News*. March 13, 2018. https://ca.news.yahoo.com/show-creator-looks-back-four-decades-degrassi-abortion-drake-165856044.html.
Betancourt, Bianca. 2018. "Here's how TV depicted abortion stories this year." *Broadly*. December 26, 2018. www.vice.com/en_us/article/yw79db/abortions-on-television-2018-black-women.

Condit, Celeste. 1990. *Decoding Abortion Rhetoric: Communicating Social Change.* Chicago, IL: University of Illinois Press.

Dickson, Jeremy. 2017. "Snake's path: Actor Stefan Brogren talks Degrassi's evolution." March 17, 2017. http://kidscreen.com/2017/03/17/snakes-path-actor-stefan-brogren-talks-degrassis-evolution.

Dionne, Evette. 2019. "How TV finally got realistic about abortions." *Bitch Media.* January 22, 2019. www.bitchmedia.org/article/how-television-depicts-abortion.

Doull, Marion, Christabelle Sethna, Evelyne Morrisette, and Caitlin Scott. 2017. "When research is personal and political: Researchers reflect on the study of abortion." In *Abortion*, edited by Shannon Stettner, Kristin Burnett, and Travis Hay. Vancouver: UBC Press: 152–71.

Fisch, Audrey. 2000. "Abortions in TV land." *Salon.* March 8, 2000. www.salon.com/2000/03/08/tv_abortion.

Johnstone, Rachael. 2017. *After Morgentaler.* Vancouver: UBC Press.

Jones, Ellen E. 2017. "The last taboo." *The Guardian.* March 13, 2017. www.theguardian.com/tv-and-radio/2017/mar/13/the-handmaids-tale-scandal-girls-jane-the-virgin-is-tv-ready-to-discuss-abortion.

Lefebvre, Benjamin. 2007. "Adolescence through the looking-glass: Ideology and the represented child in *Degrassi: The Next Generation.*" *Canadian Children's Literature* 33, no. 1: 82–106.

Levine, Elana. 2009. "Crossing the border: Studying Canadian television production." In *Production Studies*, edited by Vicki Mayer, Amanda T. Banks, and John T. Caldwell. New York and London: Routledge: 154–66.

McNamara, Brittney. 2017. "How TV gets abortion wrong." *Teen Vogue.* February 17, 2017. www.teenvogue.com/story/tv-gets-abortion-wrong.

Mohabeer, Ravindra N. 2005. "Changing faces: What happened when *Degrassi* switched to CTV." In *Growing Up Degrassi: Television, Identity and Youth Cultures*, edited by Michele Byers. Toronto: Sumach Press: 96–112.

Montgomery, Kathryn C. 1990. *Target: Prime Time.* Oxford: Oxford University Press.

O'Keeffe, Kevin. 2017. "How abortion on television has changed in the past 55 years." August 2, 2017. www.mic.com/articles/183033/how-abortion-on-television-has-changed-in-the-last-55-years.

Petchesky, Rosalind P. 1987. "Fetal images: The power of visual culture in the politics of reproduction." *Feminist Studies* 13, no. 2: 263–92.

Rankin, Lauren. 2017. "Abortion on TV and in movies is way too dramatic – Here's why." August 16, 2017. www.allure.com/story/abortion-on-tv-and-movies-is-too-dramatic.

Rosenberg, Alyssa. 2015. "TV shows distort which women get abortions – and why they get them." *The Washington Post.* December 15, 2015. www.washingtonpost.com/news/act-four/wp/2015/12/15/tv-shows-distort-which-women-get-abortions-and-why-they-get-them.

Saurette, Paul and Kelly Gordon. 2016. *The Changing Voice of the Anti-Abortion Movement.* Toronto: University of Toronto Press.

Serrao, N. 2017. "Degrassi: Next Class boss breaks down season 4's final moments." *Entertainment Weekly.* http://ew.com/tv/2017/07/10/degrassi-next-class-stephen-stohn-zig-maya.

Sisson, Gretchen. 2017. "From humor to horror: Genre and narrative purpose in abortion stories on American television." *Feminist Media Studies* 19, no. 2: 239–56.

Sisson, Gretchen and Katrina Kimport. 2014. "Telling stories about abortion: Abortion-related plots in American film and television, 1916–2013." *Contraception* 89: 413–18.

———2016. "Facts and fictions: Characters seeking abortion on American television 2005–2014." *Contraception* 93: 446–51.

——— 2017. "Depicting abortion access on American television, 2005–2015." *Feminism & Psychology* 27, no. 1: 56–71.

Stettner, Shannon, Kristin Burnett and Travis Hay, eds. 2017. *Abortion*. Vancouver: UBC Press.

Thompson-Spires, Nafissa. 2007. *Maple in My Syrup, Cheese in My Poutine: Canadian Youth Television in the United States*. PhD diss., Vanderbilt University.

Tinic, Serra. 2009. "Borders of production research: A response to Elana Levine." In *Production Studies*, edited by Vicki Mayer, Amanda T. Banks, and John T. Caldwell. New York and London: Routledge: 167–72.

Part II
Fetal materiality

At the heart of contemporary anti-abortion discourse is the emblematic fetal [handwritten margin note: connection to Doctor forcing Diane to watch puppy videos & have an ultrasound] image produced by photography and ultrasound techniques. This image is envisioned as having the capacity to shock viewers into recognition of the fetus's humanity, and consequently, the immorality and untenability of abortion. For example, the anti-abortion organisation Center for Bio-Ethical Reform funds a travelling exhibition called the "Genocide Awareness Project," consisting of graphic photographs of fetal remains and victims of genocide which has travelled to university and college campuses in Canada and the United States since 1997 (ARCC 2018). The display reimagines genocide through such comparisons as a display titled "Cambodian Killing Fields" (photograph of Cambodian genocide victims) alongside another display titled "American Killing Fields" (photograph of fetal remains). Additionally, the exhibition refigures the language of choice, juxtaposing photographs of fetal remains with those of Black victims of lynching in the United States with the caption "Racial Choice," or of Jewish victims of Nazi Germany with the caption "Religious Choice" (AbortionNo, n.d.). The stated purpose of displaying these images is because "educators properly use shocking imagery to teach about genocide," and seeing photographs of fetal remains in this context of global genocide has the capacity to show viewers that abortion is an "evil so inexpressible that words fail us when we attempt to describe its horror" (Cunningham 2012, 1). As feminist scholars have demonstrated, the image of the fetus's body is presented as ahistorical and outside of social relations; most notably, the fetus is depicted as independent from the person within whose body it resides (Mitchell 2001; Petchesky 1987; Stabile 1992; see also Chapter 1 of this book). In Part II – Fetal materiality, contributors engage with representations of the fetal body produced by both anti-abortion and pro-choice actors. These chapters assist in understanding both contemporary anti-abortion use of the fetal image as well as pro-choice representations of the fetal body that subvert the anti-abortion appropriation of the fetus and compel new interpretations of fetal materiality.

Paul Saurette and Kelly Gordon's *The Changing Voice of the Anti-Abortion Movement* (2015) is a discourse analysis of the communications strategies and rhetoric employed by major Canadian and American anti-abortion organisations from the mid-2000s to the mid-2010s. Through a comprehensive examination of websites, news releases, events, and interviews, they conclude that the common depiction of the anti-abortion movement as male-dominated, religious, focused on changing legislation, anti-woman, and fetal-centric is in fact more accurately a depiction of the American anti-abortion movement in the 1970s and 1980s (2015, 13). They call this depiction the "traditional portrait" of the anti-abortion movement in North America (Saurette and Gordon 2015, xii). In contradistinction, the contemporary anti-abortion movement in national contexts such as Canada is considerably savvier, refashioning anti-abortion arguments as progressive and feminist. It features women as spokespersons, avoids explicitly religious posturing, attempts to change the "culture of abortion," and frequently eschews the well-worn opposition between the rights of the fetus and the rights of the woman (Saurette and Gordon 2015, 316–319). Gordon and Saurette's contribution to this volume, "Representing the cause: the strategic rebranding of the anti-abortion movement in Canada," extends this work through a careful consideration of the "rebranding" strategies of the Canadian anti-abortion movement. Focusing on RightNow, one of the most recent and vocal anti-abortion organisations in Canada, they argue that the "traditional portrait" of the anti-abortion movement is a liability for contemporary activists. Intriguingly, RightNow eclipses the fetus through the argument that abortion harms women, representing both fetus *and* woman as "victims" of abortion.

On May 25, 2018, the Eighth Amendment of the Constitution of Ireland, which recognised "the right to life of the unborn" and prohibited abortion in the Republic of Ireland, was repealed and replaced by the Thirty-Sixth Amendment of the Constitution of Ireland, which included the language "provision may be made by law for the regulation of termination of pregnancy" (Tithe an Oireachtais/Houses of the Oireachtas 2018). The campaigns to retain and repeal the Eighth Amendment were fascinating because they demonstrated attachments to what Saurette and Gordon call the "traditional portrait," but they were also firmly located within the contemporary moment. For example, the "No" campaign centred women's rights and engaged social media techniques to present their position; on the other hand, the compelling narratives presented by the "Yes" campaign about women travelling long distances to have an abortion elsewhere in the UK were firmly situated within current reproductive justice strategies of abortion storytelling. Katherine Side's "Visual realignment? The shifting terrains of anti-abortion strategies in the Republic of Ireland" focuses on the use of images – specifically those that centre the fetus – in the two major "No" campaigns, Save the 8th and Love Both. Side argues that these campaigns are demonstrative of public debates in contemporary post-colonial Ireland. These campaigns are both aligned with and distinguished from the modern tactics of the anti-abortion movement internationally: they deliberately centre women and move away from explicitly religious standpoints, yet they hold on to the fetus as a central compelling image and continue to undermine the decision-making capacities of pregnant people.

Lena Hann and Jeannie Ludlow's "Look like a provider: representing the materiality of the fetus in abortion care work" shifts the emphasis of this section – the fetus – towards representations that support access to abortion. The fetal body is central to abortion clinic practice. And yet, its presence is unnameable in public when predominant arguments for abortion access centre on choice and abandon the fetus to the dense symbolic terrain produced by the visual strategies of anti-abortion activists. Abortion providers have perspicacious insight into fetal tissue, which they encounter and interact with on the levels of medical science and emotional implication on an everyday basis in their clinical work. Medical imaging plays a crucial role in abortion provision, as a tool to assist providers in determining the best way to provide abortion care, and an examination of aborted tissue consisting of fetus, embryo, or zygote is an essential component of abortion for providers, ensuring that the procedure is complete. Patients additionally come to the clinic with questions about fetal development and providers might have limited visual resources, as Parry discusses in Chapter 4. Some patients request to see aborted tissue after their procedure. As Hann and Ludlow note, within the semi-private space of the abortion clinic, important work to reclaim the aborted fetus and honour the possibility of emotional connection to the fetus has been happening for decades (Ludlow 2008, 43–44). Abortion providers' multifaceted understandings of the fetal body are essential to their practice and for addressing the position of the fetus in polarised debates about abortion, limning new possibilities for abortion-positive discourse through refusing erasure of the fetus.

The ossified binary of pro-life and pro-choice emerged out of the crucible of American political debates, particularly as they catalysed around *Roe v. Wade*, and this polarisation has had consequences globally as the primary interpretive lens through which to view abortion. Aurore Yamagata-Montoya's chapter, "Dressing the Mizuko Jizō: materializing the aborted fetus in Japan," considers an object and a ceremony in Japan which have been misinterpreted by Westerners: the Mizuko Jizō, a statuette that is publicly displayed as a protector of the aborted fetus, and the *mizuko kuyō*, a ceremony performed as conciliation to the aborted fetus. The Mizuko Jizō have attracted Western tourists' attention because of their colourful and often cute clothing, but they have also attracted specifically pro-choice Western attention as a public acknowledgement of women's relationship to their aborted fetus that is apparently untinged by shame, silence, and secrecy. Such analyses position *mizuko kuyō* as an example of a successful strategy for coping with grief (Klass and Heath 1997) or even as evidence of feminist influence that has cultivated expanded (though circumscribed) choice in Japan (Harrison 1999, 793). Yamagata-Montoya demonstrates that although American pro-choice and pro-life discourses do emerge in

Japanese understandings of the ritual, they are insufficient frameworks for analysis. She argues that the Mizuko Jizō is the manifestation of the fetus itself in public life, but that this presence cannot be understood solely as an abortion-positive presence. Instead, Yamagata-Montoya offers an analysis of the statuettes and the ritual that locates them in a globalised structure that is shaped primarily by Japanese ideals of the family and womanhood, but also American influence.

"Rattling your rage: humour, provocation, and the SisterSerpents," written by Claire L. Kovacs, is the final chapter of this section and returns to the anti-abortion use of the fetal image. This time, however, the anti-abortion fetal image is used as a weapon to combat the hypocrisy of anti-abortion activists who espouse their respect for women while advocating for legislation and cultural change that undermine women's bodily sovereignty, a subject taken up later in Chapter 15 by Jennifer Scuro. Kovacs's chapter examines the art practice of the SisterSerpents, an anonymous feminist art collective in Chicago active from 1989 until 1998 through archival and interview research. The SisterSerpents formed as a creative response to several feminist issues including access to abortion, and together they mounted exhibitions and performances, wrote public letters for the press, organised panels and community discussions, created a zine, and used guerrilla-style tactics to convey their messages to the public, particularly the American religious right. Their collective work used humour and anger to oppose misogyny and dismantle patriarchy, and this chapter looks at their notorious exhibit *Rattling Our Rage* (1990). *Rattling Our Rage* featured the fetus as a central character, a decision aimed at exposing the techniques of the anti-abortion movement as cynical exploitation of the fetus as well as challenging mainstream pro-choice advocates to similarly engage in candid conflict with the strategies of their anti-abortion opponents. Their actions were infused by righteous anger which enabled direct confrontation with the anti-abortion use of the fetal image. The SisterSerpents' tactics were located in the history of anger within feminist movements (Lorde 1984), and also prescient of the surge of feminist rage as a powerful response to misogyny and racism in the contemporary moment (Chemaly 2019; Cooper 2019; Traister 2018).

References

AbortionNo. n.d. "Genocide Awareness Project – An Initiative Against Injustice." Last accessed January 16, 2020. www.abortionno.org/college-campus-outreach-gap.

Abortion Rights Coalition of Canada/Coalition pour la droit à l'avortement au Canada (ARCC). 2018. "Analyzing the Genocide Awareness Project and the Use of Graphic Imagery by Anti-Choice Groups." Position Paper #72. Vancouver, British Columbia. Last accessed January 16, 2020. www.arcc-cdac.ca/postionpapers/72-Genocide-Awareness-Project.pdf.

Chemaly, Soraya. 2019. *Rage Becomes Her: The Power of Women's Anger*. New York: Atria.

Cooper, Brittney. 2019. *Eloquent Rage: A Black Feminist Discovers Her Superpower*. New York: St. Martin's Press.

Cunningham, Gregg. 2012. "Why Abortion Is Genocide." *Center for Bio-Ethical Reform*. Last accessed January 16, 2020. www.abortionno.org/wp-content/uploads/2012/06/whyabortionisgenocide.pdf.

Harrison, Elizabeth G. 1999. "Strands of Complexity: The Emergence of *Mizuko Kuyō* in Postwar Japan." *Journal of the American Academy of Religion* 67, no. 4: 768–796.

Klass, Dennis and Amy Olwen Heath. 1997. "Grief and Abortion: *Mizuko Kuyo*, The Japanese Ritual Resolution." *OMEGA: Journal of Death and Dying* 34, no. 1: 1–14.

Lorde, Audre. 1984. "The Uses of Anger." In *Sister/Outsider: Essays and Speeches*, 124–133. Berkeley, CA: Crossing Press.

Ludlow, Jeannie. 2008. "Sometimes, It's a Child *and* a Choice: Toward an Embodied Abortion Praxis." *NWSA Journal* 20, no. 1: 26–50.

Mitchell, Lisa M. 2001. *Baby's First Picture: Ultrasound and the Politics of Fetal Subjects*. Toronto: University of Toronto Press.

Petchesky, Rosalind Pollack. 1987. "Fetal Images: The Power of Visual Culture in the Politics of Reproduction." *Feminist Studies* 13, no. 2: 263–292.

Saurette, Paul and Kelly Gordon. 2015. *The Changing Voice of the Anti-Abortion Movement: The Rise of "Pro-Woman" Rhetoric in Canada and the United States*. Toronto: University of Toronto Press.

Stabile, Carol. 1992. "Shooting the Mother: Fetal Photography and the Politics of Disappearance." *Camera Obscura* 10, no. 1: 178–205.

Tithe an Oireachtais/Houses of the Oireachtas. 2018. "Thirty-Sixth Amendment of the Constitution Act 2018." Last accessed January 16, 2020. www.oireachtas.ie/en/bills/bill/2018/29.

Traister, Rebecca. 2018. *Good and Mad: The Revolutionary Power of Women's Anger*. New York: Simon & Schuster.

6 Representing the cause

The strategic rebranding of the anti-abortion movement in Canada

Kelly Gordon and Paul Saurette

Given the well-worn tracks that the abortion debate has followed for the last 50 years, and the fact that many of the same representational and rhetorical tendencies continue to dominate the contemporary abortion debate in the United States (particularly in the anti-abortion movement where discourse is, if anything, ever more hyperbolic), many observers assume that the Canadian anti-abortion movement is best understood as a country mouse cousin of its American counterparts: smaller, less vocal, and less influential, but otherwise similar in its beliefs and organisational, representational, and rhetorical strategies.

Building on our previous work, this chapter argues the advocacy strategies of the Canadian anti-abortion movement (which include organisational tactics as well as representational and rhetorical techniques) differ quite substantially from the traditional portrait of the movement (Saurette and Gordon 2013, 2016; Gordon and Saurette 2018). We begin by offering a brief overview of the dominant identity of the anti-abortion movement in Canada and the "brand liability" it has become for anti-abortion activists (Smith and Saunders 1990). The second section outlines a few examples of the main ways that the Canadian anti-abortion movement has sought to rebrand in response. We then offer a more detailed case study of RightNow – one the most recent new anti-abortion organisations in Canada – before offering a few concluding remarks.

Traditional anti-abortion advocacy in Canada and its contemporary challenges

Over the last decade, we've had a chance to ask many different groups of Canadians (including professional political observers, journalists, students, abortion rights advocates, medical providers, and academics, as well as the general public) to describe their impression of the anti-abortion movement and its advocacy techniques. The responses we get almost unanimously fit into what we've called the "traditional portrait" of the anti-abortion movement (Saurette and Gordon 2016).

We've termed this the traditional portrait not only because it is so dominant a representation in our culture, but also because it is a relatively accurate picture of certain, highly defining, moments of anti-abortion activism in Canada and in the US, for it does convey many of the important characteristics of the anti-abortion movement that emerged in the 1970s and became so vocal and public in Canada in the 1980s (and which have continued to grow in strength in the US to this day). In particular, the traditional portrait accurately highlights the ways in which, throughout the 1980s, the anti-abortion movement in Canada was: (i) motivated and sustained organisationally, philosophically, and discursively by religious organisations and arguments; (ii) led almost exclusively by men; (iii) largely fetal-centric in its explicit argumentation and imagery, and (iv) characterised by deep strains of anti-woman tones and rhetoric (Saurette and Gordon 2016). Indeed, the vast majority of Canadians continue to define the anti-abortion "brand" according to these characteristics.

However, there is good reason to believe that this brand represents a significant challenge for the contemporary anti-abortion movement in Canada – and thus is an important element of the representational politics of the Canadian abortion debate. As any competent strategic brand manager (whether in politics, retail, or social movements) knows, a strong brand powerfully influences the size of your actual and potential market (and thus success). In today's hyper-charged communications environment, a strong brand that resonates immediately with the existing values/preferences of its audience will gain supporters/customers; a strong brand that is actively dissonant with existing values/preferences will likely repel/lose support; and a weak brand that leaves an audience indifferent won't have much effect. The challenge for the anti-abortion movement in Canada is that the traditional portrait is a very strong brand that is very much dissonant with wide swathes of the audience they need to drum up support for their cause.

First off, on a concrete practical level the Canadian anti-abortion movement lacks both a pre-existing, large-scale base of steady support and a well-organised "political arm" (Golob 2016). Therefore, unlike the US context, "preaching to the choir" does not result in significant mobilisation gains in Canada. Moreover, overall public support for abortion rights is much higher (75–80% in most polls) and more broadly distributed than in the US. This, in part, has meant that more than 30 years after the *Morgentaler* decision, abortion rights are deeply enshrined in existing legal precedence and the background political status quo (with some exceptions). All of these facts mean that, unlike in the US – where the size and mobilisation of the anti-abortion base mean that traditional branding combined with traditional and innovative legislative and legal strategies have allowed them to make significant gains – any progress for the Canadian anti-abortion movement requires a massive influx of new supporters.

If anti-abortion activists face a much steeper hill than their American brethren in terms of their starting point, the Canadian movement also faces the problem that its overall brand, fundamental values, and traditional representational/rhetorical strategies are deeply out of step with the broader cultural/philosophical/values landscape of Canadian voters. While the traditional anti-abortion brand relies heavily on explicit appeals to religion, far fewer Canadians than Americans are religious; those that are religious are comparatively less intensely religious; and the religious community in Canada is much less politicised and politically organised (Farney 2012; Malloy 2009). Moreover, whereas the traditional brand is defined by fetal-centric arguments, several key Supreme Court of Canada decisions explicitly invalidated arguments in favour of implicit fetal personhood and fetal rights in the 1980s and 1990s, and the idea of fetal-personhood and rights has failed to become entrenched in broader Canadian values. Finally, while the traditional brand brings to mind images of exclusively male leadership and anti-woman tones/argumentation, after 40 years of growing gender equality, even mainstream Canadian conservatism has embraced gender equality (rhetorically speaking, at least) in ways that render highly problematic those traditional visual images and tones.

In Canada, then, a basic brand analysis would suggest that the traditional anti-abortion brand is likely to be ineffective in driving new support today. Since brands that embody deeply dissonant characteristics not only fail to build new support but can actually create a powerful *affective* repulsion that dramatically reduces the potential pool of new supporters (both in the moment and in the future), it is likely that the traditional anti-abortion brand identity is actually a major barrier to success for the anti-abortion movement in Canada today. Understanding the impact of the traditional representation of the anti-abortion brand identity, then, is an important element in understanding why the anti-abortion movement has been so ineffective in its advocacy over the last 25 years.

Rebranding the movement: "pro-woman," anti-abortion

If one believes that representational politics like branding matter, and that the traditional anti-abortion brand is deeply counter-productive in Canada today, an obvious question emerges: has the anti-abortion movement done anything to address this brand challenge? Over the last decade we have explored this question by systematically analysing the advocacy strategies of the contemporary anti-abortion movement in Canada, across a wide variety of media and event settings (Saurette and Gordon 2013, 2016; Gordon and Saurette 2018). The short answer is a definitive yes. We won't rehearse all those findings here. However, we do want to note several ways in which the anti-abortion movement has tried to address its brand challenges by changing its self-representation.

First, the movement has seen the creation of many new organisations that offer a very different brand platform. Established brands are like old houses – they are often solid and have many advantages like high name recognition and loyal followers. But renovating an established brand is a bit like renovating an old house – it takes a ton of work, and you don't know what you're going to find in the walls or exactly how much you're going to be able to change. For if people have a strong impression of a brand, they also have strong and deeply embedded, often subconscious, assumptions about what it stands for. Tweaking a brand here or there is sometimes possible, but doing a full-scale brand U-turn is often about as successful as the Titanic's inaugural trans-Atlantic voyage. Thus if the new idea/design is too radical a departure, brand consultants, like contractors, will often recommend simply building a new brand/house rather than trying to force-fit the old into the new. Of course, this isn't always feasible. But when the brand in question is a collective brand for a social movement made up of a variety of organisations, sometimes it is easier to simply create new organisations that can act as representational launching pads for the new brand, unhindered by the historic brand identifications that mark the older institutions.

We have found significant evidence that this is precisely what the anti-abortion movement in Canada has been doing. First, our analysis has shown that activists within the anti-abortion movement have engaged in significant intra-movement conversations about the failures of the historical anti-abortion movement and the need for profound change in the (self-)representational brand and rhetorical advocacy tactics employed by the movement (Saurette and Gordon 2016). Second, and clearly linked to this, over the last 15 years there has been a proliferation of new and vocal anti-abortion groups in Canada (perhaps most notably We Need a Law, the Canadian Centre for Bioethical Reform (CCBR), and the blog ProWomanProLife (PWPL)) that self-consciously represent themselves in very different ways than the traditional organisations. This influx, moreover, has pushed older, more established anti-abortion groups to undertake new strategic investments. According to Campaign Life Coalition vice chair, Jeff Gunnarson, while the organisation was originally founded in 1983, they have "upped [their] game" over the last decade, with membership doubling from 100,000 to 200,000 (Kingston 2019). Similarly, the Edmonton-based Wilberforce Project (previously Alberta Pro-Life) underwent a rebranding in 2012 in order to actively recruit more anti-abortion electoral candidates in the province.

The movement also seems to have bought into the idea that it needs to play down its religious identity if it hopes to persuade mainstream Canadian voters. Amazingly, in our large-scale analysis of the movement, less than 2% of the public discourse of the contemporary anti-abortion movement in Canada contains explicit or implicit references to religion or religious ideas/sources (Saurette and Gordon 2016). This doesn't mean that the movement has eschewed its religious motivations/foundations, nor that it has decoupled from it. Rather, it means that the movement has decided to sanitise those types of appeals as a way of moving away from its traditional brand identity as deeply religious.

If the movement has increasingly sought to self-represent as less explicitly religious, it has also sought to very actively rebrand in ways that eliminate the idea that it is led by old men, fetal-centric in argumentation, and anti-woman in tone. The movement as a whole has started to invest heavily in youth recruitment and training to create a new generation of anti-abortion activists in Canada. For example, the organisation National Campus Life Network (NCLN) "equips pro-life students across the country for campus life advocacy and network[s] them with each other and the broader pro-life movement" (NCLN n.d.). The group holds an annual symposium for high school and university students, is very active on Twitter and other social media platforms, and has partnered with Toronto Right to Life to create a handbook for high school anti-abortion clubs. On one hand, this has a very practical goal of creating the next generation of anti-abortion advocates. But it also has a representational goal – of allowing the movement to represent itself as driven by youthful idealism, rather than old prohibitionism.

The movement has also made significant changes to its gendered representational politics by attempting to radically transform its public face. Shifting its image away from that of a regressive, conservative movement seeking to control women's bodies and choices (something that does not resonate well in the contemporary Canadian landscape) and rebrand as modern and pro-woman, anti-abortion organisations have adopted the strategy of literally foregrounding women visually as the spokespeople and leaders of the movement. As ProWomanProLife founder Andrea Mrozek suggests:

> the beauty of being a woman who is pro-life is that it is fairly easy to annoy my opponents simply by showing up. I don't need to say all that much, when combating the anachronistic notion that "abortion is a woman's right." I simply need to stand there (with shoes on, outside the kitchen!) and ask – hey, why is that self-evident?
>
> (Mrozek 2009)

Indeed, the movement is actively cultivating a network of young, telegenic women who will be available for media commentary at a moment's notice (Hayward 2018), and today it is very rare for a male anti-abortion activist to speak publicly to the Canadian media (perhaps with the exception of the annual March for Life). The result has been that women have increasingly become the public face of the movement not only in its self-representation, but also in the bulk of the journalistic coverage of the movement since the early 2010s (Gerson 2015; Kingston 2019).

This pro-woman anti-abortion shift in visual representation has been accompanied by a significant reworking of the movement's argumentative and rhetorical techniques. Our analysis revealed that while fetal-centric arguments (often assumed to be not only the dominant, but essentially the only, argumentative strategy of anti-abortion advocates) were present in

38% of its discourse, what we term a new "abortion-harms-women" argument was much more significant (present in 43% of the discourse, and even more dominant when one analyses the amount of space each argument is actually given) (Saurette and Gordon 2013, 2016). This shift is important because these two types of arguments represent very different logics. Whereas fetal-centric arguments seek to persuade the audience that abortion is wrong because it ends the life of the *fetus* (who is cast as the victim, with the mother usually portrayed as the villain), the abortion-harms-women argument suggests that abortion is wrong because of the psychological, physical, and emotional devastation it inflicts on *women* (making both the fetus and the woman the victim ... and thus eliminating the traditional anti-woman tones). This shift towards "pro-woman" argumentation is reinforced by a variety of subtler rhetorical and representational techniques as well – ranging from the redefinition and co-optation of feminist and progressive identities to values such as equality and choice, issues such as domestic abuse, epistemological perspectives, and metaphorical tones and narratives (Saurette and Gordon 2016).

The new movement: RightNow

If the bird's-eye-view portrait above suggests a rather different contemporary anti-abortion movement than offered by the traditional portrait, a case study analysis of one of the newest anti-abortion organisations (RightNow) offers a ground-level view of the ways that one of the new players is seeking to rebrand and reposition (representationally and rhetorically, at least) the anti-abortion movement today.

The need to rebrand

The conditions of emergence of this organisation highlight a generational divide within the movement that is expressed in an active fight over both specific advocacy tactics and the broader question of whether/how the movement needs to rebrand. Although RightNow emerged on the anti-abortion scene in 2015, its co-founders have much longer histories within the movement. Alissa Golob and Scott Hayward, both in their early 30s, worked together at Campaign Life Coalition (CLC) – arguably, Canada's most established and most influential anti-abortion organisation. On their own telling, Golob and Hayward left CLC and founded RightNow because they believed that there was a significant gap in explicitly political- and electoral-oriented anti-abortion advocacy (creating a situation where there is virtually no political support for anti-abortion legislation) and because, in their view, traditional anti-abortion organisations were stuck in the past, simply continuing "to do the same things they did 30 years ago ... [failing] to acknowledge the failures they spearheaded resulting in a lack of any type of legislation" (Golob 2017). RightNow was founded to "help guide pro-lifers to win nominations. To win elections. To build a pro-life, political capital. And above all, to pass pro-life legislation both provincially and federally" (Hayward 2018). Since 2015, RightNow has been active in seven provincial elections and several riding nomination races, and vowed to target 50 "'winnable' ridings" in the 2019 federal election (Kingston 2019).

While relations between the founders of RightNow and their prior employer CLC were civil at first, their relationship quickly deteriorated. According to Golob, CLC threatened to file a lawsuit to stop Golob and Hayward from creating their new organisation (Golob 2017). The two organisations then clashed over their respective endorsements for the 2017 federal Conservative leadership. RightNow endorsed Andrew Scheer as the best political bet while CLC actively supported Brad Trost, a militant anti-abortion activist but a long shot for the leadership. Their disagreement would eventually culminate in a very public confrontation between former MP Maurice Vellacott (who accused Golob's strategy of being a misguided and impossible fantasy of political success (Vellacott 2017)) and Golob (who returned fire by accusing Vellacott of "mud-slinging to anyone who would listen" and claiming that CLC did little else than selling Easter lilies and calling it political influence (Golob 2017)).

These interactions are a particularly vivid illustration of a movement struggling with the question of if, and if so how, it should rebrand – as well as the costs of not doing so. Vellacott, the CLC's leadership, and Trost's interventions all reinforce the traditional brand. They are religious, socially conservative men in their 50s and 60s. The majority of their discourse invoked familiar tropes that buttressed those perceptions – including accusing Scheer of "cav[ing] to pressure from homosexual activists and their media allies, to abandon his principles on marriage and the natural family" (Vellacott 2017). Perhaps even more notable is that his letter was infused with what many would consider to be a condescending and patronising tone towards Alissa Golob, a woman who was in her late 20s at the time. In his letter, Vellacott refers to RightNow as "Alissa Golob's friends," and accuses them of being half-clever, drinking the Kool-Aid, and not knowing anything about how politics actually work. This type of dismissive and trivialising tone by the old stewards of the brand towards a young, successful woman (who has a long list of professional and anti-abortion credentials) only serves to reinforce the traditional portrait of anti-abortion activism – the costs of which Golob understands very well.

Rebranding religion

RightNow also embodies the fascinating ways in which different organisations within the movement are seeking to rebrand/represent the role of religion in the movement's identity, foundational beliefs, and public discourse. On the one hand, founders Hayward and Golob grew up in religious homes, with Golob attending her first anti-abortion rally at 12 years old (Kingston 2019). Throughout her time as youth coordinator at CLC, Golob openly and regularly invoked her religious affiliations at public demonstrations and anti-abortion conferences and workshops (authors' observations). On the other hand, and much like the rest of the movement, RightNow does not use religion to ground their arguments or dictate their strategic approach. In fact, Golob at times rejects the traditional notion that religion even has a place in anti-abortion activism and rhetoric. In her response to Maurice Vellacott, Golob writes, "if you think the best way forward is to do what you've always done for the last 30 years and let God take care of the rest, then our organization isn't for you" (Golob 2017). Here Golob makes clear that anti-abortion strategy should not be left up to God.

However, unlike some of the other new anti-abortion actors who have completely sanitised their public discourse from religion (Saurette and Gordon 2016, 92–117), RightNow seems to suggest that there is a third brand positioning on religion that is potentially even more effective. For RightNow invokes religion, but does so very strategically. On their webpage entitled, "Why we are different," for example, RightNow proclaims that "it is only through a diverse and inclusive supporter base, that we can reach Canadians of all ethnicities and religious and non-religious affiliations" (n.d., 2). Why this somewhat complicated positioning? Given that Golob and Hayward clearly come from Christian backgrounds, why don't they either just foreground that, or simply jettison religion since that would seem to be the most politically expedient thing to do? Why the explicit articulation of a multicultural conception of religiosity?

It seems to be based on the assumption that even though the traditional fundamentalist religious identity is a liability for the contemporary movement, having a religious identity nestled within a tolerant pluralist framework might be even more of an asset than whitewashing religion altogether. One part of this centres on the idea of adopting religious diversity as core to its vision, which seems to be based on the belief that this rebranding will allow the organisation to resonate with a hitherto untapped segment of Canadian voters: non-Christian religious communities that haven't been brought into the anti-abortion fold. According to RightNow,

> [t]he good news is that over 50% of Canadians want some sort of restriction on abortion. The bad news? Most of these Canadians don't look or think like us … This creates a bubble for us, in which we are not able to connect with other[s].
>
> (Hayward 2016)

For RightNow, building successful political support requires that the movement reach out beyond its traditional Christian base and cultivate the political support of other religious groups including "Muslims, Sikhs, Hindus, [and] atheists" (Hayward 2016). Rather than shy away from religion in public, as many activists might now suggest, RightNow is rebranding the religious orientation of the anti-abortion movement to make it "inclusive, diverse and ... here to win" by also courting the support of non-Christian religious communities (RightNow n.d.).

The only way this strategy would really work, however, is if it can avoid simultaneously offending and repelling the non- (or less) religious swathe of Canadian voters. Crucial to this, we suspect, is RightNow's belief that by *recasting* and *rebranding* their style of religion *in a pluralist and non-fundamentalist value framework*, non-religious Canadians will primarily hear the pluralist and multi-cultural tones of the framing, read it as quite different than the old fundamentalist anti-abortion religious positions of the past, and thus, at the very minimum, not treat it as something that immediately repels them from the anti-abortion position. Particularly in a context in which other progressive-sounding rhetorical appeals can also be employed (for example, when Golob, drawing on the well-worn, but still effective, representation of the movement as a civil rights issue, claims that when you are an activist "you start feeling like a true human-rights warrior, Martin Luther King-style" (RightNow 2016)).

(Young) women out front

We can also see significant evidence of "pro-woman" rebranding in RightNow's discourse. For example, on a webpage entitled, "Rep the movement," there are a variety of memes and posters that supporters are encouraged to share on their own social media platforms. One poster features the photo of a clearly distressed woman with the statement "62.2% of women said they were unable to forgive themselves after having an abortion." Another similar image was accompanied by the quote "59% of women said they felt a part of them died after having an abortion" followed by the hashtag #abortionhurtswomen. This messaging has been a consistent theme in Golob's own media strategy as well. In a 2019 interview with Macleans, for example, Golob argued, "[a]bortion is anti-woman ... It tells women that having children is a weakness, that what makes them unique is a problem" (Kingston 2019). She took this feminist messaging even further, suggesting that "[e]qual pay, flex time, and proper child care are needed ... so women don't need to choose between being parents and having a career" (Kingston 2019).

The representational politics of rebranding the movement as youthful and gender equal/woman friendly is even more evident in the public performative characteristics of the organisation. Golob had been an advocate of visually rebranding the anti-abortion movement as younger and pro-woman well before founding RightNow. At both the 2012 and 2013 March for Life youth conferences, for example, she encouraged youth to get involved in the movement because "abortionists really hate you when you are young and you are pro-life" and advised activists: "when [you] talk about abortion, talk about the psychological harm of abortion on women" (March for Life Youth Conference 2012, 2013; authors' observations). Moreover, she explicitly highlighted the rebranding importance of this – suggesting that the more loud and proud anti-abortion women there were in the public sphere, the more it would do the work of eroding the damaging and "fabricated stereotype" that "we are hateful, judgmental, and spray women with holy water" (March for Life Youth Conference 2012; authors' field notes).

The division of labour between the two co-founders of RightNow is also telling. Golob is very clearly the public face of the organisation, with Hayward remaining in the background. For example, until his widely circulated interview where he asserts that Andrew Scheer committed to a free vote on any anti-abortion legislation, we could not find one televised interview with Hayward (Browne 2019). In contrast, Alissa Golob does virtually all media interviews and public advocacy on behalf of RightNow. Since 2016, she has been featured in at least a dozen journalistic profiles of the movement, including on ViceNews, CBC, RadioCanada, and CTV, as well as many other religious publications (RightNow n.d.).

The fact that Golob is a young, well-spoken, and telegenic woman has very clearly contributed to the pro-woman branding of RightNow – with journalists often making explicit what the visuals are designed to implicitly suggest. Journalist Anne Kingston's piece is typical of this, noting that Golob "represents [the movement's] new face: an eloquent woman who argues that 'abortion culture' denies women 'choice' by pressuring them to abort, and does it with the sort of certitude that makes her a natural for CBC panels" (2019). It is not surprising, then, that during the Saskatchewan party Convention, RightNow worked with We Need a Law and the Saskatchewan Pro-Life Association to ensure that there were young, female, pro-life speakers in the break-out session and the plenary session to speak for anti-abortion policies (RightNow n.d.).

Conclusion

Perhaps the key contribution of this chapter is to show that the representational politics of the anti-abortion movement in Canada are not confined to the various rhetorical and representational techniques it uses to directly persuade its audience, but also include its most basic processes of self-portrayal. Not only is this crucial to understanding how the contemporary Canadian anti-abortion movement is championing its cause today. It also demonstrates that the new "pro-woman" rhetorical positioning we have traced is not a superficial re-working of marketing slogans, but similarly defines the movement's most basic processes of identity performance – and is thus a development that potentially holds significant implications for the struggle for abortion rights and access in the future.

References

Browne, Rachel. 2019. "Anti-abortion activists are planning to win 50 ridings for their cause in the upcoming federal election." *Global News*, August 31, 2019. https://globalnews.ca/news/5799732/canada-anti-abortion-activitists.

Farney, James Harold. 2012. *Social Conservatives and Party Politics in Canada and the United States*. Toronto: University of Toronto Press.

Gerson, Jen. 2015. "With social conservatism seemingly spent as a political force, its adherents forced to rethink their strategy." *National Post*, January 2, 2019. https://nationalpost.com/news/politics/with-social-conservatism-seemingly-spent-as-a-political-force-its-adherents-forced-to-rethink-their-strategy.

Golob, Alissa. 2016. "Why I quit my job." *Alissa Golob Personal Website*, February 2, 2016. www.alissagolob.com/why-i-quit-my-job.

——— 2017. "My response to Brad Trost and Maurice Vellacott." *Alissa Golob Personal Website*, April 6, 2017. www.alissagolob.com/my-response-to-brad-trost-maurice-vellacott.

Gordon, Kelly and Paul Saurette. 2018. "The Future of Pro-Choice Discourse in Canada." In *Abortion: History, Politics, and Reproductive Justice After Morgentaler*, edited by Shannon Stettner, Kristin Burnett, and Travis Hay. Vancouver: UBC Press, 265–291.

Hayward, Scott. 2016. "What pro-life Canadians can learn from the American election." *RightNow*, November 15, 2016. www.itstartsrightnow.ca/what_pro_life_canadians_can_learn_from_the_american_election.

——— 2018. "More pro-life MPPs than Liberals? Yes please." *RightNow*, June 10, 2018. www.itstartsrightnow.ca/blog.

Kingston, Anne. 2019. "How Canada's growing anti-abortion movement plans to swing the next federal election. *Macleans*, September 12, 2019. www.macleans.ca/politics/how-canadas-growing-anti-abortion-movement-plans-to-swing-the-next-federal-election.

Malloy, Jonathan. 2009. "Bush/Harper? Canadian and American Evangelical Politics Compared." *American Review of Canadian Studies* 39, no. 4: 352–363.

March for Life Youth Conference. May 11, 2012. Hamptons Inn, Ottawa, ON.

March for Life Youth Conference. May 10, 2013. Hamptons Inn, Ottawa, ON.

Mrozek, Andrea. 2009. "Running low in the sympathy department." *ProWomanProLife*, June 19, 2009. www.prowomanprolife.org.

NCLC. n.d. "About us." *National Campus Life Network*. www.ncln.ca.

RightNow. n.d. "About." *RightNow*. www.itstartsrightnow.ca/about.

——— 2016. "I'm sick of losing." *RightNow*, August 22, 2016. www.itstartsrightnow.ca/i_m_sick_of_losing.

Saurette, Paul and Kelly Gordon. 2013. "Arguing abortion: The new anti-abortion discourse in Canada." *Canadian Journal of Political Science / Revue Canadienne de Science Politique* 46, no. 1: 157–185.

——— 2016. *The Changing Voice of the Anti-Abortion Movement: The Rise of "Pro-Woman" Rhetoric in Canada and the United States*. Toronto: University of Toronto Press. Accessed online: www.desliris.ca/ID/451189.

Smith, Gareth and John Saunders. 1990. "The application of marketing to British politics." *Journal of Marketing Management* 5, no. 3: 295–306.

Vellacott, Maurice. 2017. "An important message from Maurice Vellacott." *Campaign Life Coalition*. www.facebook.com/CampaignLifeCoalition/photos/a.350920084948330/1556749971031996/?type=3&theater.

7 Visual realignment?

The shifting visual terrains of anti-abortion strategies in the Republic of Ireland

Katherine Side

In 2018, a visual battle was waged on the streetscapes in Ireland over the 8th Amendment. Inserted in Ireland's Constitution, *Bunreacht na hÉireann*, by public referendum in 1983, the 8th Amendment guaranteed equal rights to "life of the mother and the unborn" (Irish Statute Book [1937] 1983). Its interpretation prohibited abortion and necessitated travel to access abortion services.[1] Advocates opposed the law domestically, and then internationally, in supra-national judicial bodies and conventions (de Londras and Markicevic 2018, 91; Field 2018). In 2012, Ireland was required by the European Court of Human Rights to clarify the law. The government's response was to restrict the law further until a subsequently elected government began a process of reform involving citizen deliberation, parliamentary consideration, and a public referendum.[2]

Those who sought to retain the legal status quo embraced claims about Ireland's "collective humility, [gendered] modesty, and discipline" (Free and Scully 2018, 310). Those who sought to repeal it supported legal liberalization and distance from the country's state–church alliance. Both sides expressed their views in public campaigns. On May 25, 2018, a majority public referendum vote (66.4 per cent with 56.7 per cent voter turnout) repealed the 8th Amendment (Elections Ireland 2018). It was replaced in January 2019 with legislation and clinical guidance (Houses of the Oireachtas 2018; Institute of Obstetricians and Gynaecologists 2018).

Visual discourses in abortion are examined extensively (Parkes 1999; Hopkins, Zeedyk, and Raitt 2005; Firth 2009; Saurette and Gordon 2015; Jones 2017). I analyse the visual rhetorical strategies, including the reproduction, circulation, and display of select print visual images, in Ireland's No (retain) campaign to better understand political and communicative strategies directed at policy makers.[3] Failing to understand communicative strategies leads to possible policy erosion, typical in post-legislative periods, and minimizes the significance of legal change (Askola 2018). Analysing visual posters from two No campaigns, Save the 8th and Love Both, I demonstrate and explain the emergence of a contextually specific form of strategic visual realignment in Ireland. Observed already in Canada, the United States, and Italy, visual alignment shifts campaigning away from religious viewpoints, away from male leadership, and towards women's leadership and recognition of women's decision-making. In some contexts, visual realignment has also included shifts away from the public display of fetal-centric images (Saurette and Gordon 2017; Duerksen and Lawson 2017; Avanza 2018). Visual realignment strategies in Ireland have moved away from religious viewpoints and they include women's voices and leadership. They assume women are decision-makers about abortion. However, they also distrust pregnant people to make good decisions about their own bodies. They maintain the use of fetal-centric visual discourses and they mobilize heteroactivist organizing defined as the assertion of "the primacy of heterosexual, monogamous, and appropriately gendered marriage" and expressions of "ideological resistance" to undermine liberal laws and policies (Browne and Nash 2017, 2019, 1).[4]

Campaigning for No: Save the 8th and Love Both

Ireland's No campaigns had a visible public presence in the 2018 referendum. Two prominent groups, Save the 8th and Love Both, organized separately but sharing a central Dublin address and overlapping memberships, were both coordinated by the Roman Catholic church-affiliated Iona Institute for Religion and Society (Field 2018). Their strategies included poster and billboard campaigns, marches and rallies, celebrity endorsements, door-to-door canvassing, bus tours and roadshows, social media and video campaigning, networking and social media apps, storytelling, theatrics and street performances, consumer-oriented paraphernalia, and participation in national debates. When their intended widespread use of social media campaigning was thwarted by concerns about foreign involvement and investment and by restrictions imposed by social media giants Google and Facebook, they re-focused their efforts on poster and billboard campaigns (O'Brien 2018; O'Loughlin 2018).[5] Postering is widely used and regarded as a valuable campaign tool in referendum campaigns in Ireland. John McGuirk, conservative commentator, media advisor, and (former) communications director for Save the 8th, said, "postering helped us frame the debate … the voices on the radio match the slogans on the posters and the leaflets coming through the door. There's a great message consistency" (Leahy 2018). The No side was characterized in the media as "well-organized and well-funded" and "committed," which translated into an early lead in opinion polls (Edwards 2018; Leahy 2018).

Save the 8th was the official No campaign and was a successor to the Pro-Life Amendment Campaign (PLAC) that proposed the insertion of the 1983 amendment in the constitution (Field 2018).[6] Save the 8th operated as an umbrella organization and drew support from approximately 140 international and domestic groups (Field 2018, 620). Adopting the slogan, "Save Lives, Save the 8th," campaigners positioned themselves as the protectors of vulnerable children, women, medical practitioners, and Ireland (Browne and Nash 2020). Their main message was that the government's proposed *General Scheme* for legal abortion was "too extreme" (Department of Health 2018; Field 2018, 620). The campaign strategy favoured "simple messages" that could be "driven into people's minds" and its communications director claimed that factual information and figures, presented early, could serve as benchmarks against which all other claims were measured (Bardon 2018). Campaign posters emphasized: saving lives ("save lives, save the 8th"); protecting the disabled ("#abortiondiscriminates"); reducing harm ("abortion hurts women"); protecting the public from elected politicians ("don't give politicians total control"); and supporting patriarchal protection ("men protect lives").[7] The veracity of campaign figures and claims, when fact-checked, sometimes proved controversial (Loughlin and Ó Cionnaith 2019).

Love Both's campaign claimed to be a "nation-wide movement working to protect the life of all unborn children" (Love Both n.d.). It was characterized, by the Irish media, as "not the main group calling for a No vote," but it had a visible presence nonetheless (Baker 2018). Its bright-pink brand was intentionally continuous, visually and ideologically, with the No campaign in the 2015 Marriage Equality referendum (Browne and Nash 2020). Its messages were directed specifically at pregnant women and questioned their decision-making ability and discouraged them from travelling (Baker 2018; *The Guardian* 2018).

In the Save the 8th poster shown in Figure 7.1, the infant's startled expression aligns with text about an alleged incongruity: the visual punctum is between the image of the live infant and the suggested gestational limit for

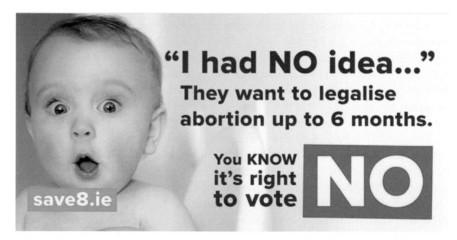

Figure 7.1 I had NO idea...

Source: Photograph from *The Nopebook* online feminist lifestyle magazine, May 24, 2018. www.thenopebook.com/activism/love-both-propaganda-irish-referendum.

legal abortion. This image was most likely purchased from a web-based stock bank of images for this specific purpose (Curran 2019). Stock images, often conservative, are intended to raise little objection; however, the image becomes contentious when it is aligned with the poster's text (Curran 2019). Combined, the text and image infer the infant's dependency, and by virtue of this, its vulnerability. However, its dependency and vulnerability are contradicted by the depiction of an autonomous infant, pictured entirely separated from a caregiver, with the "ability to communicate and interact" (Mattalucci 2012, 109; Ntontis and Hopkins 2018). In this instance, the ability to communicate also includes the ability to pass judgement on others' actions. Surprise and disbelief, expressed visually by the infant, are expected to transfer to viewers. The image and text link the infant and the six-month reference to a negotiated aspect of the referendum discourse. It reflects an agreement made by the Yes and No campaigns to use the six-month gestational marker as a common marker to reference scientific lexicon for fetal viability (McGee 2018). Visually, image and message are linked to Ireland through its adherence to agreement that is specific to Ireland's referendum, by the indication of a country code (.ie), and by the kelly-green colour brand which deviates from Save the 8th's red and white brand. The white-skinned infant also depicts a particular view of Irishness. Fact checking by a press reporter, Sarah Bardon, concluded that the poster's message was "misleading" (Bardon 2018). The proposed *Bill* (now enforced in the *Act*) always prohibited abortions when a fetus reached viability (Department of Health 2018).

Save the 8th's integrity was undermined by allegations made by a campaign supporter who falsified his credentials regarding first-hand knowledge about abortion.[8] Posters, which displayed an image of Noel Pattern (also Noel Patrún), included visual testimony from the former Ipswich (UK) hospital porter who claimed "I worked in an abortion theatre. I will never forget what I saw" (Sanz 2018). The poster cleverly used textual references to visually evoke a repertoire of fetal images which, while condemned by Save the 8th, nevertheless appeared on some of its posters and on its Instagram account (Brady 2018b). When controversy ensued about the veracity of Pattern's claim, Save the 8th deleted his testimony from their website but defended its continued use on posters: "we stand over the content of the advertisements we issued" (*Broadsheet* 2018).

Save the 8th aimed its poster campaign at the public and urged them to vote to retain the 8th Amendment. As part of a strategic visual realignment, enacted visually, the Save the 8th campaign and its posters acknowledged that abortion was a pregnant person's decision. However, it attempted to dissuade them from making that decision by judgements offered by an infant and a former hospital porter. Both images mobilized racialized discourses of Irishness that were consistent with heteroactivist organizing: the white infant depicted a particular form of national inclusion and Pattern's employment in England urged a particular post-colonial decision from which to

Figure 7.2 Love Both: Emma Maloney, Rossa Maloney.
Source: Photograph from David Hunter/Alamy Stock Photo, May 25, 2018, Maynooth. Used with permission.

distinguish a distinct position regarding abortion in Ireland from that in England (Browne, Nash, and Gorman 2018).[9]

The Love Both campaign poster shown in Figure 7.2, picturing Emma Maloney and her son Rossa (Maynooth, Co. Kildare), presented a favourable image of single motherhood. It contradicted Ireland's previous history of involuntary confinement of single mothers in mother and baby homes, country homes, industrial and reformatory schools, and laundries and the practice of "covert and legally dubious" adoption schemes (Mother and Baby Homes Commission of Investigation 2017–2019; Garrett 2000, 334). The story of mother and son is abbreviated on this Love Both poster in a recognizable Madonna-like pose with the figures enlarged. Inviting the viewers' familiarity with this pose, the figures are intended to gaze directly at viewers. In reality, because posters were hung high to avoid removal and/or defacement, the figures loomed large above viewers' heads like religious icons.

Text on some posters recounts Maloney's decision:

> I'm so thankful the 8th Amendment was there to protect me from making a quick and rash decision when I was experiencing a crisis pregnancy. I often think if I had local access to an abortion when I was feeling vulnerable I could have easily made a decision that I regretted later.

Another Love Both poster pictures Mary Kenny and her daughter Hollie (Limerick, Co. Limerick): "The time it took to plan an abortion in England was the time I needed to change my mind."

Love Both's spokesperson, Cora Sherlock, claimed its posters offered a "simple" campaign message (Baker 2018). They placed young women's voices at the forefront of public discussion, replacing the No side's previous male leadership. Both Maloney and Kenny had connections to Catholic Church organizations and participated in social media campaigns and on platforms connected to religious organizations.[10] Campaign posters for Save the 8th and Love Both were free of religious discourses, iconography, and displays. Maloney and Kenny's messages highlighted their personal decision-making abilities, which they drew on in ways that, with a No majority vote, would have denied decisions to others (Browne and Nash 2020, 124). The No campaign messages and images furthered heteroactivist tropes. They used examples of young, white women and their children to focus on the importance of love directed at pregnant mothers and children as the "proper" subjects of heterosexual love (Browne and Nash 2020, 124).[11]

Love Both's public campaign framed pregnant people as untrustworthy decision-makers (Pizzarossa 2019). Messages communicated by Maloney and Kenny implied that pregnant people's decisions were quick, rushed, and rash (*CatholicIreland.net* 2018). Even Ireland's *Taoiseach*, who campaigned for Yes, suggested that abortions "should be rare" (*Irish Times* 2018).[12] The focus on individuals and individual decision-making obscured structural considerations such as economic inequalities and constructed connections between motherhood and pregnancy as unproblematic. It reified neoliberal subjects and emphasized choice in a context that limited it (Baird and Millar 2018). Presenting abortion as harmful overlooked some other harms that people faced (Pizzarossa 2019, 49). Ironically, it highlighted vulnerability in the midst of Ireland's cervical screening scandal, where poor communication, backlogs in cervical testing and results, and inconclusive and incorrect test results ended in poor health and death (BBC 2018; Scally 2018).

Resisting visual realignment

Although women occupied leadership positions in the 2018 referendum's No campaigns, their leadership did not extend beyond its borders into electoral politics. A small but vocal group of male politicians assumed the position of the No campaign in the formal political arena, including in deliberations of the *Joint Oireachtas Committee on the Eighth Amendment* (de Londras and Markicevic 2018). This was the case even though only a single political party, Renua Ireland which had no elected representatives, endorsed the No campaign (Field 2018, 620). The party was founded, in 2015, by a formerly elected politician who was expelled from Fine Gael for opposing abortion by failing to support the *Protection of Life During Pregnancy Act* (Ryan and O'Connor 2018).

Individual adherence to religion was often less obvious than institutional adherence (Gordon and Saurette, this volume). The Iona Institute for Religion and Society, a heteroactivist religious organization that "promote[s] the place of marriage and religion in society," and asserts that "children deserve the love of a mother and father wherever possible," housed the Save the 8th and Love Both campaigns (Quinn 2019). The Institute's conservative commentators, David Quinn and Maria Steen, were both vocal in the media and campaigned for retain. However, the Irish public's shift away from the Catholic Church was unsurprising given public distrust of the Catholic Church and its national reach and international networks (Browne and Nash 2020). Association of the Catholic Church in Ireland, with sexual abuse and mother and baby home scandals, led to some characterizations of its reputation as "fatally damaged" (Smyth 2018, 135).

The public display of fetal images persisted in the 2018 campaign posters even though Save the 8th and Love Both campaigns allegedly opposed their use. Love Both used a poster image (Figure 7.3) described on its Facebook account as "an ultrasound scan of a nine-week-old baby" (*Irish Catholic* 2018). On the poster, the accompanying text imbued the fetus with personhood and directed voters to act on its behalf (Firth 2009, 55). Fetal images were used purposively to instigate parental visual recognition. They were intended to depict vulnerability, highlight "the 'wonder'" of prenatal development, instigate a rights-based discourse that encompassed fetal rights, and disparage individuals' decisions about abortion (Mattalucci 2012, 111; Saurette and Gordon 2017). Their public display also instigated cultural recognition. In Ireland, they resonated with some educational and curricular practices, including the presence of the anti-abortion organization, Youth Defence, and the US-based Precious Feet campaigns, in some schools (*Irish Independent* 2019). They resonated with the position and presence of Accord, the church-based organization established by the Irish Catholic Bishops Conference, that is the largest provider of mandatory Relationship and Sexuality Education curriculum in Catholic-ethos and secular schools at post-primary levels (Sherlock 2012, 389; McGuire 2018).

Figure 7.3 Referendum campaigning.
Source: Photograph from Andy Gibson/Alamy Stock Photo, May 7, 2018, Dublin. Used with permission.

Campaigns for the Yes and No sides drew on gendered stereotypes but they used them differently (Enright 2018). Yes campaigns advocated compassion and care for women who were forced to travel from Ireland. No campaigns advocated compassion for fetuses as "unborn." Both campaigns highlighted Ireland's post-colonial context from England (Browne and Nash 2020). Yes campaigners used a range of creative approaches to avoid continuing the abortion trail to England (Nic Ghachann 2018). No campaigns used recurring stern warnings about becoming "like England." Save the 8th claimed, inaccurately, that "In Britain, 90% of babies with Down Syndrome

Figure 7.4 Love Boats logo.
Source: Photograph from www.facebook.com/LoveBoatsIreland, 2018.

are aborted. Don't let that happen here" and, "In England, 1 in 5 babies are aborted. Don't bring this to Ireland" (*thejournal.ie* 2018a, 2018b).

The No side's heteroactivist images were also intentionally queered (Sutton and Borland 2018). For example, fetal images displayed by some No campaigners, including outside of maternity hospitals, were covered with bed sheets by hospital staff. Yes campaign groups were also involved in obscuring public displays of fetal images. Members of Radical Queers Resist covered fetal image displays with pride flags and Angels for Yes covered them with large feathered wings (Fletcher 2018).

Love Boats queered the Love Both logo with a name change, the silhouette of a ship, and the tag line, "exporting Ireland's problems" (Figure 7.4). This parodic response highlighted the hypocrisy of limiting abortion in Ireland while permitting travel elsewhere. The logo had a rainbow colour scheme that countered associations of abortion with heteroactivism and highlighted the inclusion of trans, gender-queer, and gender-diverse bodies in discussions about decision-making (Sutton and Borland 2018).

Conclusion

The No campaign suffered a resounding 2018 referendum defeat. Although it worked to visually realign its campaign messages and images by minimizing religious viewpoints and highlighting women's voices, it also elected retention of a mode of "protective paternalism" and the continued display of fetal images (Mason 2019, 686). Its messages, however, did not resonate with the majority of voters. The No campaign's heteroactivist approach did not resonate with those who had, three years earlier, supported the marriage equality referendum and the No campaign's links between whiteness, "Irish exceptionalism," and abortion did not go unnoticed (Browne and Nash 2019).

Despite their campaign defeat, some No campaign messages were translated, as political concessions, into legislative restrictions on abortion.[13] Deliberations at the *Joint Oireachtas Committee on the Eighth Amendment* indicated the extent to which No campaigns were allied with politicians, political parties, and/or state bodies (Mason 2019, 669). Restrictions that persist in post-referendum legislation include: a mandatory non-medically necessary three-day wait period that implies pregnant people cannot be trusted with decisions (Enright 2018, 2); language that rejects a redefinition of Ireland's sexual landscape by avoiding the word abortion (instead referring to "termination of pregnancy") as a decision that faces only women; and laws that criminalize assistance (but not coercion) and maintain social stigma (Shellenberg *et al.* 2011; Side 2020).[14] Furthermore, the *Act* contains no provision for travel for those who cannot leave and return without state permission or those without travel documents, reinforcing limited perceptions of Irishness (MERJ 2018). Public displays of fetal images also persist in the post-referendum period in Ireland (Hilliard 2019; Keough 2019). However, what is different about their persistence, and their location in a wider range of messages opposing abortion, is that they are no longer consistent with the state's constitutional and legal positions. Instead, they are situated in, and responsive to, an ongoing visual realignment of public representations of abortion.

Acknowledgements

Thanks to Kath Browne and Emma Campbell. Images are in the public domain; all efforts have been made to obtain necessary permission for their inclusion.

Notes

1 The referendum to insert the 8th Amendment was approved in 1983 (66.9 per cent, voter turnout was 53.67 per cent) (Field 2018, 610).
2 Abortion was legalized in 2013 where a pregnant person's life was at risk by the *Protection of Life During Pregnancy Act*, now repealed (Bacik 2013).
3 The Yes campaign's communicative strategies are analysed elsewhere (Enright 2018; Nic Ghabhann 2018).
4 The Marriage Equality referendum was approved on May 22, 2015 (62.07 per cent, voter turnout was 60.5 per cent) (Elections Ireland 2018).
5 US-based Political Social Media LLC developed apps for use in Ireland that permitted private user information to be shared with US-based conservative organizations (*Buzzfeed* 2018).
6 Save the 8th launched in January 2018; Love Both was launched in April 2018 (Field 2018).

7   Posters of white male firefighters and soldiers rescuing children from dangerous situations were condemned (Worker's Party 2018; Nugent 2018).
8   Pattern was employed as a hospital porter at the Ipswich Hospital Trust, UK. *The Irish Catholic* reprinted his false claims (Brady 2018a).
9   Distinction was also achieved through Irish-language campaigning (Nic an Bhreithimh 2019).
10 Maloney and Kenny participated in campaign-related material, including social media, *Catholic Ireland*, the *Catholic Sun*, and *Catholic News Service* (Foley 2018; MacDonald 2017). In addition to the public figures who appeared on posters, Save the 8th spokesperson Niamh Uí Bhriain and Love Both spokesperson Cora Sherlock were vocal throughout campaigning.
11 LoveBoth.ie/MyStory's web-based platform was more ethnically diverse than its public poster campaign.
12 For a critique of "rare," see Weitz, "Rethinking the Mantra That Abortion Should Be 'Safe, Legal, and Rare'."
13 For analyses of legal restrictions, see de Londras, "'A Hope Raised and Then Defeated'?" and Side, "Abortion Travel: Political Decisions, Spatial Consequences."
14 See Offences, s. 23, *Health Regulation (Termination of Pregnancy) Act, 2018*.

References

Askola, Heli. 2018. "Dropping the Ball or Holding the Line? Challenges to Abortion Laws in Nordic Countries." *Women's Studies International Forum* 66: 25–32.
Avanza, Martina. 2018. "Plea for an Emic Approach Towards 'Ugly Movements': Lessons from the Divisions within the Italian Pro-Life Movement." *Politics and Governance* 6, no. 3: 112–125.
Bacik, Ivana. 2013. "The Irish Constitution and Gender Politics: Developments in the Law on Abortion." *Irish Political Studies* 28, no. 3: 380–398.
Baird, Barbara and Erica Miller. 2018. "More than Stigma: Interrogating Counter Narratives of Abortion." *Sexualities* 22, no. 7–8: 1110–1126.
Baker, Sinead. 2018. "Love Both Launches Its Referendum Campaign and Criticises 12 Week Proposal for Abortion." *thejournal.ie*, April 8, 2018. www.thejournal.ie/love-both-campaign-launch-no-vote-3964140-Apr2018.
Bardon, Sarah. 2018. "Fact Check: Will Abortion Be Legalised Up to the Sixth Month of Pregnancy?" *Irish Times*, May 9, 2018. www.irishtimes.com/news/politics/fact-check-will-abortion-be-legalised-up-to-the-sixth-month-of-pregnancy-1.3488418?mode=sample&auth-failed=1&pw-origin=https%3A%2F%2Fwww.irishtimes.com%2Fnews%2Fpolitics%2Ffact-check-will-abortion-be-legalised-up-to-the-sixth-month-of-pregnancy-1.3488418.
BBC. 2018. "Irish Smear Scandal: Woman Who Highlighted Failures Dies." *BBC*, October 7, 2018. www.bbc.com/news/uk-northern-ireland-45778679.
Brady, Chai. 2018a. "Nurses Stress Reality of Abortion Proposal in Ireland." *Irish Catholic*. Accessed April 15, 2019. www.irishcatholic.com/nurses-stress-reality-abortion-proposal-ireland.
———2018b. "Save the 8th Denounce Graphic Abortion Images." *Irish Catholic*, May 3, 2018. www.irishcatholic.com/save-the-8th-denounce-graphic-abortion-images.

Broadsheet. 2018. "A Pro-Life Pattern." *Broadsheet*, March 8, 2018. www.broadsheet.ie/2018/03/08/a-pro-life-pattern.

Browne, Kath and Catherine Nash. 2017. "Heteroactivism: Beyond Anti-Gay." *ACME: An International Journal for Critical Geographies* 16, no. 4: 643–652.

——— 2019. "Losing Ireland: Heteroactivist Responses to the Result of the 8th Amendment in Canada and the UK." In *After Repeal: Rethinking Abortion Politics*, edited by Sydney Calkin and Kath Browne. London: Zed Books.

——— 2020. "In Ireland We 'Love Both'? Heteroactivism in Ireland's Anti-Repeal Ephemera." *Feminist Review* 124, no. 1: 51–67.

Browne, Kath, Catherine Nash, and Andrew Gorman-Murray. 2018. "Geographies of Heteroactivism: Resisting Sexual Rights in the Constitution of Irish Nationhood." *Transactions of the Institute of British Geographers* 43, no. 4: 526–539.

Buzzfeed. 2018. "The Apps for Ireland's Anti-Abortion Campaigns Allow User Data to Be Shared with the NRA." *Buzzfeed*, May 22, 2018. www.buzzfeed.com/laurasilver/ireland-anti-abortion-campaigns-apps-privacy-nra.

CatholicIreland.net. 2018. "Conference Theme of Courage Apt in Advance of Referendum." *CatholicIreland.net*, February 21, 2018. www.catholicireland.net/divine-mercy-conference-theme-courage-apt-advance-referendum.

Curran, Ann. 2019. "Sites of Production: The Use of Stock Photographs in the 2018 Irish Abortion Referendum." May 31, 2019. Canadian Association for Irish Studies Conference, Montréal, Canada.

de Londras, Fiona. 2020. "'A Hope Raised and Then Defeated?' The Continuing Harms of Irish Abortion Law." *Feminist Review* 124, no. 1: 33–50.

de Londras, Fiona and Mima Markicevic. 2018. "Reforming Abortion Law in Ireland: Reflections on the Public Submissions to the Citizen's Assembly." *Women Studies International Forum* 70: 89–98.

Department of Health. 2018. *General Scheme of a Bill, Health (Regulation of Termination of Pregnancy)*. Accessed April 15, 2019. https://health.gov.ie/blog/publications/general-scheme-of-a-bill-to-regulate-termination-of-pregnancy.

Duerksen, Kari and Karen Lawson. 2017. "Not Brain-Washed, but Heart-Washed: A Qualitative Analysis of Benevolent Sexism in the Anti-Choice Stance." *International Journal of Behavioural Medicine* 24, no. 6: 864–870.

Edwards, Elaine. 2018. "Thousands Gather for Pro-Life Rally in Dublin." *Irish Times*, May 12, 2018. www.irishtimes.com/news/social-affairs/thousands-gather-for-love-both-rally-in-dublin-1.3493432?mode=sample&auth-failed=1&pworigin=https%3A%2F%2Fwww.irishtimes.com%2Fnews%2Fsocial-affairs%2Fthousands-gather-for-love-both-rally-in-dublin-1.3493432.

Elections Ireland. 2018. *Summary of Referendums, 1937–2018*. Accessed March 27, 2019. https://electionsireland.org/results/referendum/index.cfm.

Enright, Máiréad. 2018. "The American Origins of Proposed Anti-Choice Amendments to the Health (Regulation of Termination of Pregnancy) Bill 2018." *feminists@law*, November 5, 2018. https://lawyers4choice.ie/2018/11/05/the-american-origins-of-proposed-amendments-to-the-health-regulation-of-termination-of-pregnancy-bill-2018.

Field, Luke. 2018. "The Abortion Referendum of 2018 and a Timeline of Abortion Politics in Ireland to Date." *Irish Political Studies* 33, no. 4: 608–628.

Firth, Georgina. 2009. "Renegotiating Reproductive Technologies: The 'Public Foetus' Revisited." *Feminist Review* 92: 54–71.

Fletcher, Ruth. 2018. "#Repealedthe8th: Translating Travesty, Global Conversation and the Irish Abortion Referendum." *Feminist Legal Studies* 26, no. 3: 233–259.

Foley, Ann Marie. 2018. "Divine Mercy Conference Theme of Courage Apt in Advance of Referendum." *CatholicIreland.net*, February 21, 2018. www.catholicireland.net/divine-mercy-conference-theme-courage-apt-advance-referendum.

Free, Marcus and Clare Scully. 2018. "The Run of Ourselves: Shame, Guilt, and Confession in Post-Celtic Tiger Irish Media." *International Journal of Cultural Studies* 21, no. 3: 308–324.

Garrett, Paul. 2000. "The Abnormal Flight: The Migration and Repatriation of Irish Unmarried Mothers." *Social History* 25, no. 3: 330–343.

Guardian (The). 2018. "Anti-Abortion Activists Make Final Push for Ireland's Vote." *The Guardian*, May 24, 2018. www.theguardian.com/world/2018/may/24/anti-abortion-activists-final-push-ireland-vote-referendum-love-both.

Hilliard, Mark. 2019. "Gardái Examine CCTV Over Anti-Abortion Graffiti at GP Surgery." *Irish Times*, February 18, 2019. www.irishtimes.com/news/ireland/irish-news/garda%C3%AD-examine-cctv-over-anti-abortion-graffiti-at-gp-surgery-1.3797845.

Hopkins, Nick, Suzanne Zeedyk, and Fiona Raitt. 2005. "Visualising Abortion: Emotion Discourse and Fetal Imagery in Contemporary Abortion Debate." *Social Science and Medicine* 61: 393–403.

Houses of the Oireachtas. 2018. *Health (Regulation of Termination of Pregnancy) Act 2018*. Accessed May 8, 2019. https://data.oireachtas.ie/ie/oireachtas/act/2018/31/eng/enacted/a3118.pdf.

Institute of Obstetricians and Gynaecologists. 2018. *Interim Clinical Guidelines: Termination of Pregnancy under 12 Weeks*. Dublin: Institute of Obstetricians and Gynaecologists.

Irish Catholic. 2018. "LoveBoth Campaign Condemns Poster Smearing Tactics." *Irish Catholic*, May 3, 2018. www.irishcatholic.com/loveboth-campaign-condemns-poster-smearing-tactics.

Irish Independent. 2019. "Activist Group Brings Pro-Life Campaign to Irish Schools." *Irish Independent*, December 28, 2019. www.independent.ie/ca/irish-news/education/activist-group-brings-prolife-campaign-to-schools-36864259.html.

Irish Statute Book. [1937] 1983. *Bunreacht na hÉireann/Constitution of Ireland*. Accessed May 28, 2019. www.irishstatutebook.ie/eli/cons/en/html.

Irish Times. 2018. "'Safe, Legal and Rare': Full Text of Taoiseach's Abortion Speech." *Irish Times*, January 30, 2018. www.irishtimes.com/news/social-affairs/safe-legal-and-rare-full-text-of-taoiseach-s-abortion-speech-1.3373468.

Jones, Natalie Linda. 2017. "Hanging On: Reflections on Visual Reproduction and the UK Abortion Act 1967." *Feminist Legal Studies* 25: 359–364.

Keough, Elaine. 2019. "Campaigners Protest at Drogheda Hospital Over 'First Abortion.'" *Irish Times*. January 7, 2019. www.irishtimes.com/news/health/campaigners-protest-at-drogheda-hospital-over-first-abortion-1.3750072.

Leahy, Pat. 2018. "Alarm at Apparent Lack of Urgency in the Repeal Campaign." *Irish Times*. April 10, 2018. www.irishtimes.com/news/social-affairs/alarm-at-apparent-lack-of-urgency-in-repeal-campaign-1.3456037?mode=sample&authfailed=1&pw-origin=https%3A%2F%2Fwww.irishtimes.com%2Fnews%2Fsocial-affairs%2Falarm-at-apparent-lack-of-urgency-in-repeal-campaign-1.3456037.

Loughlin, Elaine and Fiachra Ó Cionnaith. 2019. "How They Did It: Behind-the-Scenes of How the Eighth was Repealed." *Irish Examiner.* June 2, 2019. www.irishexaminer.com/breakingnews/views/analysis/how-they-did-it-behind-the-scenes-of-how-the-eighth-was-repealed-846478.html.

Love Both. n.d. "Homepage." Accessed November 2019. www.loveboth.ie.

MacDonald, Sarah. 2017. "People Only Hearing Sterilized Version of Abortion." *CatholicIreland.net.* December 5, 2017. www.catholicireland.net/people-hearing-sterilised-version-abortion-plc-conference-hears.

Mason, Carol. 2019. "Opposing Abortion to Protect Women: Transnational Strategy since the 1990s." *Signs: Journal of Women in Culture and Society* 44, no. 3: 665–692.

Mattalucci, Claudia. 2012. "Pro-Life Activism, Abortion and Subjectivity before Birth: Discursive Practices and Anthropological Perspectives." *Mediterranean Journal of Social Studies* 3, no. 10: 109–118.

McGee, Harry. 2018. "How the Yes and No Sides Won and Lost the Abortion Referendum." *Irish Times*, May 26, 2018. www.irishtimes.com/news/politics/how-the-yes-and-no-sides-won-and-lost-the-abortion-referendum-1.3509924.

McGuire, Peter. 2018. "What Are Our Children Being Taught about Sex?" *Irish Times*, April 24, 2018. www.irishtimes.com/news/education/what-are-our-children-being-taught-about-sex-1.3467341.

Migrant and Ethnic Minorities for Reproductive Justice (MERJ). 2018. "Racism and Reproductive Health: Migrant Rights and the Irish Abortion Referendum." *International Viewpoint*, May 26, 2018. www.internationalviewpoint.org/spip.php?article5535.

Mother and Baby Homes Commission of Investigation. 2017–2019. *Interim Reports on the Commission of Investigation of Mother and Baby Homes.* Accessed April 17, 2019. www.mbhcoi.ie/MBH.nsf/page/Latest%20News-en.

Nic an Bhreithimh, Lisa. 2019. "Tá: Pro-Choice Activism in the Irish Language Community." In *After Repeal: Rethinking Abortion Politics*, edited by Sydney Calkin and Kath Browne. London: Zed Books.

Nic Ghabhann, Niamh. 2018. "City Walls, Bathroom Stalls, and Tweeting the Taoiseach: The Aesthetics of Protest and the Campaign for Abortion Rights in the Republic of Ireland." *Continuum: Journal of Media and Cultural Studies* 32, no. 5: 553–568.

Ntontis, Evangelos and Nick Hopkins. 2018. "Framing a 'Social Problem': Emotion in Anti-Abortion Activists' Depiction of the Abortion Debate." *British Journal of Social Psychology* 57, no. 3: 666–683.

Nugent, Ryan. 2018. "Defence Forces Complain Over Military 'No' Advert." *Irish Independent*, May 16, 2018. www.independent.ie/ca/irish-news/abortion-referendum/defence-forces-complain-over-military-no-advert-36911481.html.

O'Brien, Ciara. 2018. "Facebook Bans Foreign Ads for the Eighth Amendment Referendum." *Irish Times*, May 8, 2018. www.irishtimes.com/business/technology/facebook-bans-foreign-ads-for-eighth-amendment-referendum-1.3487895?mode=sample&auth-failed=1&pw-origin=https%3A%2F%2Fwww.irishtimes.com%2Fbusiness%2Ftechnology%2Ffacebook-bans-foreign-ads-for-eighth-amendment-referendum-1.3487895.

O'Loughlin, Ed. 2018. "As Irish Abortion Vote Nears, Fears of Foreign Influence Rise." *New York Times*, March 26, 2018. www.nytimes.com/2018/03/26/world/europe/ireland-us-abortion-referendum.html.

Parkes, Geneviève. 1999. "Redefining the Legitimacy of Anti-Abortion Pressure Groups in Europe, Looking at France, Britain, and Central Europe." *Journal of Social Welfare and Family Law* 21, no. 3: 285–294.

Pizzarossa, Lucia Berro. 2019. "Women Are Not in the Best Position to Make These Decisions by Themselves: Gender Stereotyping in the Uruguayan Abortion Law." *University of Oxford Human Rights Hub Journal* 1: 25–54.

Quinn, David. "About the Iona Institute." *The Iona Institute*, March 19, 2019. https://ionainstitute.ie.

Ryan, Phillip and Niall O'Connor. 2018. *Leo: A Very Modern Taoiseach*. London: Biteback Publishing.

Sanz, Catherine. 2018. "Save the 8th Campaign Wrongly Described Video Speaker as Nurse." *The Times*, March 12, 2018. www.thetimes.co.uk/article/save-the-8th-campaign-wrongly-described-video-speaker-as-nurse-lrlb6lm2s.

Saurette, Paul and Kelly Gordon. 2015. *The Changing Voice of the Anti-Abortion Movement: The Rise of "Pro-Woman" Rhetoric in Canada and the United States*. Toronto: University of Toronto.

——— 2017. "The Future of Pro-Choice Discourse in Canada." In *Abortion: History, Politics and Reproductive Justice after Morgentaler*, edited by Shannon Stettner, Kristin Burnett and Travis Hay, 265–291. Vancouver: University of British Columbia Press.

Scally, Gabriel. 2018. *Scoping Inquiry into the Cervical Check Screening Programme: Final Report*, September 2018. http://scallyreview.ie/wp-content/uploads/2018/09/Scoping-Inquiry-into-CervicalCheck-Final-Report.pdf.

Shellenberg, Kristen, Ann Moore, Akinrinola Bankole, Fatima Juarez, Adekunbi Kehinde Omideyi, Nancy Palomino, Zeba Sathar, Susheela Singh, and Amy Tsui. 2011. "Social Stigma and Disclosure about Induced Abortion: Results from an Exploratory Study." *Global Public Health* 6, S1: S111–S125.

Sherlock, Leslie. 2012. "Sociopolitical Influences on Sexuality Education in Sweden and Ireland." *Sex Education: Sexuality, Society and Learning* 12, no. 4: 383–396.

Side, Katherine. 2020. "Abortion Travel: Political Decisions, Spatial Consequences." *Feminist Review* 124, no. 1: 13–31.

Smyth, Ailbhe. 2018. "The Obvious Explanations of How Power Is Held and Exercised Over Women Are Very Basic." In *Repeal the 8th*, edited by Una Mullally, 129–142. London: Unbound.

Sutton, Barbara and Elizabeth Borland. 2018. "Queering Abortion Rights: Notes from Argentina." *Culture, Health and Sexuality* 20, no. 12: 1378–1393.

thejournal.ie. 2018a. "Fact Check: Are 90% of Babies with Down Syndrome in Britain Aborted?" *The Journal*, February 3, 2018. www.thejournal.ie/factcheck-babies-abortion-3823611-Feb2018.

——— 2018b. "Fact Check: 1 in 5 Babies Aborted in England." *The Journal*, May 1, 2018. www.thejournal.ie/save-the-8th-poster-statistic-abortion-3951738-Apr2018.

Weitz, Tracy A. 2010. "Rethinking the Mantra That Abortion Should Be 'Safe, Legal, and Rare'." *Journal of Women's History* 22, no. 3: 161–72.

Worker's Party. 2018. "Tallaghat Firefighters Condemn 'Save the 8th' Firefighter Ad as 'Offensive and Misleading.'" *The Workers Party*, May 17, 2018. http://workersparty.ie/tallaght-firefighters-condemn-save-the-8th-firefighter-ad-as-offensive-and-misleading.

8   Look like a provider
Representing the materiality of the fetus in abortion care work

Lena Hann and Jeannie Ludlow

Introduction

As we drafted this essay in spring 2019, Missouri became the fifth state to pass a "Heartbeat Ban," prohibiting abortion when a fetal heartbeat is detectable by ultrasound (six to eight weeks since last menstrual period or "LMP");[1] Louisiana sent their "Heartbeat Ban" to the governor for a signature as we revised. Although these laws are often blocked by courts, they are attempts to bring an abortion ban before the Supreme Court of the U.S., "hoping to challenge *Roe*, now that the nation's highest court leans conservative" (Reints 2019). Acknowledging that the U.S. anti-abortion movement is incredibly complex, well choreographed, and well funded, we focus here on one tactic underlying the success of these, and similar, bans: they appeal, culturally, to the emotional significance of the unborn baby. Strategically invoking the fetal body, an eight-week ban becomes a "heartbeat" ban; the 2003 D&X ban becomes the Partial-Birth Abortion Ban; 20-week bans become "fetal pain bans"; and laws intended to shame people for personally and culturally complicated abortion decisions are called "PreNDA" bills – Prenatal Nondiscrimination Acts. One source for the deployment of the fetal body in anti-abortion legislation is the 1992 Supreme Court decision in *Planned Parenthood of Southeastern Pennsylvania v. Casey*; Section 3205 of *Casey* required, as part of "informed consent" for abortion, "detailed descriptions and pictures of the fetus at two-week gestational increments from fertilization until full-term" (Wharton, Frietsche, and Kolbert 2006, 325 n. 40). Thus, *Casey* mandated a long-standing tactic of anti-abortion activism: using representations of the fetal body, pre- and post-abortion, to dissuade people from choosing abortion.[2]

The U.S. pro-choice movement has no strong or effective narratives to counter this tactic. In the mid- to late twentieth century, as feminist journalist Roberta Brandes-Gratz explains, images of "dead women" were deployed to balance the emotional impact of "dead fetus[es]" (Giloolly 1995). More recent pro-choice tactics invoke science: obstetrician/gynaecologist Jen Gunter recommends that "heartbeat" bans be renamed "fetal pole cardiac activity" bills, in the interest of scientific accuracy, since the seven-week embryo doesn't yet have a heart (Gunter 2016). Gunter's argument is scientifically sound but ultimately ineffective because it does not address the cultural significance of the fetus. Many families in technological societies have seen an ultrasound image of a tiny pulsation and thought (or been told), "there's the baby's heartbeat!" Those who have not had this experience may well have seen media representations of it. As many feminist critics have explained, increased technologization of pregnancy has changed the cultural significance of the fetus (Dubow 2011; Duden 1993; Hartouni 1992; Kimport *et al.* 2013; Little 1999; Mason 2002; Mills 2005; Newman 1996; Petchesky 1987; Reagan 2010; Stabile 1992; Weitz 2008). Redefined social understandings of fetus and baby de-emphasize distinctions and, consequently, serve anti-abortion movements internationally; Katherine Side's chapter in this volume, for example, examines the anti-abortion deployment of the fetus/baby relationship in Ireland. Curiosity about the fetus is not, however, limited to those who oppose abortion. Indeed, several chapters in this volume, by Manon Parry, Sucharita Sarkar, and Aurore Yamagata-Montoya, suggest that pro-choice people are interested in talking about the fetus, although we are not often given the opportunity to do so, and Rachel Marie-Crane Williams's chapter graphically represents the stigmatizing power of such silencing. We argue that in order for the abortion rights movement to respond to "heartbeat bans" and other anti-abortion invocations of the fetus, we must have more multifaceted and nuanced conversations about the fetus and abortion.

One of the most obvious sources for models of these nuanced conversations is the abortion clinic. Abortion providers – anyone whose healthcare-related work contributes to people's abortion experiences – already have these conversations with co-workers, patients, and their loved ones. In-clinic conversations about the fetus often begin during employee training and include examination of and discussions about post-abortion fetal parts, in order to determine whether an abortion is complete. With patients, conversations range from "I want you to get this clump of cells out of me before it becomes something real" to "I would like to write a letter asking the baby for forgiveness before I have my abortion" (Ludlow 2008a). Because providers work in one of the few settings that engages simultaneously with the scientific realities of the zygote, embryo, and fetus and the emotional significance of the fetus, they are a powerful source of strategies for these conversations. We are two among a handful of provider-scholars – academic researchers who have worked or currently work in abortion care and utilize overlapping lenses of abortion practice and academic theories/methods in our scholarly work – and we have given a lot of thought to the significance of the fetus in abortion conversations. In this chapter, we offer perspective on fetal tissue/bodies and abortion, echo calls by provider-scholars for nuanced and normalizing conversations about abortion, provide models from clinical experience for these conversations, and suggest ways for activists and advocates to think and talk about abortion that honour a variety of lived experiences with and emotional responses to the fetus.

Experiencing abortion   *misconception: abortions are uncommon*

Approximately 926,000 abortions are performed in the U.S. each year, and each one results in the removal of embryonic or fetal tissue from the pregnant person's body.[3] Almost 70%, or approximately 640,000, of abortions are performed in-clinic. Providers remove embryonic/fetal tissue from the uterus and a staff person examines the tissue to ensure nothing has been retained in the patient's body that could cause infection. The remaining 30% of abortions in the United States are induced by medication, and the pregnancy or fetal tissue passes at home, where the aborting person can potentially see it.

Clinic work taught us that very small, identifiable fetal parts (arms, legs, hands, feet) begin to develop around nine weeks LMP; this tissue breaks up easily during in-clinic aspiration abortion procedures. Prior to this, most aborted pregnancy tissue resembles a wet cotton ball and translucent tissue. As gestation increases, fetal parts become more identifiable and the fetus begins to resemble a small baby. Unless someone works in an abortion care facility or is a patient who views their post-abortion fetal tissue, most people will never have access to what real aborted fetal tissue looks like at each stage of gestation.[4]

Two-thirds of abortions are performed before eight weeks LMP, which means one-third of all abortions occur after fetal parts begin to develop. This is important to consider as pro-choice rhetoric has long discounted *pro-choice is often rebuttal to pro-life* anti-abortion imagery while proclaiming the fetus is not a baby, but rather just a clump of cells or "tissue" (Ludlow 2008a). This does not capture the reality of all abortions and is flatly untrue for fetuses after nine weeks LMP. Similarly, this dismissal does not reflect the lived experiences of abortion providers who often feel like they must keep the visual reality of abortion a secret to protect the pro-choice movement.

Outside of medical textbooks, only one set of pro-choice, scientifically accurate images of aborted fetal tissue exists, created at the Center for Choice II (CFC2) in Ohio (Ludlow's home clinic) more than 25 years ago. These photographs,[5] collected in *A Guide to Fetal Development for Abortion Providers* (Derenge and James 1993), are accessible in only some U.S. clinics by staff and some patients, if that clinic happens to utilize the photos for patient counselling, education, or viewing.[6] The guides were developed in the early 1990s after patients kept asking to see, touch, and say goodbye to their tissue. Eventually, CFC2 self-published the *Guide* and made it available to other clinics, at cost. In 2016, Hann interviewed Sara Derenge, one of the creators of the *Guide*. "Our clinic philosophy was that women need to know what is going on with their bodies, and be *using fetal imagery for good and informing patients*

able to make their own choice. This [*Guide*] is just another piece of that," Derenge said. When asked if their clinic had concerns that anti-abortion activists would misuse the images of aborted fetal tissue to push their own narratives, Derenge replied, "They've already done that. Protestors have the giant posters of full-term fetuses. The book shows actual size and actual tissue and what it really looks like."

Derenge shared a story about the *Guide*: in the mid-1990s, protestors who regularly harassed staff and patients wanted to see inside, assuming it was an "abortion mill." Derenge said the staff invited the protestors in for conversation and then showed them the fetal development book:

> [The protestors] said, "You actually show them this?" Yes, we do. They were jaw-dropped, astonished. [They said], "That's just amazing that after you do that [show the photos of aborted fetal tissue], that the woman is okay. She must really be doing something that she wanted to do." I think it was more peaceful ... the protestors were less aggressive after that.

Derenge noted that some independent and feminist abortion clinics strove to conceptualize new ways of understanding abortion and that honesty and transparency were important to these efforts. Hann's research with 22 independent abortion clinics around the U.S. found that many still had copies of *A Guide to Fetal Development for Abortion Providers*. Several staff (including Hann) reported reading the guides during staff training, although many had no idea where they came from or the rich history of their development and dissemination around the country.

Provider-scholars and abortion care nuance

Provider-scholars have long called for more nuanced thinking about fetuses in mainstream abortion discourse, modelled on how providers think through, and make sense of, their work. Academics, advocates, and activists would do well to look to abortion providers (specifically independent providers)[7] and provider narratives to frame new understandings of pro-choice discourse and the fetus. These provider narratives are often at odds with mainstream pro-choice discourse, which creates tension between providers and activists, advocates, and academics. Provider-scholar Lisa Harris, MD, PhD, challenged pro-choice discourse over a decade ago by arguing that silence around the reality of abortion and fetal tissue, especially in the second trimester, is dangerous to abortion providers, the patients they serve, and the abortion rights movement as a whole (2008). More recently, she has outlined the ways that pro-choice refusal to acknowledge the material reality of the fetal body in abortion threatens to corroborate anti-abortion accusations that providers are immoral, dishonest, and untrustworthy. She writes about providing second-trimester abortions,

I must ... honour that my lived experience of abortion work also includes experiencing it as violent, as something that really does "stop a beating heart," as something morally complicated, and which for me raises real questions about human life.

(2019, 191)

Harris' frank invocation of the (sometimes physical and sometimes symbolic) "beating heart" of the fetus stands in stark contrast to Gunter's insistence that there is no heart there.

Abortion providers denounce the assumption that the fetus is an undesired by-product of the fight for abortion rights. Lisa Martin and provider-scholar colleagues propose the "dangertalk" framework to categorize themes that arose in Providers Share Workshops to illuminate the importance of centring provider narratives and experiences within the abortion rights conversation (2017). Dangertalk is defined as "the perspective of individuals within a movement who self-censor authentic experiences that feel dangerous to a movement they support and love" (Martin *et al.* 2017, 80). Many abortion providers remain silent about everyday aspects of their lived experiences, in order to avoid antagonism within the pro-choice movement. The movement then perpetuates stereotypes and misinformation that are detrimental to understanding the reality of abortion care. Ludlow calls these silenced aspects of abortion provision "the things we cannot say," arguing that political constraints on what providers are allowed (or comfortable) to say publicly have led to a predominance of tragic or traumatized public narratives of abortion experience (2008b). The "things we cannot say" are often the most normal and most common aspects of abortion experience; that abortion results in fetal remains is one of these. Harris, Ludlow, and other provider-scholars have called for more research on provider perspectives on abortion care, with special attention paid to the rewards of this work instead of just the challenges. Creating spaces for providers to have honest and complex conversations, and then duplicating these spaces in advocacy circles, will serve to increase nuanced understanding of abortion more broadly, as well as the more deeply stigmatized elements of abortion work – like fetal tissue – more specifically.

Hann's research analyses abortion providers' experiences with fetal remains, in order to understand how working with tissue affects post-abortion viewing opportunities for patients; this work culminated in a new guide, *Patient-Centered Pregnancy Tissue Viewing: Strategies and Best Practices for Independent Abortion Providers* (Hann 2020). In interviews with clinic staff, Hann found that many lean against the confines of pro-choice discourse; providers navigate nuance and complexity with women and pregnant people from every walk of life, from every complicated background, and in every pregnancy decision. This is true whether they are citing politically safe anecdotes from their abortion care experiences or pulling the curtain back on some of the lesser-known but important components of their work, including the relationship patients and providers have with the fetus. *Patient-Centered Pregnancy Tissue Viewing* helps providers to situate their role in providing honest and accurate information about fetal tissue behind clinic walls within the greater landscape of abortion narratives. It includes a brief history of how fetuses have been visualized and understood over time, followed by a synthesized literature review about seeing fetuses via ultrasound and post-abortion tissue viewing, as well as in cases of still-birth, and providers' roles in these situations. One section is dedicated to the findings from Hann's research on tissue viewing strategies across multiple independent clinics in the United States. This research also suggests strategies that advocates and activists can use in non-clinical spaces to speak about the fetus and abortion in more nuanced ways.

Steps towards multifaceted conversations about the fetus in abortion

When providers' and clinic workers' practices shape advocacy, activism, and academic work, that work will be better situated to honour a variety of abortion experiences, both physical and emotional, and to reflect the diverse cultural significances of the material fetal body. In this section, we suggest ways to mobilize providers' experiences in non-clinical settings.

Engage abortion providers

Fetal tissue viewing was created out of patient needs and requests, and providers' desires to meet those needs. Providers who facilitate tissue viewing report that it generates transparency and honesty in their work, which helps destigmatize abortion in their dynamics with patients as well as internally (Hann 2016). Some providers worry about risk in showing fetal tissue, but they confront so many risks in their work that they pro-actively choose to move forward anyway, prioritizing being transparent and patient-centred over potential anti-abortion manipulation of their work. Still, the only accurate and pro-choice images of aborted fetal tissue exist in clinic spaces (Derenge and James 1993; Hann 2020). How can activists and advocates help extend these providers' perspectives into the movement at large? They can engage professionals who discuss fetal tissue on a regular basis and understand it scientifically and symbolically, using their knowledge as a basis for consciousness-raising within the movement.

Shout Your Abortion (SYA) has revitalized the consciousness-raising model of bringing people together to discuss reproductive issues via book clubs, TV watch parties, open mic nights, and other social gatherings (2019). What started as a hashtag social media phenomenon grew into a vibrant, glossy coffee-table book unapologetically displaying pro-abortion art, abortion stories, and provider profiles (Bonow and Nokes 2018).[8] In March 2019, the TV show *Shrill* by SYA co-founder Lindy West premiered on Hulu. The main character, Annie Easton, had an abortion in the first episode, a decision that allowed Annie to exert ownership over other parts of her life (Bryant *et al.* 2019). Shout Your Abortion encouraged people to host SYA book clubs and *Shrill* watch parties to celebrate abortion and discuss it with friends, family, and acquaintances; they provided small grants to laypeople and organizations hosting these gatherings.

Ideally, abortion advocates could utilize this social gathering model to engage in honest and nuanced discussions about fetuses and abortion. One powerful new documentary – *Our Bodies Our Doctors* – presents abortion provider experiences. One scene features discussions and examination of fetal tissue from clinicians' perspectives (Haaken and Cress 2018). This is one of the only accurate portrayals of early gestation aborted tissue available to the public; screening it can begin important conversations with pro-choice allies. Shout Your Abortion or other reproductive justice organizations could provide additional resources for accurate information that honours both scientific and emotional understandings of the fetus. Abortion rights organizations could invite providers to strategy meetings and onto advisory boards and boards of directors, mindfully including provider voices and serving to strengthen abortion provision and access. Similarly, if academics' scholarly analyses could be influenced by providers' knowledge and, in turn, be shared with providers in accessible, applicable ways, we would all benefit. The experiences and input of providers can help activists, advocates, and academics reflect on their own assumptions about the provision of abortion care and analyse the ways they reproduce mainstream pro-choice discourse that may be at odds with the needs and experiences of providers and of those who seek abortion care. This is especially true when considering the role of the fetus in abortion care work.

Evaluate discomfort

Providers have written about their own discomfort talking about elements of their work that do not fit in with the mainstream conversation on abortion, like the provision of later abortions, working with ambivalent patients, and seeing fetal parts. These hidden elements of abortion care have been named in a variety of ways: "acknowledging the ickies," "the things we cannot say," and "dangertalk" (Johnston 2002, 165; Ludlow 2008b; Martin *et al.* 2017). The presence of fetal tissue is a natural outcome of abortion. When clinic staff see, handle, and talk about tissue, when they answer patients' questions about or requests to see or touch aborted fetuses, it can feel dangerous, like an industry secret that must not be shared outside clinic walls. These conversations about the fetus happen daily within many abortion clinics, while mainstream pro-choice discourse deems the fetus "just a clump of cells" and calls anti-abortion fetal imagery inaccurate and grotesque. If pro-choice advocates could come to terms with the reality of fetal tissue and listen to the experiences of providers and patients who find value in considering the fetus, one manifestation of abortion stigma could be challenged. Discomfort with fetal tissue is normal because there are few neutral images of it accessible to general audiences. Still, ignoring it only digs a deeper hole to be filled with negative representations of abortion and aborted fetuses. Many clinicians have already committed to the deep work of thinking about these complex issues in values clarification exercises within their workplaces; abortion advocates can do the same in their circles, be it in official organizational capacities or in social venues. Some fetal tissue discussion prompts might include:

1. Describe the first time you saw fetal tissue. When, where, and in what context did you see it? (Real life or photos? At work or in the media? etc.)
2. What did the fetal tissue look like? How was it represented? Who was representing it?
3. What feelings did you have about it at the time and what do you think impacted those feelings? What feelings do you have about that situation now?
4. Think about fetal tissue that looks like "just a clump of cells" compared to a gestation where you can see fetal parts. Would your feelings change based on the gestation of the tissue, reason for abortion, or other factors?
5. What are five words you would use to describe fetal tissue in the abortion rights movement?

(Hann 2020)

Value complexity and allow tension

Anyone who discusses the questions above in a group will likely hear different opinions and reactions regarding fetal tissue. The next step in exploring these experiences is to avoid the impulse to categorize feelings about the fetus. Provider-scholars like Harris encourage us to hold complexity and tension at the same time as morality and certainty; to consider abortion outside a purely political context (2019). Johnston reminds us that many people seeking abortion care do not see their experiences as political (2002). A patient who requests to view their post-abortion fetus may just want to see what came out of their body mere seconds ago, or they want to confirm for themselves what abortion "really" looks like, as a means of self-empowerment instead of just trusting (or denying) that the images portrayed by anti-abortion protestors are true. They could be surprised in various ways by the sight of small identifiable hands or feet while simultaneously grateful for the opportunity to see them. By holding these experiences in tension without seeking to resolve them, we can consider the fetus without erasing the pregnant person who made the informed choice to see their fetus after the abortion. We can honour the agency of that person to make decisions that are best for them. Valuing complexity and allowing tension means we cannot control for disgust or regret, just like we cannot control for elation, confusion, sadness, or pleasure; instead we can acknowledge the range of human experiences and give each person space to have their own. This is where mainstream advocacy can utilize provider experiences and narratives to strengthen abortion discourse. We can be empowered by, not afraid of, the wide-open landscape available to us in thinking and talking about fetal tissue with those who find it important.

Acknowledge the fetus

When people have abortions, they know they are ending pregnancy; acknowledging that the pregnancy is an embryo or fetus is honest, transparent, and scientifically accurate. This is not to say that every person wants to think deeply or even talk about their fetus, nor should they be required to, but for those who do, we need to provide opportunities for that experience beyond the clinic walls. When we speak about our research or our abortion experiences, people regularly share their pregnancy, abortion, and miscarriage stories with us. Many describe wanting to see the fetus and how it made them feel to be allowed or denied that opportunity. One family friend who experienced several miscarriages shared that the hospital denied her the ability to see her fetal tissues. This felt like a betrayal; something that was in her body moments ago no longer belonged to her. Someone with medical power could prevent her from seeing part of her body and remove an avenue towards closure that she deeply desired. She felt that this denial was paternalistic and cruel, and that it was justified by a general sentiment that aborted or miscarried fetuses are disgusting or traumatic. According to providers who facilitate post-abortion tissue viewing, this access to information – about pregnancy, bodies, curiosity, closure – can be one of the most validating aspects of a patient's abortion appointment. Advocates, activists, and academics can help counter the anti-abortion sentiment cultivated around fetuses for decades by refusing to dismiss the fetus as gross or disturbing. Creating new meaning via sharing more nuanced experiences with fetuses both validates those who have had the experiences and unapologetically claims the fetus as an element of abortion care. Provider Peg Johnston writes that "normalizing abortion is the anti[-abortion movement]'s worst nightmare"; more public discussion about the fetus normalizes the lived experiences of abortion patients and providers alike (2002, 161).

"Look" like a provider

Provider-scholar Krista Jacobs wrote in 2002 about the ways those seeking abortion care "had been looking to the mainstream media as [their] source of information about what it means to be pro-choice, rather than to individuals and direct service providers within the pro-choice movement itself" (178). Abortion providers have access to hundreds and thousands of patient abortion experiences and as many fetal tissues removed during those pregnancies. Providers and staff are also people who have had pregnancies, abortions, miscarriages, and children. To "look" like a provider means to reflect inward on one's values and experiences, see them as valid, and work to create space for others to think through complex issues and lived realities while accessing the care they need. The movement can help ensure that the reality and complexity of all abortion experiences – not just the politically convenient ones – are represented in ways that benefit providers, patients, and the movement as a whole. In our efforts to protect pro-choice messaging, we have silenced and overlooked some abortion experiences; in doing so, we have inadvertently provided space for abortion stigma to flourish. If we are going to resist anti-abortion laws that exploit the fetal body, we must open our minds and hearts to the diversity of patients' and providers' experiences and reactions to the fetus.

Notes

1 The other states: Mississippi, Kentucky, Alabama, and Georgia (Reints 2019).
2 See Ludlow, this volume.
3 Guttmacher Institute, "Fact sheet: Induced abortion in the United States." All statistics about abortion in this section are from this source.
4 There is limited research on how often patients ask to see their post-abortion fetal tissue. This service varies by abortion provider (Ludlow 2008a; Wiebe and Adams 2009; Hann 2020).
5 The *Guide* includes photos of post-abortion tissue at each gestational age (by week) taken, with patients' consent, at CFC2.
6 The D and X ban (so-called Partial Birth Abortion ban) in 2003 renders the post-18-week LMP photos in the CFC2 *Guide* out of date.
7 Independent clinics are those not affiliated with the Planned Parenthood system in the U.S. We call for attention to independent providers' voices because they provide 60% of all abortions (Madsen, Thibodeau, and Schubert 2017) and their ways of speaking about abortion may be less constrained by governmental threats of defunding that circumscribe Planned Parenthood's employees' voices.
8 For more on the "pro-abortion" movement, see Tarico, "Why I am pro-abortion, not just pro-choice."

References

Bonow, Amelia and Emily Nokes, eds. 2018. *Shout Your Abortion*. Oakland, CA: PM Press.
Bryant, Aidy, Alexandra Rushfield, and Lindy West. 2019. "Annie." *Shrill* season 1 episode 1. Hulu.
Derenge, Sara and Nancy L. James. 1993. *A Guide to Fetal Development for Abortion Providers*. Toledo, OH: Center for Choice II.
Dubow, Sara. 2011. *Ourselves Unborn: A History of the Fetus in Modern America*. Oxford: Oxford University Press.

Duden, Barbara. 1993. *Disembodying Women: Perspectives on Pregnancy and the Unborn*. 1991. Trans. Lee Hoinacki. Cambridge, MA: Harvard University Press.

Gillooly, Jane, dir. 1995. *Leona's Sister Gerri*. ITVS video production. PBS distribution.

Gunter, Jen. 2016. "Dear Press, stop calling them 'heartbeat' bills and call them 'fetal pole cardiac activity' bills." *Dr. Jen Gunter* blog. December 11, 2016. Accessed May 21, 2019. https://drjengunter.com.

Guttmacher Institute. 2017. "Fact sheet: Induced abortion in the United States." Accessed June 2, 2019. www.guttmacher.org/fact-sheet/induced-abortion-united-states.

Haaken, Jan dir. and David Cress prod. 2018. *Our Bodies Our Doctors*. Specular Productions, LLC.

Hann, Lena. 2016. "Providing the option to look: Independent clinic workers' approaches to fetal viewing practices." Unpublished dissertation, Community Health, University of Illinois. http://hdl.handle.net/2142/93055.

—— 2020. *Patient-Centered Pregnancy Tissue Viewing: Strategies and Best Practices for Independent Abortion Providers*. Minneapolis, MN: Abortion Care Network.

Harris, Lisa. 2008. "Second trimester abortion provision: Breaking the silence and changing the discourse." *Reproductive Health Matters* 16, 31(Supplement): 74–81.

—— 2019. "The moral agency of abortion providers: Conscientious provision, dangertalk, and the lived experience of doing stigmatized work." In *Ethical Issues in Women's Healthcare: Practice and Policy*, edited by Lori d'Agincourt-Canning and Carolyn Ells, 189–208. New York: Oxford University Press.

Hartouni, Valerie. 1992. "Fetal exposures: Abortion politics and the optics of allusion." *Camera Obscura* 29: 130–49.

Jacobs, Krista, ed. 2002. *Our Choices, Our Lives: Unapologetic Writings on Abortion*. Lincoln, NE: IUniverse Star.

Johnston, Margaret R. 2002. "Opting out of the abortion war: From the Birmingham Bombing to September 11th." In *Our Choices, Our Lives: Unapologetic Writings on Abortion*, edited by Krista K. Jacob, 153–69. Lincoln, NE: IUniverse Star.

Kimport, Katrina, Ushma D. Upadhyay, Diana G. Foster, Marry Gatter, and Tracy A. Weitz. 2013. "Patient viewing of the ultrasound image prior to abortion." *Contraception* 88: 666–70.

Little, Margaret Olivia. 1999. "Abortion, intimacy, and the duty to gestate." *Ethical Theory and Moral Practice* 2: 295–312.

Ludlow, Jeannie. 2008a. "Sometimes it's a child *and* a choice: Toward an embodied abortion praxis." *Feminist Formations* 20, no. 1: 26–50.

—— 2008b. "The things we cannot say: Witnessing the trauma-tization of abortion in the United States." *Women's Studies Quarterly* 36, nos. 1/2 (Spring): 28–41. https://doi.org/10.1353/wsq.0.0057.

Madsen, Nikki, J. Thibodeau and E. Schubert. 2017. *Communities Need Clinics: The Role of Independent Abortion Care Providers in Ensuring Meaningful Access to Abortion Care in the United States*. Minneapolis, MN: Abortion Care Network.

Martin, Lisa A., Jane A. Hassinger, Michelle Debbink, and Lisa H. Harris. 2017. "Dangertalk: Voices of Abortion Providers." *Social Science & Medicine* 184: 75–83. doi: 10.1016/j.socscimed.2017.05.001.

Mason, Carol. 2002. *Killing for Life: The Apocalyptic Narrative of Pro-life Politics*. Ithaca, NY: Cornell University Press.

Mills, Catherine. 2005. "Technology, embodiment and abortion." *Internal Medicine Journal* 35: 427–28.

Newman, Karen. 1996. *Fetal Positions: Individualism, Science, Visuality*. Writing Science. Edited by Timothy Lenoir and Hans Ulrich Gumbrecht. Stanford, CA: Stanford University Press.

Petchesky, Rosalind Pollack. 1987. "Fetal images: The power of visual culture in the politics of reproduction." *Feminist Studies* 13, no. 2: 263–92.

Reagan, Leslie. 2010. *Dangerous Pregnancies: Mothers, Disabilities and Abortion in Modern America*. Los Angeles, CA: University of California Press.

Reints, Renae. 2019. "These are the states that passed 'Heartbeat Bills.'" *Fortune Magazine*. May 31, 2019. http://fortune.com.

"Shout Your Abortion." 2019. Accessed June 2, 2019. https://shoutyourabortion.com.

Stabile, Carol A. 1992. "Shooting the mother: Fetal photography and the politics of disappearance." *Camera Obscura* 28: 179–205.

Tarico, Valeria. 2016. "Why I am pro-abortion, not just pro-choice." *Free Inquiry*. July 8, 2016. https://secularhumanism.org/2016/07/cont-why-i-am-pro-abortion-not-just-pro-choice.

Weitz, Tracy. 2008. "Abortion and ultrasound: Women's preferences for 'looking' and the law." Abstract. *Contraception* 78: 188–9.

Wharton, Linda J., Susan Frietsche, and Kathryn Kolbert. 2006. "Preserving the core of *Roe*: Reflections on *Planned Parenthood v. Casey*." *Yale Journal of Law and Feminism* 18, no. 40: 325.

Wiebe, Ellen R. and Lisa C. Adams. 2009. "Women's experience of viewing the products of conception after an abortion." *Contraception* 80, no. 6: 575–7. doi: 10.1016/j.contraception.2009.07.005.

9 Dressing the Mizuko Jizō

Materialising the aborted fetus in Japan

Aurore Yamagata-Montoya

Introduction

If you walk through Japanese temples or shrines, you are likely to encounter ranks of cute statuettes, most of them dressed up in red bibs and hats or handmade clothes. What you are actually witnessing is the materialisation of fetuses. Whereas other chapters in this volume show that in North America, there is still the same struggle as in the 1980s to find "positive" images and symbols of abortion, this chapter highlights the materialisation of the fetus and the recognition, in Japan, of the maternal–fetal relationship even after an abortion has taken place, through the ritual of *mizuko kuyō*.

Mizuko kuyō was, and still remains despite its decreased practice, the "major form of ritualization to commemorate abortion" in Japan (Hardacre 1997, 14). The term *mizuko* literally translates as "water babies" and refers broadly to aborted or miscarried fetuses and stillborn babies. A *kuyō* is a religious memorial service, usually for ancestors. *Mizuko kuyō* is associated with Buddhism, but can also be found in Shintō, Shugendō, new religions, and spiritualisms (Hardacre 1997, 2). Although presented as the "*mizuko* boom" in the Japanese media, since its emergence in the 1970s, *mizuko kuyō* has remained a minority phenomenon practised by only 40 to 45% of the religious institutions (Hardacre 1997, 92), and estimated to be requested by around 15 to 20% of abortion recipients (Hardacre 1997, 251). In Japan, abortion is legal in the first five months of pregnancy and has been widely practised since the 1950s. The number of reported abortions peaked in the mid-1950s and started to decline for the next two decades when contraception became more widely available. After 1975, the numbers rose slightly again, though mainly for younger women (Hardacre 1997, 57–8). Today, abortion remains a common method of contraception in Japan, and the Japanese fetal mortality rate (including miscarriage and abortion) stood at 12.5% in 2013 (Moto-Sanchez 2016, 320). This is much higher than any other industrialised country.

The ritual of *mizuko kuyō* differs depending on the area and specific temple traditions: using either a single large or smaller individual statues, and with or without *ihai* (memorial tablet), *kaimyō* (posthumous Buddhist name), and/or *tōba* (wooden slat placed on the grave), the ceremony is carried out upon request, on regular dates throughout the year, or on traditional Buddhist holidays (Brooks 1981, 121). The ceremonies carried out on the temple grounds during festivals gather up to several hundred people. The most widespread and visible rite is the erection of a statuette, most often a Mizuko Jizō, on the temple grounds. Jizō, the bodhisattva associated with travellers, has also become the protector of children, especially dead children, protecting them in their journey to the afterlife (Wilson 2007, 5). Despite the large array of rites for *mizuko*, the individual Jizō statuettes have become emblematic of the *mizuko kuyō* and associated mostly with abortion. It is this part of the ritual that is of most interest to this chapter because of how it materialises the fetus.

Large-scale religious facilities can have thousands of statues, but it is far more common to have a grouping of a hundred or fewer (Hardacre 1997, 200). The statues are often lined up, with each line somewhat elevated from the one in front, so as to give full visibility to all. Brooks describes the 6,000 statuettes of Shiunzan Jizō Temple as having "calm, innocent faces, red bibs and caps, and their hands are held gently together in a gesture of prayer," but this description could apply to nearly all Mizuko Jizō (1981, 125). Within the same grounds, all are made from the same mould and look alike, yet they are individualised through the clothing and other accessories often given to them by practitioners.

This chapter first presents how the Japanese ritual has been misinterpreted by Westerners who have been looking at it through the pro-choice and pro-life binary. This dualistic lens does not take into consideration the specificities of the Japanese context, such as the stigma attached to birth outside wedlock and the co-existence of, and constant negotiation between, secrecy and visibility. I then move on to argue that *mizuko kuyō*, especially through the Jizō statuettes, materialises the fetus in a way that is different from medical imaging. The next section provides evidence for the ritual as key to normalising abortion. The acknowledgement of the fetus' materiality contributes to defining abortion as a part of responsible family planning and a way of avoiding family stigma. The last section looks at the materialisation of the fetus as child through the dressing of the Mizuko Jizō. This part of the ritual acknowledges women's relationships to their aborted fetuses, though in highly normative ways.

Through the Western lens

The moral framework through which abortion is perceived in Japan varies greatly from that of the West.[1] If abortion is largely tolerated in Japan, having children born outside of wedlock is not socially acceptable. Because the *koseki* (family registry) records babies given up for adoption at birth, abortion is the only way to avoid the social stigma of childbirth outside wedlock for both the pregnant woman and her family on whose *koseki* she is registered until she gets married (Hardacre 1997, 68).

If in the West, religious moral precepts have been central in articulating the pro-life discourse (see Gordon and Saurette's chapter in this volume about the relationship between the Canadian anti-abortion movement and religious activist groups), in Japan religious beliefs have not pushed towards a banishment of abortion, but rather towards the abortion recipient seeking forgiveness from the aborted fetus through *kuyō*.[2] So, although abortion is not morally condemned, women who resort to *mizuko kuyō* indirectly recognise their guilt and repentance.

The dominant positions regarding abortion in the West (pro-life *and* pro-choice) cannot be readily applied to this ritual. Both pro-life and pro-choice advocates appropriate elements of the Japanese context into their own discourses. On one hand, the Japanese media have defined the ritual in fetal-centric terms, as well as simplifying abortion seekers as "young, selfish women" (Gordon and Saurette identify this discourse in the contemporary anti-abortion movement in Canada in this volume). The visual depictions during the "*mizuko* boom" also match the pro-life imagery of the fetus (see, for example, Ludlow's chapter in this volume which describes such images in the U.S.), which is closer to a newborn baby than the "real" representation of the fetal tissue as described by Hann and Ludlow in this volume or the "babies in bottles" encountered in the medical museums studied by Parry in this volume. We understand then how the statuettes appeal to Western pro-life defenders who find an echo of their own graphic representations in this ritual that recognises women's guilt. In addition, the incarnation of the fetus in a statuette looking like a fully formed child and the caring mother–child relationship the practitioner can construct with its Mizuko Jizō, by dressing it and giving it presents, participates in the creation of the aborted fetus' personhood that matches pro-life discourses. Even so, the Japanese religious ritual does not question abortion. On the contrary, debate sparked in Japan about how the religious institutions and individuals involved in it make money from it (LaFleur 1992).

On the other hand, pro-choice advocates have imported the ritual abroad as a way to empower women.[3] In Japan, women's choice does not stop with the decision to have an abortion or not, but also extends to what happens after: to practise or not practise *mizuko kuyō*, how to practise it (by selecting a certain temple or shrine and a certain type of ceremony), how visible it should be, and how to dress the Mizuko Jizō; more widely, dressing (or not dressing) the *mizuko* symbolises the kind of relationship, if any, they wish to have with the aborted fetus. Women in Japan have the opportunity to publicly acknowledge their abortion and the materiality of the fetus. However, whereas the materiality of the fetus is recognised, it is done in normative ways that define the person who had an abortion as a mother and represents the fetus as a child to be taken care of.

Many pro-choice Westerners oppose *mizuko kuyō* to the "culture of secrecy and shame around abortion" experienced in the United States (Wilson 2007, 227). However, the Japanese situation is not as straight-forward as presented from abroad. Secrecy co-exists – at times somewhat paradoxically – with the visibility of abortion and *mizuko kuyō*. Issues of anonymity and visibility have to be constantly negotiated. Indeed, the choice of a temple to perform *mizuko kuyō* will give the practitioners more ano-nymity or visibility, depending on the temple's policy and the type of ritual. A private ritual ensures maximum discretion, whereas participation in a *mizuko* festival will reveal the reason for their presence. Whatever degree of secrecy is chosen, some kind of identification is usual (Brooks 1981, 126). Thus, practitioners requesting more anonymity need to travel to a more dis-tant temple so as both not to be seen practising *kuyō* and for relatives and acquaintances not to be able to read their name engraved on the Mizuko Jizō. Hardacre simplifies the situation by opposing two groups in terms of age and visibility/secrecy (1997). She separates younger women, searching for anonymity far from home, from older women who "feel the desire to register publicly their belief that they did not abort unfeelingly or callously" (Hardacre 1997, 16). If such polarisation does not reflect the reality of all women's needs and experiences, it also shows how women's agency can work to navigate the complex line between secrecy and visibility.

Materialising the fetus through the Mizuko Jizō

The fetal-centric discourses dominant in the media at the time of the "*mizuko* boom" (mid-1970s to late 1990s) were a central element in pla-cing the aborted fetus in a highly visible position. The number of reported abortions in Japan peaked in the mid-1950s and started to decline for the next two decades when contraception became more widely available. Paradoxically, *mizuko kuyō* became widely known and practised when the abortion rates were already decreasing. It is not related, then, to higher numbers of abortions, but to its better visibility – its "commercialization" and "marketing," in the terms of Hardacre (1997). *Mizuko kuyō* emerged alongside the "occult boom" in the 1970s in which the media was a central element to its development. Television programmes with spiritualists were shown during prime time and several researchers refer to the broadcasting of a *mizuko kuyō* ceremony on TV in 1975 as the starting point of the ritual's broad interest and practice (Brooks 1981, 120). That is not to say that abortion was not represented in Japan before, but the few films and novels mentioning abortion in the post-war decades tended to focus on the pain and suffering women endured because of abortion, such as *Pigs and Battleships* (1961).

The representation of the aborted fetus identified by Hardacre in the fetal-centric and misogynistic discourses of the Japanese media (1997, 91) is not dissimilar to the unborn baby images based on Nilsson's fetal photographs that Ludlow identifies within the U.S. pro-life movement. This shared imagery may have contributed to the appropriation of the ritual by anti-abortion Western movements. However, whereas in the West the fetus was identified as an "autonomous space-hero" (Petchesky 1987, 281), in Japan this image of the fetus is associated with a "floating" spirit, contributing to the sensationalism of the message specific to the Japanese media that constructed the fetus as vengeful spirit. Medical imagery is not used in the Japanese media with a heroic identification of the fetus but rather dresses it with a negative yet powerful identity. The Jizō statues materialise the fetus in a different way. The image of the fetus as evil spirit is replaced when doing *kuyō* by that of the fetus as a child to care for. The appeased Mizuko Jizō has peaceful features, far from the "evil spirit" described in the media.

The ritual of *mizuko kuyō*, like the Western pro-life discourses, separates the fetus from the feminine body. It literally stands on its own, like a newborn would, going even further than the usual Western anti-abortionist representations that display a floating unborn child similar to the fetal photographs. The Mizuko Jizō is not only a fully formed being, but it is also standing on its own two feet, independent from the pregnant body. The statuette does not represent the unborn "baby" but rather an older individual. Some statues adorn the adult-like features of Jizō, while others have child-like faces that enable an easier identification of the statuette with the fetus-child, giving it a posthumous, though normalised, visual representation very different from the "sonographic detailing of fetal anatomy" (Petchesky 1987, 277).

The medical imagery of the fetus may be lacking in the case of aborted pregnancies and, when the fetal tissue is not shown, the Mizuko Jizō is the only material remnant of the fetus. The Mizuko Jizō offers a sensory experience of the fetus more developed than the visualisation that Petchesky identified in medical imagery (1987). The 3D materiality of the statuette allows it to be touched, dressed, and talked to. Indeed, Japanese women appropriate the Mizuko Jizō, and through it their aborted fetus, by dressing it in a similar way in which fetal pictures have become part of the tradition of family photographs which enabled women to appropriate and "become custodian[s] of the image" that makes the fetus real (Petchesky 1987, 75). Japanese women are the custodians of their fetuses. The actress Jennifer O'Neill describes the overwhelming emotion of this visual tableau: "I tried to digest the display of love and loss that spilled across the field before me. My mind suddenly filled with the images of babies who might have filled the empty picture frames" (Wilson 2007, 179). However, I do not believe that the "picture frames" are empty. The ritual of *mizuko kuyō* enables women to acknowledge the materiality of the aborted fetus. In Chapter 8, Hann and Ludlow have highlighted the need for a "real" representation of fetal tissue after abortion, and a wish from some patients to see it. They recognise the emotional significance of the fetus which does not end suddenly with the abortion. Mizuko Jizō offer a possibility to extend the materiality of the fetus, beyond the medical representations that fetal pictures (before abortion) or fetal tissue (after abortion) can provide. The statuettes offer a less "real" but no less emotionally invested representation that oscillates between the biological reality of the fetus (shown in medical museums as described by Parry in this volume) and the more diverse artistic images (such as those described by Ludlow, Byers, Sarkar, Kovacs, or Latimer in this volume).

Mizuko kuyō: normalising abortion

The medical imagery of the fetus enters the family home and becomes an emblem of family togetherness during the pregnancy. The fetus gains space in the photo album that used to be reserved for the newborn child before the development of ultrasound imagery. On the contrary, the Mizuko Jizō does not enter the confined space of the house. The statuette stands "alone," separated from its "family."[4] The materialisation of the fetus as Mizuko Jizō does not grant it entrance into the sacred space of the family; rather, it stays on the margins.

As I noted above, abortion is a way to avoid the pregnancy being listed in the *koseki* and is considered in Japan as part of responsible family planning and a way to avoid bringing shame upon the family. Hardacre's analysis of responses to letters published in advice columns since the postwar years shows that abortion was and still is socially more acceptable than a child born out of wedlock, although a moral judgement is expressed towards the couple, and especially the woman (1997). Economic hardship and the negative influence a new child might have on the already existing family are also socially accepted reasons (Hardacre 1997, 73). In other words, abortion is tolerated as long as women do not reject motherhood completely, but rather one specific pregnancy that can endanger her current or future family (Underwood 1999, 761). Abortion is then a way to protect the family. Despite Prime Minister Abe's preoccupation with the lack of children being born, the legitimacy of the children and the reproduction of the model of the traditional *ie* (stem family) are of central importance. Moreover, the well-being of the spouse and current children is more valuable than the size of the family. Abortion is then normalised not only by the large number of procedures carried out since the 1950s and the increasing visibility since the 1970s, but also through the socially accepted reasons, i.e. abortion as a way to protect the family.

This meaning of abortion diverges from the West where it is seen as a threat to the family. In Japan, where living and education costs are high and a major concern for parents, family planning is seen as essential for the well-being of the – often small – family. *Mizuko kuyō* has even become a ritual to unite members of the family, be they from the same or different generations. Whereas the ritual is mainly carried out by women or couples, men and whole family groups also partake in *mizuko kuyō*, indicating an "acceptance, legitimation, and routinisation of the practice" (Hardacre 1997, 247). In these cases, the secrecy, if any, includes the male partner and/or the family members. The ritual is usually designed for one *mizuko*, but some religious facilities offer to pray for more than one fetus at a time, be it several abortions experienced by the same woman or for all the *mizuko* of past generations of the family, gathering together members of the family to perform *mizuko kuyō*, especially mother–daughter pairs (Hardacre 1997, 162). The materialisation of the fetus as Mizuko Jizō allows for inter-generational and multi-generational gathering around abortion. Individuals physically gather around the statue to commemorate the fetus like they would gather around the cradle of a newborn baby. The existence of this shared ritual contributes also to the better visibility and acceptance of abortion in Japan.

Dressing the *mizuko kuyō*: women's relationships to their aborted fetuses

From the mid-1970s, the Japanese print media promoted a discourse about abortion and *mizuko kuyō* that identifies the pregnant woman as a "mother." This terminology is used to emphasise the guilt of the woman who had an abortion in her negation of the role she should have filled. Elizabeth Harrison argues that *mizuko kuyō* is not a fully empowering experience for women, but rather comforts them in the expected role of mothers. The relationship between the woman who had an abortion and the Mizuko Jizō is copied on the one between a mother and child, thus defending a fetal-centric perspective and normative social interactions and gender roles. By taking care of the statue, the woman "re-conceives herself as the mother of the child-who-never-was" (Harrison 1996, 259).

The care of the Mizuko Jizō – through the ritual, dressing it, and giving it gifts – acknowledges a potential relationship between pregnant person and fetus. In the West, this relationship is embraced in the case of intentional pregnancy that results in a healthy born child, for whom the fetal image becomes the first family photograph. But in cases of abortion, miscarriage, or stillbirth, the pregnant woman's relationship to the fetus is silenced and disappears with the material evidence of the fetus (fetal images and fetal tissues).

One way of taking care of the Mizuko Jizō is by dressing it. It gives the fetus a personhood otherwise negated by the religious institutions, because the aborted fetus is often nameless. Zwi Werblosky and Raphael Jehuda quote a manual for priests that indicates how to give posthumous names depending on the age or cause of death (stillbirth or miscarriage) (1991). However, this manual doesn't provide any indication for aborted fetuses. They remain nameless, simple *mizuko*. Nonetheless, some temples sell *tōba*, but instead of the *kaimyō*, the priest simply writes "*mizuko kuyō*" and the practitioner adds his or her name in the margin (Werblosky and Jehuda 1991, 309). As with the statues, the practitioner, often a woman, is the one identified by name, lending it to the nameless fetus, as a parent would pass down his/her surname to a child.

The aborted fetus who has gained a child-like figure through the statue is also given personhood through individualised clothing. The statuette, at the difference of a single large statue of Jizō, enables parents to pray to it more individually but also to personalise it. The "mother" dresses the *mizuko* like she would her child with clothes selected or made especially for it. This act of dressing the *mizuko* creates a caring link between the woman and her aborted fetus. Once again, the Western opposition cannot be readily applied here. This act both empowers women using pro-choice arguments to encourage the practice, and re-creates a normative caring mother–child relation between the woman and the aborted fetus represented through the statue.

More commonly, Mizuko Jizō wears a red bib and cap but they are sometimes dressed more fashionably and with childish patterns or items. A journalist reported in an English-language newspaper: "I've even seen bibs with alphabet patterns and Hello Kitty on them" (Chavez 2012). Brooks mentions statuettes dressed in "raincoats, baseball jackets, knitted shawls, or baseball shirts" (1981, 125). Figure 9.1 shows three Jizō in raincoats amidst the more traditional red bibs.

Figure 9.1 Raincoat Jizō.

Source: Photograph by Aurore Yamagata-Montoya, 2011. Digital photograph, private collection.

Mizuko Jizō also receive offerings matching the identification of the statu-ette with a young child: juices, candies, toys, and stuffed animals. During the *mizuko* festival at Enman'in (Shiga prefecture), "the grounds of the temple were decorated as for a fair, with numerous vendors of clothing, food, and children's snack items suitable as offerings to *mizuko*" (Hardacre 1997, 175). At Zōjō-ji (Tokyo prefecture), the statuettes are accompanied more often by a colourful toy windmill than the traditional flowers that adorn ancestors' graves. The aborted fetus is treated like a child and the *mizuko kuyō* facilities sometimes resemble a playground. Buying children items and making offerings ("presents") to the Mizuko Jizō contribute to the materi-ality of the fetus and enforce a normative mother–child relationship.

Women, who are at the core of this ritual, are under the authority of the often male clergy for many aspects of the *mizuko kuyō*. However, Harrison corrected the belief that women were passive participants and has stressed women's agency (1995, 67). I argue that the choice of dressing the *mizuko* in non-traditional clothes is a way to exercise their agency. Indeed, the non-traditional clothes chosen – as well as the stuffed animals and small toys – are part of the *kawaii* subculture, which emerged from and is driven by young women. However, although agency is exercised by choosing non-traditional, non-religious items, we have to remember that the *kawaii* aes-thetic celebrates feminine social behaviour and physical appearances as being "sweet, adorable, innocent, pure, simple, genuine, gentle, vulnerable, weak, and inexperienced" (Kinsella 1995, 220). Therefore, women do not present themselves as empowered but as child-like and non-threatening to the family and to society in general. The guilty but repentant woman constructs with her materialised fetus a socially approved relationship.

Conclusion

This chapter has highlighted how the ritual of *mizuko kuyō* contributes to the materialisation of the fetus in Japan. It does so in a different way from the medical imagery shown in the Japanese media that largely contributed to the development of the ritual in the 1970s. The popularisation of the Jizō statuettes offers a normalised representation of the fetus as an independent child with peaceful features standing on its own.

Mizuko kuyō was key in the normalisation of abortion as a way to protect the family. The ritual is considered an ordinary and necessary component of responsible family planning. *Mizuko kuyō* contributes to the normalisation of the woman seeking abortion as responsible, yet repentant and guilty at the same time. Inter-generational and multi-generational groups of individ-uals of a family gather around the materialised fetuses, further contributing to the widespread acceptance of abortion as ordinary and non-threatening.

The materialisation of the fetus through the statue not only comes from religious facilities' initiatives, but also practitioners who request the ritual and actively participate by dressing the Mizuko Jizō. The dressing and taking care of the statue create a relationship between the "mother" and her aborted fetus. Practitioners of *mizuko kuyō* become custodians of their materialised aborted fetus.

As I have shown, the Japanese social and moral frameworks through which abortion is viewed diverge widely from the Western pro-life and pro-choice binary. Westerners have tended to interpret the ritual of *mizuko kuyō* through their own position and each side has claimed it in support of their arguments. However, *mizuko kuyō* is neither pro-life nor pro-choice. It enables us to think about abortion through a different prism and although it cannot – and should not – be readily applied in other countries, it offers interesting new perspectives going beyond the binary opposition. To conclude this chapter, I would like to mention three of them, drawn from the arguments of this chapter. First, the visibility of a ritual and the materialisation of the aborted fetus does not entail the end of all secrecy surrounding abortion. It has to be constantly negotiated in the different steps of the process and by each practitioner. Second, the acceptance of abortion does not have to go against traditional family values. Third, the materialisation of the fetus, different from medical imagery, acknowledges a potential relationship between the pregnant woman and the fetus, even after abortion, but does not necessarily empower women or give them the freedom to choose what kind of relationship. The materialisation of the fetus in the Japanese context of *mizuko kuyō* can help us think about abortion anew.

Notes

1 Throughout this chapter, I use the term "West" to include North America and Western Europe as sharing a debate on abortion based on moral and religious criteria, while remaining aware that it is a generalisation of various local realities. I am also aware that the literature cited is predominantly North American and refers usually to the U.S. positions on abortion.
2 We have to note, however, that the reality of spirit attacks by aborted fetuses is denied by 45% of religious institutions surveyed in 1986 and two surveys carried out in 1983 and 1984 show that not all women who do *kuyō* believe in it either. The reasons for commemorating the aborted fetus are not so simplistic and monolithic (Hardacre 1997, 92 and 96).
3 Jeffrey Townsend Wilson (2007) developed extensively how the ritual is imported and adapted in Japanese-American communities, but also how it is appropriated in the United States by non-Buddhists for mostly therapeutic reasons.
4 There are some exceptions to this practice. For example, at Ishiyamadera the practitioners can buy a small statue of Kannon dedicated in the name of their *mizuko* which will then be placed in the family altar (Hardacre 1997, 243).

References

Brooks, Anne Page. 1981. "*Mizuko Kuyō* and Japanese Buddhism." *Japanese Journal of Religious Studies* 8, no. 3/4: 119–47. www.jstor.org/stable/30233267.

Chavez, Amy. 2012. "A Guide to Jizō, Guardian of Travellers and the Weak." *Japan Times*, March 31, 2012. www.japantimes.co.jp/community/2012/03/31/our-lives/a-guide-to-jizo-guardian-of-travelers-and-the-weak/#.XNv2OI4zaM8.

Hardacre, Helen. 1997. *Marketing the Menacing Fetus in Japan*. Berkeley, Los Angeles, CA; London: University of California Press.

Harrison, Elizabeth. 1995. "Women's Responses to Child Loss in Japan: The Case of *Mizuko Kuyō*." *Journal of Feminist Studies in Religion* 11, no. 2: 67–93.

―――― 1996. "*Mizuko Kuyō*: The Reproduction of the Dead in Contemporary Japan." In *Religion in Japan: Arrows to Heaven and Earth*, edited by Peter Francis Kornicki and Ian James McMullen, 250–66. Cambridge: Cambridge University Press.

Kinsella, Sharon. 1995. "Cuties in Japan." In *Women, Media and Consumption in Japan*, edited by Lise Scov and Brian Moeran. Honolulu, HI: Hawai'i University Press.

LaFleur, William R. 1992. *Liquid Life: Abortion and Buddhism in Japan*. Princeton, NJ: Princeton University Press.

Moto-Sanchez, Milla Micka. 2016. "Jizō, Healing Rituals and Women in Japan." *Japanese Journal of Religious Studies* 43, no. 2: 307–31.

Petchesky, Rosalind Pollack. 1987. "Fœtal Images: The Power of Visual Culture in the Politics of Reproduction." In *Reproductive Technologies: Gender, Motherhood and Medicine*, edited by Michelle Stanworth, 57–80. Cambridge: Polity in association with Blackwell.

Underwood, Meredith. 1999. "Strategies of Survival: Women, Abortion, and Popular Religion in Contemporary Japan." *Journal of the American Academy of Religion* 67, no. 4: 739–68.

Wilson, Jeffrey Townsend. 2007. "Mourning the Unborn Dead: American Uses of Japanese Buddhist Post-Abortion Rituals." PhD diss., University of North Carolina at Chapel Hill.

Zwi Werblowsky, Raphael Jehuda. 1991. "*Mizuko Kuyō*: Notulae on the Most Important 'New Religion' of Japan." *Japanese Journal of Religious Studies* 18, no. 4: 295–354.

10 Rattling your rage
Humour, provocation, and the SisterSerpents

Claire L. Kovacs

Genesis of the SisterSerpents[1]

The SisterSerpents slithered into being on July 4, 1989, meeting in secret, "hiding from ostentatious, bombastic forms of patriotism" happening outside (Mesing 1991, 11). Made up of a constantly shifting roster of women, the first generation of vipers was small – a painter, a graffiti artist, a mail art specialist, and a photographer. Thinking about ways to utilise art as a weapon of social change, they looked to combine humour, anger, and art in equal measure to combat misogyny in the world. Writing about the genesis of the collective in the Serpents' *MadWoman* zine, Snake1 writes:

> The number one aim of this collective of rad fem arty types was to express, without compromise or self-censorship, our anger at how women are treated. We felt certain we were not the only women feeling angry and we wanted to create an opportunity for ourselves and other women to express this outrage … above all we felt that keeping a sense of humor and using humor is vital. If people laugh with you it's the first step to convincing them to agree with you.
>
> (SisterSerpents papers 1993, 3–4)

The SisterSerpents harness anger and rage as a catalyst in their work, which connects to a long history of feminist interventions. This rage can also be a stimulus for contemporary activists and artists in their own work against anti-abortion agendas. In her recent book *Good and Mad: The Revolutionary Power of Women's Anger*, Rebecca Traister writes that "rage can be a powerful tonic" (2018, 2). In a 1981 keynote address on the role anger can play in addressing racism, Audre Lorde speaks of anger as something that when "focused with precision … can become a powerful source of energy serving progress and change" – a change, she reminds us, that is not a simple or temporary shift in thinking, but "a basic and radical alliteration in those assumptions underlining our lives" (2007, 127). María Lugones builds on the work of Lorde and others as she makes distinctions between first-order anger that often confounds and subordinates and second-order anger, the anger that Lorde (and later Traister) speaks of that transforms oppression and transmutes fear into power (2003). Taking up the mantle from Lorde and Lugones are recent texts such as Brittney Cooper's *Eloquent Rage* and Soraya Chemaly's *Rage Becomes Her*, which focus on the ways in which women can harness their rage, untethering it from expectations of gender roles, and utilising it to our advantage (Cooper 2019; Chemaly 2019). Even *Shout Your Abortion*, a movement whose goal is to centre stories, destigmatise abortion, and give voice back to those whose abortion stories are theirs to tell, gives space for a panoply of emotions, including anger. It is within the same framework from which the SisterSerpents find their centre in rage and anger.

The group was the brainchild of Jeramy Turner, who put a classified ad in the local paper asking for artists who wanted to form a politically minded art group. Feminism, a central tenet of the yet-to-be-named SisterSerpents, was not the main organising catalyst for Turner's classified ad. However, the Supreme Court's ruling on *Webster v. Reproductive Health Services* issued out the day before their first meeting, which gave the states more ability to legislate restrictions in access to abortion care, gave the group plenty of fodder for conversation. United in their convictions against the decision, the Serpents decided to start with the issue right in front of them. The choice to start with a response to the *Webster* decision was not one that was laboured over; it was, as Turner notes, "spontaneous … and unplanned." ① → a small group fighting a larger one

From this small generation, the SisterSerpents' ranks grew, as did their → impromptu practice and praxis. Calling it "pestering," they combatted misogyny and actions / the patriarchy through curatorial work, performances, lectures, letters to activities the press, a zine (*MadWoman*), and guerrilla tactics – including posters and neon stickers on ads, lampposts, and the walls of Chicago. The Serpents strike at what they call "palatable misogyny" ② culturally acceptable modes of sexism that pervade women's lives. The Serpents utilised art as a mode of bellicose cultural discourse. ② → seen in Fuck a Fetus

Anonymity was also essential for the group, because as Serpents Naomi Cohn and Turner note:

COHN: It was … this ability to multiply yourselves beyond. If people assumed that we were more-many and more-powerful than we were, awesome.

TURNER: They were frightened of us. And when I say "they" I mean men and women and people in power. A lot of people were frightened of us. And we were proud of this.

This fear was likely stoked by the creation and dissemination of their manifesto which bluntly states that "Our art is merely and marvellously our weapon," and that "anonymity does not imply a low profile. We are present anywhere and everywhere (so watch what you say and do, our numbers are growing)." Stating a two-fanged approach, they note that their actions are warnings to our oppressors, that we are a force that will not be ignored. But more importantly, our actions are encouragement for women, to rid ourselves of the shackles on our brains, to release our splendid imaginations, and discover our own voice and needs in the process.

(Bradley n.d., 8)

It is the rage, the anger, the fury of the SisterSerpents' work that is just as resonant as the well-placed, sly humour. And in many circumstances, it was this refusal to kneel – their rejection of nuance and refusal to pull back or to mitigate their anger – that was the source of much of the ire and criticism that was pointed towards the work of the Serpents. Like many women who dare to show their unmitigated fury, the Serpents were cast as irrational, shrill, and a perversion of societal norms.

SisterSerpents against fetal worship

The SisterSerpents engaged in guerrilla-style tactics to intervene on the streets of Chicago. Their collages of found text and image, layered with created text, were photocopied as posters that were wheat-pasted around the city, in their zine, *MadWoman*, and in programmes for performances organised by the Serpents. In addition to wheat-pasting posters, the Serpents would also intervene in public spaces through stickering. The stickers, meant to quickly respond to and critique contemporaneous culture, would be placed on advertisements to call out and critique ad campaigns, on anti-abortion signage, or just on the streets – reminding passers-by that the Serpents were there and watching.

Early on, likely with the *Webster* decision still fresh in their minds, the Serpents created a commentary on the absurdity of fetus worship that would become one of their most infamous posters (Figure 10.1).

Measuring 18" × 23", the poster centres on a soft-focus photograph of a nine-week, five-day-old fetal specimen in its placental sac from the Museum of Science and Industry Chicago.[2] The top of the poster reads, "For all you folks who consider a fetus more valuable than a woman," while text continues around the fetal specimen, exhorting said viewers to have a fetus replace a woman within typical misogynist gendered roles for women, including: "Have a fetus cook for you" and the eponymous "Fuck a fetus." Cohn and Turner talk about the genesis of this poster:

COHN: I do remember the Fuck a Fetus [poster] and the fetus exhibit as very powerful, and that clearly came straight from, "Oh, fetuses have been elevated above women in status."

TURNER: [Snake2] didn't go and take [the photos] for us, she had two things in her apartment: a huge box of rubber snakes, which is how we got our name, because we would always put snakes up with the posters, and the

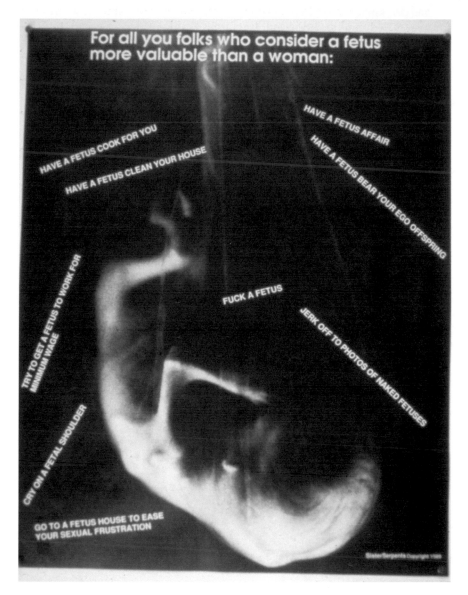

Figure 10.1 SisterSerpents, "Fuck a Fetus" poster, 1989. Photograph and collage.
Source: Courtesy of the Women and Leadership Archives, Loyola University Chicago.
Reproduced by permission of the artists.

other was a huge box of these shiny huge colour prints of close-ups of the fetuses from the museum. [Snake2] brought forth this black and white soft-focus fetus and we stuck it on the wall. I think we were probably eating and drinking, and we had this thing on the wall in front of us. Just instantly [we started thinking about] all [the] folks that consider a fetus more valuable than a woman and what [to] do with it. It was very spontaneous, very instantaneous … [This] was not against abortion rights. It was not against abortion curtailment. It was against the denigration of women in comparison to an unborn … That the women were valued so much less … So that was the premise of it. We didn't sit down and discuss a premise of it. We never had those kinds of conversations. People just understood and we all agreed. There wasn't a need to convince anybody, amongst us.

The "Fuck a Fetus" poster (as it became known) found its way onto walls all over Chicago (Figure 10.2), mailed to collaborators to be posted in other cities, and shared with comrades nationally and internationally.

A copy ended up in the hands of Lou Acierno, director of the New York City-based collective ABC No Rio, and he decided immediately that he

Figure 10.2 SisterSerpents, "Fuck a Fetus" poster, installed on the streets of Chicago, c.1989.

Source: Courtesy of John M. Flaxman Library Special Collections, School of the Art Institute of Chicago. Reproduced by permission of the artists.

wanted to do an exhibition of their work. Reflecting on the poster, Acierno appreciated their extreme presentation, noting that many liberals have anxiety about being too extreme, and that the poster itself became a provocation (Hanson 1990). Writing about responses to it in 1990, John Stevenson notes that even within feminist circles there was a sense that the poster was a bridge too far: "Some feminists feel the poster targets the fetus itself, or at least takes right-to-lifers too much on their own terms, seemingly validating their professed concern for the unborn." But he was quick to point back to the Serpents' purpose: "For its creators, such criticisms miss the poster's mocking humour" (Stevenson 1990). Stevenson missed the importance of the Serpents utilising the same imagery as the anti-abortionists – a point to which we will soon return. Ann Kuta, the associate director of the Chicago chapter of the National Organization of Women, had a more accepting perspective, pointing out that, "Frankly, they're a lot less confrontational than the pro-life people who stand outside of clinics. Anyone who wants to be offended should stand outside an abortion clinic on a Saturday morning" (Hanson 1990).

The poster even made its way into the May 1990 issue of *Industrial Worker* as the issue's centrefold, placed there by the Ann Arbor Industrial Workers of the World Collective. The response to the poster by IWW readership was swift and mostly negative. In a series of letters to the editor in the July 1990 issue, one is left with the sense that those writing to the publication missed the sense of irony and humour conveyed in the poster, calling into question the feminist and pro-choice intentionality of the work (Industrial Worker 1990). Attempting to let their readers in on the joke, the July issue also included excerpts from an article on the ABC No Rio iteration of the exhibition *Rattle Your Rage*, and tried again in the October 1990 issue with a long letter entitled "Sister Serpent Is All of Us," which called out the unconscious misogyny of the letters. But this poster, and the spectrum of responses it would elicit, was just the beginning, as it played a major role in the SisterSerpents' exhibition, *Rattle Your Rage*.

Rattling their rage

Curating exhibitions was another mode that the Serpents utilised to engage the public in discourse around misogyny. Their first exhibition was a small affair, a window installation at the Guild Complex in Chicago in August 1989. Their next exhibition, *Rattle Your Rage*, was held at Chicago Filmmakers from March 8 to April 1, 1990, and then travelled to ABC No Rio Gallery in New York from April 6 to June 30 of the same year. The Serpents created a call for "angry," "feminist," and "professional" works, which eventually came in not only from Chicago, but also New York, San Francisco, Florida, Cleveland, and elsewhere, and an exhibition postcard advertised both venues.

In the exhibition's first iteration, the collective rented space from Chicago Filmmakers, and in proposing the show to the gallery, the SisterSerpents outlined their purpose:

> Our aim is to raise our voices in rage, using visual art as our interpreter. We hope to represent work that is complex as well as angry, powerful at the same time as expressing oppression.
>   We aim to shock, disarm, and stimulate our audience.
>   ...
>   We expect the art to be quite radical and controversial.
> (SisterSerpents papers 1993)

In their proposal to ABC No Rio, the Serpents were even more explicit in the central role that anger played in the exhibit:

> This is not simply a forum for women's self-expression. Rather, we aim to exhibit the ART OF RAGE, the art that has the strength and veracity of a street demonstration in the anger it expresses, the relentlessness, and the joy that comes from speaking fiercely in our own voices.
>   ...
>   This will be a clear, uncompromising voice of rage, but one that is as complex as the many facets of women's oppression. This will not be a show that insists on a specific style, but the messages from the work and from the accompanying statements will be clearly directed to the urgency for revolt.
> (ABC No Rio Archive n.d.)

Intentionally angry, threatening, and jolting, the exhibition included work by thirty-two artists from around the country that were intentionally radical and controversial. The exhibition was designed to provoke. The moment a visitor entered the space they were confronted with what came to be known as the "fetus wall" (Figure 10.3). The wall built off the "Fuck a Fetus" poster, replicating it as wallpaper, and combining it with another iteration of the poster complete with rubber snakes, and additional photos taken by Snake2 and modified by the Serpents, including fetuses with Hitler moustaches, smoking, and wearing a nose ring.

When speaking about how the "fetus wall" came into being, Turner remembers that they needed to fill the large space at Filmmakers and decided to begin the exhibition with their now-notorious poster. The resulting installation turns to eleven the rhetoric about fetuses being more valuable than the women that carry them. Explaining the poster, the group issued the following statement: "Our poster points to the current fanaticism we call fetus worship, which preposterously elevates a fertilised egg to the status of 'unborn child' and relegates women to the role of parasitical host" (Stevenson 1990).

Figure 10.3 SisterSerpents, installation photo of "Fetus wall" from *Rattle Your Rage*
at Chicago Filmmakers, 1990.

Source: Courtesy of the Women and Leadership Archives, Loyola University Chicago.
Reproduced by permission of the artists.

Context of other fetal works

In 1990, Lucy Lippard mused about why so few women artists were taking
up the abortion issue, calling on them to move beyond the coat hanger,
asserting, "The fetus still reigns. We have to get the little bugger on our side,
transform its unborn bathos into the misery of the unwanted child as well
as the horrors of the exploited woman's body" (Lippard 1990). While not
used as part of the abortion debate until the 1980s, fetal specimens have a
long history of display as well as use in rhetorical and artistic strategies.[3]
By the seventeenth century, fetal remains had come to play a prominent
role within the Wunderkammer aesthetic, and by the nineteenth century,
specimen collections became critical to the emergence of modern biology.
By the mid-twentieth century, fetal remains were routinely collected and
preserved – a normalised and unremarkable practice.

   Fetuses made their way into popular culture in the mid-1960s when the
pioneering photographic images of Swedish photographer Lennart Nilsson
were published in *Life* magazine. These photographs of fetal post-mortems
extend a centuries-old tradition of fetal representation, reanimating the specimen in jars for a mass audience. Staged in much the same manner as earlier
Fetal displays, the fetuses in Nilsson's photographs are posed to resemble

living entities.[4] What separates the work of the SisterSerpents' "Fuck a Fetus" poster and the "fetus wall" of *Rattle Your Rage* from these earlier endeavours is that the Serpents were heeding Lippard's call (albeit retro-actively) to "get the little bugger on [their] side."

Response to *Rattle Your Rage*

As one might imagine, *Rattle Your Rage*'s intentional centring on women's fury drew a variety of responses. Writing about the ABC No Rio iteration, Arlene Raven channels the importance of anger to the SisterSerpents:

> The anger that is central to SisterSerpents' analysis and mission is among the most controversial emotional positions that women can assume … SisterSerpents encourage women to "rid ourselves of the shackles on our brains, to release our splendid imaginations." Anger takes women out of roles as nurturers, peacemakers, or preservers of social systems. Anger also accompanies most women's moves towards liberation. Women moving from deforming self-hatred to personal creativity and power can be raw and strident. But from this fit of fury can come col-lective strength and the shape of a new destiny.
>
> (Raven 1990)

The exhibition drew the ire of the American Family Association, who sent letters to members of Congress and published flyers decrying the National Endowment for the Arts (NEA) for supporting such an offensive exhibit. However, in a move out of the elision playbook, the NEA did not fund the exhibit. The SisterSerpents rented gallery space from Chicago Filmmakers, who did receive funding from the category of Media Arts "for exhibitions of independent film and video, and provision of access to film editing equipment" – in other words, the NEA grant had nothing to do with the rented gallery space (NEA 1989, 90). The indignation was carried on by the Heritage Foundation and misrepresentation of the NEA's role in funding the SisterSerpents even made it into George F. Will's column *The Last Word* in *Newsweek* (Will 1994). Reflecting on the NEA affair, Naomi Cohn is still amused: "It is still just so charming to me. It was just less than ten women saying what they thought, and it was so threatening. I mean I still get such joy out of that."

The criticism did not stop with the written word. During *Rattle Your Rage*, a vandal smashed the front window of the Gallery, and as a result, Chicago Filmmakers asked the SisterSerpents to hang tarpaulins over their "fetus wall" for the remainder of the exhibition, the Serpents acquiescing to an act of self-censorship to maintain the gallery space (Figure 10.4).

In addition, Chicago Filmmakers put up a notice disclaiming any "direct involvement or curatorial input of anyone affiliated with Chicago Filmmakers" (Stevenson 1990). In discussing the exhibition with Joyce

Figure 10.4 SisterSerpents, installation of "Fetus wall" censored from *Rattle Your Rage* at Chicago Filmmakers, 1990.

Source: Courtesy of the Women and Leadership Archives, Loyola University Chicago. Reproduced by permission of the artists.

Hanson for an article, Chicago Filmmakers' director Brenda Webb reflected on her reservations about the exhibition ahead of the opening:

> "Rattle Your Rage" is about violence against women, not about abortion. But the main reason I had doubts was the fetus poster. Frankly, that's why I was hesitant to support them. Personally, I found the poster to be offensive, but I didn't want to get myself in a position of suppressing or censoring them.
>
> (Hanson 1990)

The iteration at ABC No Rio was not without its problems. Turner reflects on an example of censorship that happened in the New York City space:

> When we did the ABC No Rio show, we tacked up posters and fliers, interspersed with the "fine art" pieces and sculpture, on every available surface: ceiling, floor, entire high-ceilinged walls.
>
> The show was scheduled to be up for a month [and] we were planning to keep this chaos of a show up for the entire time. ABC would have performances and theatrical pieces on some scheduled evenings. During our show run, there was a theatre piece scheduled, a one-man performance about porn addiction, written and performed by an "ex" porn

addict. When he saw this exhibit up in his performance space he was incensed. He said he could not possibly perform with this work on the walls.

One work that the performer took umbrage with was Lisa Broderick's *Pro Choice* which included a photograph of a bloodied, naked woman dead from an illegal abortion, an image commonly used in the 1970s in the push towards *Roe v. Wade*. The text below the image warns, "Women die when abortion is illegal." Turner continues:

> ABC No Rio, punk, radical, ABC No Rio decided that what we should do is to cover the entire exhibit in brown paper – sounds familiar, doesn't it? – during the times when this man's play was being performed. That way he wouldn't have to see any of these offending images, and particularly, not that one, which I recall had to come down during his performances, because it was so disturbing to him it bored a hole right through the brown paper.
>
> So, maybe six times, Mary Ellen and I would cover everything up, take the offending item down, and then, the next day, take all the paper off and rehang the poster!

A bit of graffiti scrawled on the wall of the exhibition, "The media would have you believe that it's always madness, never misogyny," seems an apt metaphor for the pressure the Serpents felt that resulted in a capitulation and self-censorship (Raven 1990).

Relationships to anti-abortion rhetoric

While the Serpents were intentionally engaging in provocation by situating the fetus wall right at the entrance to *Rattle Your Rage*, they were also, intentionally or unintentionally, directly combatting an evolving use of the fetus in anti-abortion rhetoric, applying Rosalind Pollack Petchesky's principle that "a picture of a dead fetus is worth a thousand words" (Pollack Petchesky 1987, 263). Anti-abortion propaganda was part of a trend in the 1980s to take up images derived from or inspired by Nilsson's photographs.[5] Such uses of fetal imagery do exactly what the SisterSerpents' use of the fetus is working to counteract: the effacement of women's reproductive bodies and treating a woman instead as an incubator for the fetus, claiming personhood for the fetus and in so doing effectively erasing the woman's identity and humanity (Newman 1996, 8).

The image of the fetus was such a viable metaphor for anti-abortionists that in February 1991, just months after *Rattle Your Rage* closed, *Harper's* published a Volvo ad which equated the image of the fetus with an endangered childhood in need of protection (in this case, moving safely from one place to another, buckled into a Volvo) (Taylor 1992). The 1980s also saw the beginnings of the use of tiny feet, portrayed on lapel pins or bumper stickers, to stand as a symbol of the fully formed humanity of early human life. Functioning as a synecdoche, feet were deliberately chosen to make the fetus appear gestationally advanced, visually appealing, and emotionally sympathetic. Such uses of fetal imagery efface women's reproductive bodies and the image of the solitary fetus commits an erasure of the woman's body.

The metonymy of a fetus as an "unborn baby" was constructed in public imagination through the dissemination of photographs of a late-second-stage or third-stage fetus, often photographed independent of its placenta and umbilical cord, instead focusing on the hands and feet. Most often it was a carefully chosen selection of a series of photos of a nineteen-week-old fetus that was the most widely disseminated version. This is also the same gestational age of one of the specimens from the Museum of Science and Industry (eighteen weeks, six days) that was photographed by Snake2, and utilised on the fetus wall within *Rattle Your Rage*.

With such rampant use of images of fetuses in anti-abortion rhetoric, it is little wonder why the Serpents, whose practice embodied provocation, decided to open their exhibition with a wall of fetuses, modified to fit their own rhetorical style and purpose: to counter a dialogue of "fetus worship." Through their active political discourse – in galleries and on the streets – they engaged in a righteously aggressive campaign to bring attention to the pervasive cultures of misogyny and patriarchy that still poison our environment today. They captured the anger and frustration of women's lives, using humour and "pestering" to get in the viewer's face and make them engage, whether they wanted to or not. Their work combatting "fetal worship" provides an important framework from which to better understand the discourses around access to abortion care and bodily autonomy in the late 1980s and early 1990s. Furthermore, the Serpents' uncompromising and unapologetic tactics provide an example of the ways that women can and should utilise their righteous rage to call attention to these issues, still so relevant in the contemporary moment.

Notes

1 This chapter is dedicated to Mary Ellen Croteau, a fierce SisterSerpent who "died as she lived, with dignity and on her own terms" on February 16, 2019. Rest in Power + Peace, Mary Ellen.

A note on the anonymity of the SisterSerpents' collective: I will refer by name to the SisterSerpents who have acknowledged that they were part of the collective and given their permission to be directly referenced. Other Serpents discussed who have not given permission to reveal their identities will be referred to as Snake1 and Snake2.

I want to wholeheartedly express my appreciation to SisterSerpents Naomi Cohn, Mary Ellen Croteau, and Jeramy Turner for their generosity in sharing their experiences and wisdom with me through interviews and emails. I would also like to thank the staff at the following archives for lending their research expertise in this project: ABC No Rio Archive; AIC Ryerson and Burnham Libraries; Chicago Artist Files, Harold Washington Library Center, Chicago Public Library; Museum of Contemporary Art Chicago Library; SAIC Flaxman Special Collections; and the Women and Leadership Archives, Loyola University of Chicago. Gratitude, also, to my fellow participants in the 2018 NEA/Newberry Summer Institute on Art and Public Culture in Chicago, audience members in the Augustana College Women + Gender Studies Tea Talks series, and the 2018 Feminist Art History Conference at American University attendees, and my fellow participants in this publication for their feedback on the various stages of this essay.

    Quotes from emails and interviews have been edited for concision and clarity.

2 Like many institutions, the Museum of Science and Industry Chicago holds a pre-natal specimen collection. The twenty-four human embryonic and fetal specimens range in development from twenty-eight days to thirty-eight weeks.

3 For a discussion of contemporary museums' engagement with displays of abortion, see Manon S. Parry's chapter in this volume.

4 For an example of earlier fetal displays, see Gijsbert M. van de Roemer, "From Vanitas to Veneration: The Embellishments in the Anatomical Cabinet of Frederick Ruysch."

5 See also the work of Lena Hann and Jeannie Ludlow, this volume, which addresses the lack of neutral images of the fetus available to the general public.

References

ABC No Rio Archive. n.d. New York.

Bradley, Amanda. n.d. "Serpentine Artists Hiss at Misogyny." *The Daily Northwestern*, 8. Box 1, Folder 19. Women and Leadership Archives, Loyola University of Chicago, SisterSerpents Papers.

Chemaly, Soraya. 2019. *Rage Becomes Her: The Power of Women's Anger*. New York: Atria.

Cooper, Brittney. 2019. *Eloquent Rage: A Black Feminist Discovers Her Superpower*. New York: St. Martin's Press.

Hanson, Joyce. 1990. "Art with a Bite: SisterSerpents vs. Sexism." *New City*, March 15, 1990. Pamphlet: SisterSerpents (P-35304). Art Institute of Chicago, Ryerson and Burnham Libraries.

Industrial Worker. 1990. "Sister Serpent Is All of Us," October 1990. Box 1, Folder 11. Women and Leadership Archives, Loyola University of Chicago, SisterSerpents Papers.

Lippard, Lucy. 1990. "Sniper's Nest." *Z Magazine*, October 1990. Box 1, Folder 20. Women and Leadership Archives, Loyola University of Chicago, SisterSerpents Papers.

Lorde, Audre. 2007. "The Uses of Anger: Women Responding to Racism." In *Sister Outsider: Essays and Speeches by Audre Lorde*, 2nd ed., 124–33. New York: Ten Speed.

Lugones, María. 2003. "Hard-to-Handle Anger." In *Pilgrimages/Peregrinajes: Theorizing Coalition Against Multiple Oppressions*, 87–98. New York: Rowman & Littlefield Publishers.

Mesing, Suzanne. 1991. "SisterSerpents Strike Abortion Foes." *New Directions for Women*, February 1991. Box 4 – Exhibition Files 1991. School of the Art

Institute of Chicago Flaxman Special Collections, Randolph Street Gallery Papers (Flaxman), Box 4 – Exhibition Files 1991.

National Endowment for the Arts. 1989. "Annual Report."

Newman, Karen. 1996. *Fetal Positions: Individualism, Science, Visuality.* Stanford, CA: Stanford University Press.

Pollack Petchesky, Rosalind. 1987. "The Power of Visual Culture in the Politics of Reproduction." *Feminist Studies* 13, no. 2: 263–92.

Raven, Arlene. 1990. "ABC No Lady." *Village Voice,* June 19, 1990. Box 1, Folder 19. Women and Leadership Archives, Loyola University of Chicago, SisterSerpents Papers.

Roemer, Gijsbert M. van de. 2010. "From Vanitas to Veneration: The Embellishments in the Anatomical Cabinet of Frederick Ruysch." *Journal of the History of Collections* 22, no. 2: 169–86.

SisterSerpents papers. 1993. Women and Leadership Archives, Loyola University of Chicago. *SisterSerpents Present MadWoman.* Spring 1993. ABC No Rio Archive.

Stevenson, John. 1990. "SisterSerpents' Hiss and Hers." *In These Times,* April 4, 1990. Box 1, Folder 11. Women and Leadership Archives, Loyola University of Chicago, SisterSerpents Papers.

Taylor, Janelle S. 1992. "The Public Fetus and the Family Car: From Abortion Politics to a Volvo Advertisement." *Public Culture* 4, no. 2: 67–80.

Traister, Rebecca. 2018. *Good and Mad: The Revolutionary Power of Women's Anger.* New York: Simon & Schuster.

Will, George F. 1994. "The Last Word: Washington's Works of Art." *Newsweek,* January 10, 1994. Box 1, Folder 21. Women and Leadership Archives, Loyola University of Chicago, SisterSerpents Papers.

Part III

Abortion storytelling and memoir

Speaking honestly and openly about abortion is a political act of resistance that has the power to contest abortion stigma and normalise a common medical procedure. This is particularly salient within the contexts discussed by contributors to this volume so far, where anti-abortion activists control how abortion is visualised by exploiting the multivalence of the fetal image to such a degree that abortion is an unspeakable topic experienced by many but still publicly concealed. Currently there is a groundswell of abortion storytelling online, often in response to legislative debates about restricting abortion, abortion myths, and abortion stigma. Contemporary storytelling exists within a historical legacy of storytelling as a means to communicate the urgency of safe and legal abortion access. Diane Schulder and Florynce Kennedy's *Abortion Rap: Testimony by Women Who Have Suffered the Consequences of Restricted Abortion Laws* (1971) reproduced testimony from 314 people, mostly women, who contested the constitutionality of New York's abortion laws in January 1970. *Abortion Rap* contains stories of the harrowing and dangerous reality of illegal and unsafe abortion: risk of infection, infertility, and death; sexual harassment and rape; as well as shame and stigma. Intentionally disturbing the reader through horrifying details, the court transcriptions are in themselves a compelling argument for safe and legal abortion access. Echoes of *Abortion Rap* have been heard more recently on the Facebook page In Her Shoes – Women of the Eighth. The page was established on January 14, 2018 by Erin Darcy to educate the public through telling stories about the effects of the Eighth Amendment in Ireland on women forced to continue an unwanted pregnancy, travel to the UK to have an abortion, or take abortion pills acquired online that are illegal (Darcy 2018). And yet abortion storytelling is also rooted in second-wave feminist consciousness-raising groups, as a first step towards politicisation through normalising women's private lived experiences and speaking about them. Contributors in Part III – Abortion storytelling and memoir consider how speaking personally about abortion is an act that continues to form the bedrock for political organising, particularly in times of decreased access to abortion and conservatism in places like the United States. Examining abortion storytelling and memoir in contexts that range from decriminalised safe abortion with unequal access (Canada) to legal and safe abortion in specific cases (India) to illegal and unsafe abortion (Poland), contributors demonstrate the capacity of narrative to expand abortion access and understanding, while also considering its limitations.

A position of "pervasive negativity" towards abortion is something that regrettably transcends the differences between reproductive rights movements focused on privacy and choice, and reproductive justice movements focused on liberation and justice, according to Carly Thomsen (2013, 150). This negativity contributes to abortion stigma. A substantial number of stories about abortion contribute to this negativity, because they have been told for the purposes of garnering support for legal and safe access and aim to expose the terrifying consequences of unsafe and illegal abortion. However, Thomsen asks her readers to consider what it might look like to refuse abortion negativity and "celebrate" abortion access within a critical reproductive justice framework, suggesting that these stories have the capacity to not only expand how abortion is commonly understood but also to create more critically engaged and responsive movements for abortion access (2013, 156). T.L. Cowan's "Abortion for beginners" is a celebratory love story with abortion as its love object. Written in the style of a comedic performance essay, this chapter queers abortion as an aperture into possibilities yet to be imagined. Anchored by three "abortion films" – *The Silent Scream* (Dabner 1984), *Dirty Dancing* (Ardolino 1987), and *Cabaret* (Fosse 1972) – Cowan offers a subversive narrative of her childhood as the daughter of ardent anti-abortion activists. For Cowan, abortion opens up a world of queer erotics and status as a child. Tracing this openness through a narrative of her life told through the three films, Cowan's chapter explores her becoming into a life rendered impossible by her childhood – a pro-choice queer feminist.

Heather Latimer's "All politics are reproductive: abortion and environment in Marianne Apostolides' *Deep Salt Water*" analyses Apostolides' memoir as a model of what Donna Haraway calls "tentacular thinking" (2016, 30). Tentacular thinking is a binary-busting reworlding which refuses the artificial divisions between "nature" and "society" that support capitalism, progress, and modernisation and instead envisions a better way of thinking with and beside human and non-human kin (Haraway 2016, 50–51). Apostolides' *Deep Salt Water* locates her abortion alongside environmental crisis and climate change, centred especially on water as foundational to life (2017). Latimer argues that Apostolides' memoir is an intervention that disrupts the humanist futurism that underpins well-known debates about abortion, as well as the anthropocentric ways that abortion is represented. Through Apostolides' tentacular thinking, new questions are raised about the ethics of human reproduction within a global context of climate emergency, and abortion is reframed as a natural act that is planetary. Such thinking supports efforts to expand reproductive rights into reproductive justice frameworks, locating human reproduction in relation to its effects and interdependence on the environment and non-human beings. The understandings of abortion that are produced through the connections that Apostolides makes – between her aborted fetus and a fish, or the ocean and her body – remind the reader that although human reproduction has massive implications for the planet, it is one kind of reproduction amongst many. These new understandings produced through her memoir are valuable ways for considering how movements for reproductive justice and climate justice can form solidarities and nonhuman-centred ways of thinking about reproductive politics.

Sucharita Sarkar's "From compulsion to choice? The changing representations of abortion in India" takes this section of the volume in a different direction. Considering how online and print feminist storytelling about abortion illuminates a multifaceted and contradictory legislative terrain in India, Sarkar examines how abortion memoir informs visual art and activist campaigns that support not only abortion access, but also a better understanding of abortion in India. Sarkar analyses the tensions that emerge between the Medical Termination of Pregnancy Act of 1971, which legalises abortion in certain situations, and the Pre-Natal Diagnostic Techniques (Regulation and Prevention of Misuse) Act of 1994, which criminalises the culturally sanctioned act of sex-selective abortion. Government efforts to raise public consciousness of the latter act have resulted in some confusion regarding the legality of abortion in India, where up to 85% of individuals may not know that abortion is legal but do know that sex-selective abortion is illegal (Nidadavolu and Bracken 2006, 160–1). Thus, online campaigns to educate the public about the legality of abortion in India that use ordinary stories about abortion, such as the *Youth Ki Awaaz* (Voices of Youth) website and Facebook page, perform important political work in educating the public about abortion access. Likewise, feminist artists draw from women's stories of compelled sex-selective abortion as relevant research to inform their visual art practice. Sarkar argues that the political role of abortion storytelling cannot be underestimated for its ability to accurately convey information about abortion legislation in India, but additionally, to expose the shortcomings of the legislation and advocate for legislative change informed by reproductive justice politics.

Filmmaking has been an invaluable technique to educate viewers about a range of issues related to abortion for decades; in the Weimar Republic, Hans Tintner directed *Cyankali [Cyanide]* (1930), based on Friedrich Wolf's play, which condemned the legal prohibitions on abortion in Germany at the time. Inspired by consciousness-raising as a method of generating theory, feminist documentary filmmakers have positioned testimony in a central political role to argue the inhumanity of illegal and unsafe abortion and advocate for improved access, and changed legislation. In the United States, there has been a spike in documentary films about abortion in response to abortion bans in states like Alabama, which juxtapose women's stories of unwanted pregnancy against anti-abortion activist strategies; Jennifer Scuro examines *Jackson* (Crow 2016), an example of these new American films, in the following section. Dagmara Rode's "*Underground Women's State*: Polish struggles for abortion rights" is an inquiry into the use of feminist documentary filmmaking for abortion storytelling in Poland, where abortion is illegal in all circumstances except for cases of rape, risk to the health or life of the pregnant person, and fetal anomaly. *Underground Women's State* (Snochowska-Gonzàlez and Zdrojewska 2009) is a film about the "abortion underground," a decentralised network that provides illegal abortion access that ranges in levels of safety, usually depending on cost. The film was unsuccessful in 2009, as it was funded through crowdfunding websites, attained only limited distribution, and was not especially effective in generating empathy from its audience, according to filmmaker Claudia Snochowska-Gonzàlez. However, Rode argues that the film prefigures contemporary abortion activism in Poland, which has seen massive public protest in response to proposed bills to enact total abortion bans in 2016 and 2018. Her chapter considers how reproductive justice frameworks informed the film and have since been taken up in Poland, resulting in the expansion of abortion storytelling.

References

Apostolides, Marianne. 2017. *Deep Salt Water*. Toronto: BookThug.

Ardolino, Emile, dir. 1987. *Dirty Dancing*. Santa Monica, CA: Lionsgate, 2019. Blu-ray video.

Crow, Maisie, dir. 2016. *Jackson*. New York: A Girl Friday Films Production in association with Reel Peak Films, Last Clinic Film, LLC., 2018. DVD video.

Dabner, Jack Duane, dir. 1984. *The Silent Scream*. Brunswick, OH: American Portrait Films. Video.

Darcy, Erin. 2018. "In Her Shoes – Women of the Eighth." Facebook [Community], January 14, 2018. www.facebook.com/InHerIrishShoes.

Fosse, Bob, dir. 1972. *Cabaret*. United States: Warner Archives, 2018. Blu-ray video.

Haraway, Donna. 2016. *Staying with the Trouble: Making Kin in the Chthulucene*. Durham, NC: Duke University Press.

Nidadavolu, Vijaya and Hillary Bracken. 2006. "Abortion and Sex Determination: Conflicting Messages in Information Materials in a District of Rajasthan." *Reproductive Health Matters* 14, no. 27: 160–171.

Schulder, Diane and Florynce Kennedy. 1971. *Abortion Rap: Testimony by Women Who Have Suffered the Consequences of Restricted Abortion Laws*. New York: McGraw-Hill.

Snochowska-Gonzàlez, Claudia and Anna Zdrojewska, dirs. 2009. *Underground Women's State*. Warsaw: Entuzjastki Film Group, 2009. DVD video.

Thomsen, Carly. 2013. "From Refusing Stigmatization Toward Celebration: New Directions for Reproductive Justice Activism." *Feminist Studies* 39, no. 1: 149–158.

Tintner, Hans, dir. 1930. *Cyankali*. Avondale, AZ: Rarefilmsandmore.org, 2015. DVD video.

11 Abortion for beginners

T.L. Cowan

Abortion has always been special to me. I was raised in a small town in Ontario, just a few hours' drive north of Toronto. Until Grade 6, I went to a local, rural public elementary school; during these years I was very aware that I was one of a few Catholic kids in the school, and certainly the only kid I knew besides my own brothers and sisters whose parents were obsessed with abortion. I mean, they really hated abortion and really loved unborn fetuses and took us kids to all kinds of rallies. Our house was full of anti-abortion pamphlets, information packages, and fundraising swag. They held meetings. I read all of the materials, heard all of the speeches, and memorised the gory details. I knew about suction abortions and saline abortions and D&Cs. I knew about a heartbeat at 10 weeks or 12 weeks, and how big the feet were again at such-and-such week. But it was wasted learning. No one in my peer group cared a bit about abortion.

In the mid-1980s, our parents transferred us to the Catholic school, an hour-long bus-ride away.[1] At first, I thought that perhaps in a Catholic school there would be kids like me with parents like mine and I expected abortion would be something we'd talk about *all the time* and I was looking forward to it. Abortion was the thing I knew most about in the world, and I was ready to be an expert. I was disappointed to discover that, even in Catholic School, none of the other kids wanted to talk about abortion unless a person was lucky enough to know someone whose older sister had had one. (This happened to me twice, and let me tell you, it was *thrilling*. I had so much specialised knowledge to share.) But I was still the only kid in my class for whom abortion was the only current event worth knowing about. At home, when we watched the news, it was to follow the Real Crime story of abortion clinic celebrity murderer Dr Henry Morgentaler. We even knew people who were in jail for various crimes against abortion, and sometimes there would be stories on TV about them, the heroes of the day.[2] We were the only family I knew for whom the primary destination in The City (Toronto) was the Morgentaler abortion clinic on Harbord Street. No Eaton's Centre or *Cats* at the Elgin Theatre for us. Our big city family activity was meeting up with our parents' friends, and slowly walking back and forth on the sidewalk, carrying mangled fetus signs and singing church songs. From time to time someone would get carried away by the activist spirit and try to storm the door, or chain themselves to the door, or start yelling and charge the doctors and nurses or the people going in to get abortions. And sometimes there were large marches of thousands of adults and children, which started at the Ontario Legislature, Queen's Park, and snaked around downtown Toronto. By the time I was a teenager, I was familiar with the route. At least once I coaxed some other teenagers into a speed-marching-while-carrying-a-mangled-fetus-sign race. Who cares that I was wearing a pink-cotton, drop-waisted, ankle-length sundress that I sewed myself? I won that march. But mostly our Toronto time was spent walking back and forth on a sidewalk to the tune of "Peace Is Flowing Like a River."

Unsurprisingly, perhaps, it was while slowly walking back and forth in front of the Harbord Street clinic that I saw lesbian feminists for the first time. This was early on, when I was somewhere around 6 or 8 maybe. The lesbian feminists were marching on the other side of the street, in what I now know is called a counter-protest. They were carrying NO WIRE HANGERS signs. I learned much later that this was a motif borrowed from the famous scene in *Mommie Dearest* (1981). There were dozens or even hundreds of them, *all of those women together*, and I couldn't take my eyes off of them. They took my breath away. After that first time, I spent every hour of every day fantasising about them and hoping I would see them again. I looked forward to the next trip to Toronto and was always on the lookout for them. I imagined everything about them: how they all knew each other, what kind of food they ate, where they bought their clothes, where they got their hair cut, what their houses looked like, and that perhaps they even lived together *in apartments*. I loved the idea of living in an apartment, I loved these women, and I loved abortion for bringing them to me.

I guess I was 11 or so when the film *The Silent Scream* (1984) was released and began to make its way around the anti-abortion venue circuit of high schools, community centres, and church basements, screened for the purpose of scaring teenagers and swaying popular opinion in the years leading up to the big Supreme Court abortion case in Canada. For some time, and I am not sure how long, my parents toured *The Silent Scream*, and would leave our house in the evenings to give a screening (a *screaming*) and, I suppose, to lead a post-screening (post-*screaming?*) discussion. I'm sure I've seen *The Silent Scream*, probably projected onto our living room wall, but the only memories I have are of the voice of the narrator, the great anti-abortionist Barnard Nathanson, at once alarmist and patronising. I have a foggy memory that, a few years later, *The Silent Scream* may have been shown in my Grade 8 Catholic School sex ed class, and that when I heard the rumour that this was going to happen, I casually bragged, "Oh, I've already seen it."

But I have earlier, vivid memories of the existence of the film because it opened a magical window for me – the window into babysitters. I don't know how often my parents screened this film. In my mind, it went on for months, or even years. Most keenly, I remember feeling with certainty and pride that they were doing something far more impressive and professional than usual: in the early evening, they both got dressed up in smart clothes for these nights out and practised their speeches. Watching them get ready to go out gave me a warm feeling of middle-class comfort, like this is what it would be like to have parents with money and education, with careers. I had always been ashamed of our family – the fact that we had very little money and that my mom stayed home. I *desperately* wanted her to stop having babies and to go back to school or at least to get a job. On *Silent Scream* nights, not only did my parents leave the house looking classy, they also hired babysitters to look after us. This was, without a doubt, the highlight of my childhood. It's likely that it was mostly older ladies from the church who would stay with us, but I've grafted a better memory. I'm sure there were at least a few *Silent Scream* nights in which we got an actual teenaged-girl babysitter. I know it's not unusual for pre-teen queers to fall in love with the gum-chewing volatility of their babysitters. But how many of you can say that you experienced the hot bliss of your first lez crushes while your parents were out showing what is perhaps the most obscene anti-abortion horror film of all time?

While I feel sorry for all the people who sat through those screenings, all I care to remember are those hair-sprayed and frosted goddesses sitting on our couch eating chips and letting me stay up late as long as I had my pyjamas on. Is it possible that their boyfriends came over? Did they talk on the phone? Whatever did they say to me? I don't remember any of these details. All I remember is that I was ecstatic with their proximity – that they were *in my house* and that their jeans were skin tight. These girls were in high school and I loved them. They were magical creatures of glossy disdain, and abortion brought them to me.

The years following the *Silent Scream* babysitter window passed in a haze of misery. The only exception was a few months of 1987, when I won several regional public speaking competitions for my speech, "The Life of an Unborn Child." It was written and performed from the point of view of a cheerful fetus who does not get aborted. With this public speaking success under my belt, I raked in enough award money to buy myself a peach and white floral knock-off Laura Ashley dress for Grade 8 graduation. Once again, abortion was good to me.

Later that same year I turned 13 and got a job as a chambermaid and waitress at a nearby summer resort. I was by far the youngest person working there. I forged an exciting life for myself – arriving home by my curfew but then sneaking out of my bedroom window to sprint back to the party in the staff cabin. I made new friends. I found alcohol and cigarettes. I could not believe my luck. If you have ever had the good fortune to be the youngest person in the secret world of small-town under-age party life, you might appreciate how it felt like I was doing everything right when, later that year, the movie *Dirty Dancing* (1987) came out, and affirmed all of my life choices. Just as a reminder: *Dirty Dancing* is a sexy movie set in the staff cabin of a summer resort, with an abortion at its narrative centre.

It would be impossible to overstate the importance of *Dirty Dancing* for me. It truly was the most vital and happiest thing in my life for years. Like everyone, I had the soundtrack on cassette, and I listened to it millions of times, dreaming of adversity and forbidden romance. Come the summer of 1988, I was back working at the resort and we dirty danced our way through every night. Grinding is still actually the only way I know how to dance.

Let's think about *Dirty Dancing* as an abortion movie. In the opening scene, we learn that Baby is on vacation at a resort with her educated, stylish parents and her clueless, vain sister. Right away on the first night, Baby escapes the resort's boring scheduled guest activities and discovers the staff cabin and the dirty dancing. That scene of discovery, when the doors burst open and everyone is just all over each other; it's what I had always hoped people would do, if given the chance. But Baby is humiliatingly square – she's easily shocked and bad at moving her hips. However, very soon after this humiliation, the luckiest thing happens to Baby: she finds Penny crying in a heap and learns that she needs an abortion but that it's impossible because it can only happen on a night when Johnny and Penny have a dancing gig at another resort and no one else can fill in for her because everyone else has to work. But Baby can do it because *she doesn't have to work*! Do you remember the dance lesson scenes in the studio with Penny and Baby? Penny's bodysuit. Baby's knotted T-shirt and leotard. All of that steamy femme-on-femme screen time. Brought to us by abortion. The next fabulous thing to happen to Baby is that Penny's abortion goes *all wrong* and Baby has to be very brave and get her doctor father to come to help to save Penny's life. And then, as a reward for being so brave, Baby gets to lose her virginity! As it has been for me, abortion was so lucky for Baby.

By the time I got to university, I upgraded my love-affair with abortion. In frosh week, I learned that a girl could ask for the morning-after pill in Student Health Services and I could not get my hands on it soon enough. My whole first year, I did nothing but take the morning-after pill. I was hooked on the smallest of abortions. I don't know if I was ever even pregnant, but I craved that crampy, decisive discharge for its own sake. While everyone else was into beer and hash, I was into vodka and morning-after pills. My addiction to the morning-after pill lasted only as long as my brief experiment in heterosexuality, and I am grateful to that period of my life for all of those sweet little abortions.

The morning-after pill was my gateway drug to becoming a lesbian, among other things. I am the cautionary tale. It's what patriarchal anti-abortionism (I know, they mean the same thing) has always feared: that if women could have abortions, they might not need men at all. The cultivation of heritage patriarchy – which keeps the old seeds alive, growing those ideas over and over again, year after year – produces a perverse fruit: a genetic obsession with outlawing queers and abortion. And, indeed, queers and abortions, we are the same thing. Living in a family that taught me to hate queers as much as abortion, I needed to become an abortion before I could become a queer. I imagined myself *never having been born, never having existed*, in order to make a life full of queer impossibilities.

This is a little bit like what happens with my favourite abortion crush of all time, the flaky and ambitious Sally Bowles (famously played by Liza Minnelli) in *Cabaret* (1972). Released just a year before *Roe v. Wade* in the United States, *Cabaret* uses abortion procedurally, as a way to keep the movie interesting, innovative, both future-oriented and complicit. Narratively, it allows Sally to keep on living an unexpected life. Unlike *Dirty Dancing*, abortion doesn't drive the plot in *Cabaret*. Instead of screening abortion, *Cabaret* off-screens abortion. After a decadent and drawn-out three-way affair, Sally finds out she is pregnant. Instead of moving back to England with her gay boyfriend, Brian, to live out her days in a *dinky little cottage in Cambridge with a playpen in the bedroom and diapers on the towel rack and a life of hating each other*, she trades in her prized fur coat for an abortion. The abortion happens offstage and is marked only by Sally arriving back to the apartment without her fur.

As she walks away from Brian, Sally is thinking ahead to her next audition. Choosing to stay in Weimar-era Berlin with Nazism on the rise, Sally is thinking only of her own momentum. Without looking back, she gives a backwards wave, and flashes her shocking green fingernails one last time, saying, *It may not amount to anything, but you never know*. This line offers the gift of uncertainty, of Sally's tentative, capricious, immoral, and possibly reprehensible future. This is an abortion in pursuit of a future of stupid decisions, mistakes, risks, failures, great loss, and potential. There are many kinds of girls in this world and Sally Bowles is one of those kinds; for girls like me who identify with Sally – her desperation, her big dreams, her hustle – there's never been a better abortion.

Acknowledgements

Thank you to Sarah Sharma, Alex Tigchelaar, Jas Rault, and Rachel Hurst for multiple readings and help with this piece.

Notes

1 In 1984 Catholic schools became fully funded by the Province of Ontario.
2 In 1983 Morgentaler opened an abortion clinic on Harbord Street in Toronto; until 1988 when he won *R v. Morgentaler* (his second constitutional challenge of Canada's federal abortion laws), this clinic operated illegally. From 1969 to 1988 federal abortion laws dictated that abortions could be performed only when a committee of doctors agreed that continuing the pregnancy would put the woman's life or health at risk. Even after 1988 the clinic remained an anti-choice protest destination; it was firebombed in 1992.

12 All politics are reproductive

Abortion and environment in Marianne Apostolides' *Deep Salt Water*

Heather Latimer

In response to this edited collection's goal of examining how writing and art can make abortion more visible, audible, and palpable, this chapter analyses Marianne Apostolides' memoir of abortion, *Deep Salt Water*, a poetic and moving meditation on the interconnected topics of reproduction and climate change (2017). It argues that in connecting these two topics *Deep Salt Water* is able to disrupt the political and cultural contexts that popularly frame abortion, and which are dominated by anti-abortion discourse and imagery, by representing abortion as a natural act. While it may seem counterintuitive to claim that abortion is natural – after all, we usually define something as natural precisely because it is *not* the result of human action – *Deep Salt Water* places abortion within larger conversations about the reproduction of interspecies life, representing it as an act that is part of the everyday passage of time on earth. It therefore represents abortion as natural in two senses of the word: first, as something that is "in accordance with or determined by nature," and second, as something that is "legitimate" (Merriam-Webster 2019). In other words, it places reproductive politics within the context of environmental politics by linking Apostolides' abortion to a larger set of questions about the ethics of reproducing humans and non-humans alike. It therefore situates abortion within the realm of ecology, or within "the web of relationships and interconnections among organisms and their 'homes' (their communities and biophysical environments)" (Di Chiro 2010, 200). As I will detail below, representing abortion in this manner disrupts the humanist-driven, "pro-life" futurism that often saturates discussions of abortion, while also maintaining a commitment to reproductive justice, which is the right "to maintain personal bodily autonomy, have children, not have children, and parent the children we have in safe and sustainable communities" (SisterSong n.d.). To that end, *Deep Salt Water* stakes a claim for the legitimacy of abortion by repositioning the human as one being among many, and by expanding reproductive justice to include the reproduction of non-human communities and ecosystems.

Although *Deep Salt Water* has been praised as unique in bringing together what appear to be disparate topics (Forget 2017), I suggest that abortion and climate change are related in how they each reveal the links between the politics of gender, the politics of reproduction, and the politics of production, or how we create and maintain the social institutions that surround the work of producing, raising, and caring for people (Sturgeon 2010, 104). For instance, both demonstrate that our individual choices are always imbricated in and by gendered political contexts (and vice versa), and both suggest that the reproduction of individuals, communities, and larger social systems are interwoven. Reproductive politics *are* environmental politics, as feminists of colour, Indigenous feminists, and racialised feminists from the Global South have pointed out for years (Danforth 2010; Di Chiro 2008; SisterSong n.d.; Silliman *et al.* 2004). For instance, efforts to sustain healthy communities and to control the means of reproduction entail a necessary connection between reproductive issues and environmental issues (Sturgeon 2010, 103). "Reproduction is a materialist and a planetary issue" (Sturgeon 2010, 108). This essay builds from these insights in order to claim that *Deep Salt Water* offers a timely and significant reframing of abortion by reinforcing this connection without falling into tired, conservative tropes about "human nature," which are often used to hold up the nuclear family as sacred or divine in anti-abortion arguments. Instead, *Deep Salt Water* refuses to separate individual reproduction from planetary reproduction without centring the heteronormative, nuclear family as "the telos of the social order," or fetishising the fetus as a symbol for the future itself (Edelman 2004, 11).

In this sense, *Deep Salt Water* is in conversation with the work of posthumanist and new materialist feminists who trouble the human/non-human divide in the politics of reproduction. These theorists claim that divisions between human and non-human, biology and politics, nature and culture, are both untenable and hierarchical, and they refuse to see the environment as some surface or terrain "out there" upon which we happen to "find ourselves" (Colebrook 2013, 51). They also reject the idea that nature and matter are passive or inert, and see them as active in their own right. In doing so, they seek to redefine what is or is not labelled life, living, or alive, by casting all matter and all bodies, including human and non-human, not simply as objects of knowledge, but as vital agents of their own (Oppermann 2016, 27). Similarly, *Deep Salt Water*, as "an imaginative expression of all the human body shares with the earth it inhabits," suggests that it is the human who is vast and timeless, and nature that is affective and intelligent; and, as outlined above, situates abortion as one reproductive choice among many within this dynamic relationship (Alvarez n.d.). It demonstrates that we exist in a "continuous process" of "making and unmaking each other" that can be both life sustaining and life ending (Lewis 2019a); in *Deep Salt Water*, no reproductive choice is pure or neutral, and every reproductive choice is interlinked with the world in that "life doesn't disappear" when we die (Apostolides 2017, 122). Rather, time moves "like the power of undertow," bringing into focus that life and death are always colliding (Apostolides 2017, 16).

In order to unpack how *Deep Salt Water* represents abortion in relationship to larger questions about life, death, and the environment, this essay works through a series of arguments. First, it engages with the work of Donna Haraway, Noël Sturgeon, and other theorists invested in thinking about reproduction within a multispecies context, in order to claim that *Deep Salt Water* represents reproduction as an ongoing, planetary process rather than a personal event. Then, it argues that Apostolides is able to do something truly remarkable with her poetics: write a memoir of abortion that is not focused on the singularity of human life or of human relationships, and thereby disrupt the way that reproduction is usually conferred with the cultural burden of signifying human futurity (Edelman 2004, 13). Finally, it claims that writing such as Apostolides' can help us to reshape or reframe our approach to abortion politics at a time when access to abortion is under renewed attack in the US and elsewhere (see Hann and Ludlow, Chapter 8 in this volume), and when it seems that we have little left to gain by holding fast to the dominant discourses and frames traditionally used to fight for abortion rights.[1]

All politics are reproductive

At its core *Deep Salt Water* links reproductive choices, acts, and practices to the ethics of living under the strain of environmental change at our current moment, a time now commonly referred to as the Anthropocene, and defined as the period where human activity is the dominant factor impacting the environment. The text makes clear that reproductive practices are an integral part of environmental destruction and climate change, and that any conversation about environmental ethics must include one about human reproduction. As Apostolides states, "thematically, the book is asking how we arrive at our ethical selves through awareness of the consequences of our actions – through the ability to hold the vastness of time within our mortal bodies" (Apostolides and Maroney 2018). This is the "profound level at which the two main stories of the book – the abortion and human destruction of nature – dissolve into each other" (Apostolides and Maroney 2018).

Feminist theorists concerned with the health of multispecies life on earth also explore the link between reproductive and the environmental ethics, noting that our accepted ideas of what is appropriate or "natural" about pregnancy, family formation, or marriage, for example, are linked to environmental issues. These theorists argue that "embedded in the contemporary appeals to the natural status of reproduction are deep attachments to political positions" (Sturgeon 2010, 103). And, like Apostolides, they look at how these deep attachments are part of the "vastness of time," by seeing reproduction as an ontological framework rather than a private, personal event, or thing. Noël Sturgeon, for instance, argues that the reproduction of people, economies, and environments all centre around gendered arrangements of work and sexuality, in that the heteronormative, middle-class, suburban, and consumer-driven family unit is celebrated as the Western norm, despite being a contributing factor to our current environmental crisis (Sturgeon 2010, 107). This happens through the focus on fuel-intensive transportation via suburban living, the long-distance shipping of consumer goods from stores involved in globalised production, and the gendered promotion of women as "shoppers," to give three examples. Even further, a burden is placed on this family unit to guarantee human survival in the face of environmental degradation, through neoliberal notions of consumption and choice, which obscures the very activities and arrangements that caused the crisis in the first instance (Sturgeon 2010, 107). This is why Sturgeon argues that nurturing and supporting children, finding adequate health care, accessing clean air, food, water, and housing, and earning a living wage are all part of the "intertwined reproduction of environment, communities, and individuals" (Sturgeon 2010, 103). Reproduction – and here I mean the reproduction of social groupings, ecosystems, or economic structures as much as of human beings – comes with consequences for the environment.

Sturgeon questions what might happen, however, if we refused to separate human fertility from the fertility of the earth, "not by promoting an ancient pagan set of practices and beliefs, but by examining the reciprocal relationship between the reproductive capacities of humans and what gets called 'the environment'" (2010, 108). This question is taken up by several other theorists as well (Clarke 2018; Haraway 2016; Murphy 2018), all of whom demonstrate that "reproduction is always and relentlessly individual and social and biological and cultural and political in complexly entangled ways" (Clarke 2018, 22). For instance, Michelle Murphy argues that we need a reproductive politics where reproduction is "not just a baby," but also considers "which kinships, supports, structures, and beings get to have a future and which are destroyed … its ambit extends into air, water, land, and a mesh of life forms into the multigenerational future" (2018, 109–10). Similarly, Donna Haraway calls for a displacement of humanism from the centre of reproductive politics, especially when thinking about our environmental crisis. In her most recent work, for instance, Haraway suggests we "make kin, not babies" as part of learning how "to live and die well with each other in our thick present" (2016, 1).

Instead of focusing solely on the human in their reproductive ethics, therefore, all of these theorists promote a multispecies reproductive justice, which is about "sustaining the conditions necessary for collective thriving" and "sustaining community beyond biology" (Strathern *et al.* 2019, 162). However, this call for sustainability is not a call for population control, or an abandonment of reproductive rights, including the right to abortion. As Haraway states:

> I don't think it would ever be possible to populate the earth with 7–11 billion human beings and their associated pathogens, exploited food animals, endless mining, ruined waters, species extinctions, and

degraded crops without violently breaking the control by both individuals and Peoples, and especially women's control, of their own sexuality and generations, including numbers and kin practices.

(Strathern *et al.* 2019, 171)

What this means is that controlling women's and other pregnant people's ability to decide how and when to have or not have children has been a fundamental part of creating our current environmental crisis, and returning that control needs to be a fundamental part of dealing with that crisis. This is because our current environmental degradation came into being through centuries of colonialism and capitalism, ideologies and ways of living that are reproductive at their core.[2] I think this is what Haraway is trying to make clear when she suggests, following Jason Moore, that capitalism is not an economic system or a social system, but "a way of organizing nature" (Clarke 2018, 12). This is why it is through changing our relationship to nature, through reworlding, as she puts it, that one must go about reorganising capital. Rethinking reproductive politics is a key step in this reworlding.

It is with this idea in mind, of multispecies reproductive justice as a kind of reworlding, that I now turn to *Deep Salt Water*, a book that claims that within "the world of the Anthropocene," we, as humans, "must arrive at ourselves as ethical creatures through our own efforts to see how our actions affect the world" (Apostolides and Maroney 2018). As I will detail below, in tackling the topics of abortion and climate change together, Apostolides is able to demonstrate, like the theorists outlined above, that all reproductive choices are more than personal or private decisions. Even further, she is able to highlight why enlarging the spectrum of reproductive justice to include the reproductive stakes of human and non-human communities alike is a significant step in reimagining the hierarchies of the world outside of the binaries of human and animal, nature and culture. In turn, this reimagining allows us to reframe abortion within a larger conversation about belonging and "relatedness" that refuses to see kinship as strictly biological, or human.

Deep Salt Water

Deep Salt Water is a hybrid of poetry, prose, and science writing. Apostolides moves between lyricism, abstraction, and straightforward text, recounting her past, as is typical of memoir, but she also speculates on the future, and engages in what we might label magic realism, as she considers the connections between her own life and the life of the planet. Two narratives run parallel throughout the text: one detailing the relationship Apostolides had with the man with whom she became pregnant, the other between Apostolides and her aborted fetus, whom she brings to life in the memoir and names Blythe. The text is then divided into thirty-seven discrete pieces or vignettes, a number that mirrors the length of a full-term pregnancy, and these vignettes are grouped into three "trimesters," or sections. The first trimester is the most abstract and poetic, the second trimester tells the abortion story itself, and the third trimester fleshes out the book's themes. It takes time for the reader to get the basics of Apostolides' story, but eventually we learn that at age twenty-three she met a man, fell in love, became pregnant, and had an abortion. They split up; she married, had two children, and divorced. After seventeen years they reconnected, and this serves as the impetus for *Deep Salt Water*, although it is the abortion itself that is the focus, and how abortion can be understood within larger questions about the connection between human and non-human life.

In order to get at these larger questions Apostolides eschews the prose typical of a memoir and instead stretches "syntax to the point where logic breaks," asking readers to feel and experience the themes rather than telling them about her abortion in a direct manner (Maroney and Apostolides 2018). The first page is typical of her writing style, and begins with Apostolides describing Blythe as a "fish in her body," and her abortion as a "gush of ocean":

#1

Blythe was a fish in my body. Her eyes are open in the murk. My water broke and the whole sea spilled. It came without warning: the gush of ocean. A sac of grief floods cities and women. I flow like sleep until I'm emptied. Now I'm bone, and the hard-round planet will push to be born.

(2017, 11)

Here, and throughout the book, Apostolides conflates the body with the sea. Later on, for instance, she will describe Blythe's "fins" as rippling as she laughs, calling her my "small but perfect fish" (Apostolides 2017, 21), and she will also continue to equate herself with the ocean's power, noting that "the same life that gives breath can take it away" (2017, 46). As she explains in an interview with Eric Maroney, this mixing of personal experience with oceanic metaphors and imagery is purposeful: "As I composed a personal scene, I'd imagine its equivalent dynamic in the ocean … not overthinking, not drawing direct parallels, but creating a medium in which 'meaning' (across multiple currents) can be absorbed, almost subconsciously" (Apostolides and Maroney 2018). For readers, this medium can be disorienting and difficult, but is ultimately successful, as Apostolides explores the complex and profound ways the body and the sea are connected. In fact, María Alvarez suggests the book's "emotional strength" lies in this relationship: "The weaving of Apostolides' personal pain with the metaphoric pain of the ocean allows the reader to enter the world of the text through various points of empathy" (n.d.).

Apostolides opens up points of empathy by creating "a sense of submergence" in her writing in order "to release [the reader] into the book's themes and emotions, rather than an engagement head-on with the ethical and personal issues that constellate around the topics" (Apostolides and Maroney 2018). While there are several ways she does this – through the use of fantasy in bringing Blythe to life, for example – what I want to concentrate on in this essay is how Apostolides communicates what she says is the underlying theme of the book: "namely, that ethics is awareness of consequence – steady awareness, in the face of our mistakes – and the resulting alteration of our future behaviour" (Apostolides and Maroney 2018). What she means here is not that she regrets her abortion. In fact, she writes that the abortion was not a mistake, even if the pregnancy was an accident. Rather, what she is suggesting is that her abortion shaped her life in ways she hadn't anticipated. As she writes, "we need to remain aware of the intensity of this act, and that through this awareness we arrive at a deeper sense of wholeness" (Lang 2017). She further explains that she needed to "reach a place of awareness. Not *forgiveness*. [She'd] committed no sin. But awareness" (Lang 2017). In other words, her abortion, much like her growing understanding of climate change, reminds her that small actions often have large consequences. And also, significantly, that at all times we are making choices about life and death. For instance, the choice to *have* a child is a kind of choice of death as well, in that the only thing we can be certain of when we have a child is that at some point that child will die (Morgenstern 2018, 12). Or, in the words of Haraway, we are already living and dying together in a complex web of kinship regardless of our attempts to imagine ourselves as autonomous, independent beings with endless or boundless futures. This is why Apostolides writes that "the only protection" from death is to "not be born" (2017, 28). Later on, she takes this one step further by suggesting that it was actually the abortion that brought Blythe to life, not the pregnancy. She states, "it's the abortion – the *surgical* abortion – that made her a child" (2017, 56).

In exploring this paradox – that the only protection from death is to not be born, that death is what brings us to life – Apostolides realises there are no neutral reproductive choices or positions. Thinking about the other decisions she may have made to stop from getting pregnant, for instance, she notes that birth control pills in our water waste have affected the fertility of fish. As she writes, "Our birth control pills have made them sterile; sometimes 'males' make eggs in their testicles. Due to the synthetic hormones in urine, fish take in estrogen though their gills. But I'm not 'polluting.' I'll only discard one embryo, and the pills I take will be for the cramping" (2017, 63). Playing with what it means to pollute the world with different kinds of waste, as well as the different roles and responsibilities we all have for that waste, fetal and otherwise, Apostolides interrogates the notion of moral pureness. This interrogation runs throughout the text, and is akin to Alexis Shotwell's position in *Against Purity*, who writes that to be against purity is not to be for pollution, necessarily, or for harm, sickness, or premature death, but "is to be against the rhetorical or conceptual attempt to delineate and delimit the world into something separable, disentangled, and homo-genous" (2016, 15). Similarly, *Deep Salt Water* reinforces our interconnect-edness and inseparability. Apostolides makes this explicit when she suggests that it is possible to experience grief or guilt about an abortion, for instance, and not question the rightness of the decision, just as it is impossible to not be complicit in the degradation of the planet through climate change: "We cannot be pure" (Apostolides and Maroney 2018). In fact, I think this is what Apostolides means when she writes that the biggest "quandary" she hasn't been "able to rest" about her abortion is that the decision had to be hers alone, even if the baby that might have been born would have been shared (2017, 62). Someone must choose for everyone. As Hann and Ludlow explore in Chapter 8, what this suggests is that abortion can be simultan-eously lifesaving and violent. It is precisely by "holding these experiences in tension," as Apostolides does, that we can consider fetal life "without erasing the pregnant person" (Hann and Ludlow, Chapter 8 in this volume).

In this case, understanding the tension that arises when someone must choose for everyone means seeing that all reproductive decisions are pol-itical, not just the decision to end a pregnancy. *Deep Salt Water* makes it clear that reproductive justice is not only about access to birth control, abortion, or reproductive health care; it is about the political and cul-tural contexts in which certain relationships are reproduced, and made to flourish, whilst others are left to die. The book speaks to this larger def-inition when Apostolides points out, for instance, that the ocean is dying because of our efforts to live longer, reduce suffering, and improve our diets. "We only intended to make ripe tomatoes," she writes, yet we have pumped carbon into the atmosphere and nitrogen into the oceans (Forget 2017). Apostolides asks, how can we rank these things? "I 'murdered' a fetus. I fed my children. To feed my children, farmers sprayed: soft rain came down in the moonlight of chemicals. Maybe a mother was killed by a drone, like a bee or collateral" (2017, 110–11). And, at another point, reflecting on how the shipping industry has affected the oceans, she imagines the "tons of metal bearing down, a hull of crates all crammed with bananas. They feed that mush to babies; it's safer" (2017, 29). Holding together these chains of interrelated actions and events requires a concerted effort to think about whose lives, and whose "safety," are prioritised in our reproductive pol-itics, and it asks us to think about whether safety is even an admirable, or realistic, goal for our reproductive ethics. It requires us to "stay with the trouble," as Haraway puts it, "of living and dying in response-ability on a damaged earth," by learning "to be truly present, not as a vanishing pivot between awful or edenic pasts and apocalyptic or salvific futures, but as mortal critters entwined in myriad unfinished configurations of places, times, matters, meanings" (2016, 2, 1). *Deep Salt Water* makes this effort by reminding us that individuals do not exist apart from their relationship with other beings and things, both human and non-human. This, more than anything else, is what makes the text powerful, as its exploration of life and death on earth reframes kinship outside of strictly biological terms, and therefore abortion outside of strictly human terms. In other words, by focusing on the reproductive stakes of human and non-human communities simultaneously, *Deep Salt Water* reframes abortion within a larger conversation about belonging and "relatedness" that refuses to see kinship as something that is created solely by ancestry, genealogy, or birth.

Conclusion

Haraway suggests that we engage in something she calls "tentacular thinking," or thinking with and alongside the earth's critters – bacteria, fish, moss, reefs, and insects, for instance – as a way to learn how to live and die together, for how to become compostable together, as she puts it (2016, 30). Apostolides' text engages in tentacular thinking in obvious ways, by pairing the ocean and the body, the fetus and fish, for example, but also it is tentacular in its representation of abortion as mysterious, powerful, even spiritual. Apostolides asks,

> What is the language to talk of abortion? The language of rights is too limited: its logic and lawfulness place it firmly within the mundane. The mysterious crux of abortion, therefore, is denied. But the language of "ethics" is slippery, sliding – so easily – inside the throat of religion.
> (2017, 41)

This is why she says that "abortion exists in the realm [she] call[s] 'spirit'," noting that it is a concept she can only hold inside her body, rather than "her brain" (2017, 122). She expands further when she suggests that abortion and climate change "exist at the limit of human understanding" (Apostolides and Maroney 2018). As she puts it, she can approach these issues "from a personal standpoint (with abortion) or a scientific standpoint (with climate change). Ultimately, though, they draw us toward the horizon of meaning; this is where a different kind of seeking must begin" (Apostolides and Maroney 2018). It is in this different kind of seeking that we find the tentacular thinking that makes her realise that abortion, for her, can be both a form of death and a natural act; we must "hold the mystery" of the act, "just as we hold the mystery of birth" (Apostolides and Maroney 2018).

This mystery reminds us "birthing and unbirthing the world are overlapping projects" (Lewis 2019b, 126). And, at a time when abortion rights are under new assault in the US, and elsewhere, this strikes me as a radical claim, because seeing the ways that we are birthing and unbirthing the world at the same time might be one way to resist the humanist, heteronormative futurism that is integral to pro-life discourse, and which privileges fetal life at all costs (Latimer 2013). This, in turn, might also be one way to disrupt the reliance on defensive arguments, which have become the default position of the pro-choice movement, and which only ever positions abortion as a traumatic, sad, choice, rather than an integral part of decision making about life on earth. It might allow us to fight the assumption that the "fetus belongs [solely] to anti-abortion discourse" by fighting the either/or thinking at the heart of contemporary reproductive politics (Hann and Ludlow, Chapter 8 in this volume). In creatively refiguring abortion, therefore, *Deep Salt Water* offers a different and more expansive response than how abortion is usually understood socially and legally. It reflects, as Haraway puts it, that the most important thing about making kin and making kind, as categories of care, or as relatives without ties by birth, what she calls lateral relatives, is that this is what can stretch the imagination and change the story (2016, 103). Arguably, Apostolides does just this in *Deep Salt Water*: changing the dominant story of abortion and stretching the imagination by asking to imagine reproduction outside of the human, abortion outside of choice, and by shifting the terms of the debate from morality to ecology.

Notes

1 As several authors in this volume outline, recent laws in the US have effectively banned abortion in some states, and have also outlawed insurance coverage for many forms of birth control, and proposed jail sentences for women who have abortions, or even miscarriages.
2 The interconnected ideologies of racism, nationalism, and imperialism rest on the notion that "race can be reproduced" (Weinbaum 2004, 4).

References

Alvarez, Maria Isabel. n.d. "Deep Salt Water." Review of *Deep Salt Water*, by Marianne Apostolides. *Colorado Review*. Accessed June 1, 2019. https:// coloradoreview. colostate.edu/reviews/deep-salt-water.

Apostolides, Marianne. 2017. *Deep Salt Water*. Toronto: BookThug.

Apostolides, Marianne and Eric Maroney. 2018. "Interview with Marianne Apostolides." Interview by Eric Maroney. *Colorado Review*, January 18, 2018. https://coloradoreview. colostate.edu/interview-with-marianne-apostolides.

Clarke, Adele E. 2018. "Introducing Making Kin Not Population." In *Making Kin Not Population*, edited by Adele E. Clarke and Donna Haraway, 1–40. Chicago, IL: Prickly Paradigm Press.

Colebrook, Claire. 2013. "Framing the End of the Species." *Symplokē* 21, no. 1–2: 51–63. https://doi:10.5250/symploke.21.1–2.0051.

Danforth, Jessica (Yee). 2010. "Reproductive Justice: For Real, For Me, For You, For Now." www.jolocas.blogspot.ca/2011/11/reproductive-justice.html.

Di Chiro, Giovanna. 2008. "Living Environmentalisms: Coalition Politics, Social Reproduction, and Environmental Justice." Environmental Politics 17, no. 2: 276–98. https://doi.org/10.1080/09644010801936230.

———. 2010. "Polluted Politics? Confronting Toxic Discourse, Sex Panic, and Eco- Normativity." In *Queer Ecologies: Sex Nature, Politics, Desires*, edited by Catriona Mortimer-Sandilands and Bruce Erikson, 199–230. Bloomington, IN: Indiana University Press.

Edelman, Lee. 2004. *No Future: Queer Theory and the Death Drive*. Durham, NC: Duke UP.

Forget, André. 2017. "Marianne Apostolides' Deep Salt Water." Review of *Deep Salt Water*, by Marianne Apostolides. *Canadian Notes & Queries* 100, Fall 2017. Last modified February 3, 2018. http://notesandqueries.ca/reviews/marianne-apostolides-deep-salt-water-reviewed-by-andre-forget.

Haraway, Donna. 2016. *Staying with the Trouble: Making Kin in the Cthulucene*. Durham, NC: Duke University Press.

Lang, Carla. 2017. "Deep Salt Water: Month One." *Room Magazine*. Accessed June 1, 2019. https://roommagazine.com/blog/deep-salt-water-month-one.

Latimer, Heather. 2013. *Reproductive Acts: Sexual Politics in North American Fiction and Film*. Montreal: McGill-Queen's University Press.

Lewis, Sophie. 2019a. "A Radical Defence of Abortion." *Verso Books*, June 4, 2019. www.youtube.com/watch?v=jMGptJXz618.

——— 2019b. *Full Surrogacy Now: Feminism Against Family*. New York: Verso.

Merriam-Webster. 2019. "Natural." Merriam-Webster Dictionary. www.merriam-webster.com/dictionary/natural.

Morgenstern, Naomi. 2018. *Wild Child: Intensive Parenting and Posthumanist Ethics*. Minneapolis, MN: University of Minnesota Press.

Murphy, Michelle. 2018. "Against Population, Towards Afterlife." In *Making Kin Not Population*, edited by Adele E. Clarke and Donna Haraway, 101–24. Chicago, IL: Prickly Paradigm Press.

Oppermann, Serpil. 2016. "From Posthumanism to Posthuman Ecocriticism." *Relations* 4, no. 1: 23–37.

Shotwell, Alexis. 2016. *Against Purity: Living Ethically in Compromised Times*. Minneapolis, MN: University of Minnesota Press.

Silliman, Jael *et al.* 2004. *Undivided Rights: Women of Color Organize for Reproductive Justice*. Cambridge: South End Press.

SisterSong. n.d. "Reproductive Justice." Accessed June 1, 2019. www.sistersong. net/reproductive-justice.

Strathern, Marilyn, Jade S. Sasser, Adele Clarke, Ruha Benjamin, Kim Tallbear, Michelle Murphy, Donna Haraway, Yu-Ling Huang, and Chia-Ling Wu. 2019. "Forum on *Making Kin Not Population*: Reconceiving Generations." *Feminist Studies* 45, no. 1: 159–72. https://doi:10.15767/feministstudies.45.1.0159.

Sturgeon, Noël. 2010. "Penguin Family Values: The Nature of Planetary Environmental Reproductive Justice." In *Queer Ecologies: Sex, Nature, Politics, Desires*, edited by Catriona Mortimer-Sandilands and Bruce Erikson, 102–30. Bloomington, IN: Indiana University Press.

Weinbaum, Alys Eve. 2004. *Wayward Reproductions: Genealogies of Race and Nation in Transatlantic Modern Thought*. Durham, NC: Duke University Press.

13 From compulsion to choice?

The changing representations of abortion in India

Sucharita Sarkar

In an abortion story posted on the *Youth Ki Awaaz* (Voice of Youth) website, an anonymous woman writes:

> While I felt relieved after the procedure, I also felt a sense of guilt, even though I knew I had made the right decision given my circumstances … I was glad to be not pregnant anymore, but I also felt a sense of loss … When it comes to abortion, there are many more grey areas than a binary understanding of "pro-choice" or "pro-life" would have us believe.
>
> (Anonymous 2015)

Representations of such contradictory and fraught abortion experiences – and also the symptomatic anonymity of such narrators – are often encountered in India, and these "grey areas" need to be studied in the context of India-specific abortion legislations, practices and prejudices. Whereas the abortion discourse in the west has been centred around the pro-choice vs. pro-life debate, in India, the contemporary discourse is underpinned by the two separate legislations regarding abortions. The first is the Medical Termination of Pregnancy Act, 1971, through which the Indian government legalised abortion conditionally; this was amended in 2002 and modified further through the MTP Rules and Regulations, 2003 (hereafter referred to as the MTP Act). The second legislation, enacted to control and eliminate the culturally accepted practice of sex-selective abortion or female feticide, is the Pre-Natal Diagnostic Techniques (Regulation and Prevention of Misuse) Act, 1994, which was amended in 2003 to the Pre-Conception and Pre-Natal Diagnostic Techniques (Regulation and Prevention of Misuse) Act (hereafter referred to as the PCPNDT Act). These legislations separately address two significant reproductive justice problems prevalent in India: the insistence on representing abortion as sin by socio-religious conditioning, and the cultural valorisation of sons, which leads to discrimination against, and death of, daughters (even in the fetal stage). The MTP Act recognises women's right to choose abortion and the PCPNDT Act aims to control female feticide. In practice, however, the coexistence of the two acts often serves to undermine the effective understanding and implementation of each. Ironically, the legalisation of abortion under the MTP Act often provides loopholes and routes for the continuation of female feticide, despite the existence of the PCPNDT Act. Parallelly, the social awareness generated by the PCPNDT Act – which equates female feticide with murder – contributes to persistent stigmatisation of *all* abortions, including abortions legally allowed by the MTP Act.

This chapter positions the changing representations of abortion in India in the context of these two abortion legislations. I will analyse the cultural biases underpinning these legislations, and the confusions generated by their overlapping and conflicting domains. Then, I will explore the emerging representations of abortion in select feminist print and online memoirs and campaigns, and visual art projects. I hope to understand how these newer representations contest the shaming and silencing of women in prevalent abortion practices, and how they communicate the abortion laws as well as expose their gaps. The chapter concludes by attempting to critically assess the impact and reach of these new abortion representations.

MTP and PCPNDT Acts: cultural biases and confusing representations

At present, the MTP Act legalises abortion of fetuses up to twenty weeks only by registered medical practitioners in specific instances: if there is risk to "the life" or the "physical or mental health" of the mother, or risk that the child will be born "seriously handicapped"; or if it is a pregnancy resulting from rape; or if a "*married* woman" is pregnant because of a contraceptive "failure," which may "constitute a grave injury to the physical or mental health of the pregnant woman" (The Gazette of India 1971, 238; emphasis added). The MTP Act, by validating the life, health and (to a certain extent) choice of the woman, attempts to address the traditional biases against abortion that deny women control over their own bodies. The Hindu belief in reincarnation presupposes the personhood of the fetus, and the Hindu concept of karma (each of our actions has a suitable reaction) necessarily posits induced abortion as a sin, unless it is performed to save the mother, because "it would be a sin upon the child to be born and kill in [sic] mother in the process" (Subramuniyaswami 1993). The MTP Act's emphasis on saving the mother's life and health may be traced to this Hindu sanctioning of abortion in exceptional cases only. Most Hindu scriptures, however, reinforce the representation of abortion as a sin. For instance, the *Atharva Veda* 6:113.2 criminalises the "embryo-slayer" as the greatest of sinners (Whitney and Lanman 1905, 363). Mainstream cultural representations, as visibilised in popular Hindi films and television shows, also persistently stigmatise abortion by filtering it through shame and violence. Films like *Raazi* (2018) term abortion as "*qatl*" (murder), while in *Kya Kehna* (2000) the female protagonist chooses not to abort when she dreams of the child-god

Krishna calling her *"Maa"* (Mother), thus insidiously promoting Hindu notions of fetal personhood (Nagpal 2018).

In an apparent contradiction, Hindu scriptures and rituals also persistently prioritise sons and devalue daughters. The *Atharva Veda* 6:11.3 has a prayer to the gods for the birth of sons: "May he put elsewhere woman-birth; but may he put here a male" (Whitney and Lanman 1905, 289). Such scriptural passages – and there are several – reflect and entrench son-preference and the undesirability of daughters in Indian patrilineal families. Social practices like dowry (compulsory giving of assets to the groom by the bride's family) and the structural inequities of patrilineal families and widespread violence against women in both domestic and public spaces make daughters a source of financial and emotional anxiety. Thus, scriptures and systems combine in cohesive and contradictory ways to produce an environment where female infanticide became a common, although covert, practice in certain regions across India (Bhatnagar, Dube and Dube 2005; Aravamudan 2007). With the import of fetal sex-determination technologies from the west in the mid-1970s, the illegal practice of female infanticide morphed into the still-legal practice of female feticide, because "killing a baby after it was born might generate a sense of guilt and invite punishment, but aborting a child in the womb was an unseen and comparatively safe act" (Aravamudan 2007, 32). To curb this widespread anti-woman practice, it became necessary to legislate the PCPNDT Act, which regulates that all pre-natal diagnoses, like ultrasonography and amniocentesis, be performed only for "purposes of detecting genetic abnormalities" or other fetal disorders, and prohibits "sex-selection" practices or the communication of the fetus' sex (National Commission for Protection of Child Rights 1994, 2–6).

Even after the implementation of the PCPNDT Act – which also insists that ultrasonography clinics compulsorily declare that revealing the sex of the fetus is illegal – female feticide continues to be a rampant, though covert, practice. The fuzzy terminology of the MTP Act generates confusion and loopholes: "contraceptive failure" can legally be used as a reason for any abortion by married women, including sex-selective abortions. On the other hand, reproductive justice activists opposing female feticide often represent sex-selective abortion as "murder" to discourage parents. Such activism against sex-selective abortions often unintentionally criminalises *all* abortions. Surveys of "anti-sex-selection messages" used by government agencies to publicise the PCPNDT Act on radio and television have revealed a "disproportionately large number" of "medical images," such as magnified visuals of fetuses, or "violent" content about "murder of girls and killing of females" framed in visuals of "splashes of blood" (MacPherson 2007, 415). Another study observed how public service anti-sex-selection posters "implored the audience to make the 'right' choice when considering sex determination and sex selective abortion" but "did not include information about when a woman may legally have an abortion" (Nidadavolu and Bracken 2006, 165). Medicalised, violent fetal imagery that metonymises the pregnant woman to her uterus diminishes or erases the socio-cultural context of the PCPNDT Act, while the omissions about safe and legal abortion information generate confusion about the MTP Act.

Community-based studies suggest that up to 85% men and women "may be unaware that abortion is legal in India," although awareness about "legislation pertaining to sex determination" is "far greater" (Nidadavolu and Bracken 2006, 160–1). It is not only governmental public service messages that aggravate the existing confusion and ignorance about abortion rights. A recent television talk show on Sony Entertainment broadcast an episode about a mother's "moral dilemma" in aborting a fetus diagnosed with congenital disability: the pre-episode advertisement declaimed, "Mother asked to kill her own child" (Ravi 2018). Such representations conflate fetal personhood, an extra-legal misreading of abortion as murder, and a hyper-mediatised policing of abortion decisions located in a culture of persistent woman-shaming. The impact of such discriminatory and erroneous representations can be gauged in an #AbortTheStigma YouTube video where a random selection of seven educated urban young men and women in New Delhi are quizzed about abortion awareness and support. Six out of seven believed that abortion was illegal; all felt that abortion was not openly talked about; all except one described abortion negatively as "cruel and stupid," "killing a life," and "against humanity" (Youth Ki Awaaz 2015). These deep-rooted and extensive misconceptions indicate the urgent need for a multi-pronged facts-based and rights-based counter-discourse.

A feminist abortion counter-discourse also needs to consider the lacunae and biases of the MTP Act itself. Although the MTP Act legislates that married women do not need partner consent to undergo abortion, the omission of unmarried/divorced/widowed/queer women and the framing of abortion as a compulsion (permitted under extenuating circumstances only by medical experts) reveal entrenched heteropatriarchal biases and a continuing disabling of women's agency. The law's biases reflect, and are amplified in, the lived social situations of abortion-seeking women. Abortion by choice, especially in single women, continues to be religio-culturally stigmatised as a sin, while abortion of unwanted female fetuses is often a compulsion forced on disempowered mothers by their son-desiring conjugal families. The relentless scrutiny and social shaming of pregnant single women often compel them to approach informal, unsafe abortion providers "for confidentiality and secrecy" (Visaria *et al.* 2004, 5048). The question of choice is problematised when mothers internalise son-preference and appear complicit in sex-selective abortions. Some urban, educated, privileged mothers claim: "Unless I have a son, I cannot be happy. I want a son" (Aravamudan 2007, 89). Such justifications for repeated sex-selective abortions need to be understood intersectionally, in the context of the overdetermined choices, strategic compliance and relative vulnerability of women in familial constellations of power and powerlessness.

This is the messy terrain – fraught with compulsions, confusions and stigmatisations – that reproductive rights activists have to navigate in India: how to promote awareness of abortion choices and rights while still combating sex-selective abortions? The MTP Act and PCPNDT Act often work at cross purposes because they are erroneously conflated in popular understanding. Hence, there is a need for clarity of information about, and distinction between, both Acts. A joint report of two feminist human rights organisations, Asia Safe Abortion Partnership (ASAP) and Creating Resources for Empowerment in Action (CREA), affirms this need to unpack the "unfortunate entanglement" of sex-selection and safe abortion rights (ASAP 2015, 4). Abortion researchers suggest that "the possibility of misinformation is particularly great" because all abortions are associated with "a culture of silence" (Nidadavolu and Bracken 2006, 162). In this context, the dissemination of accurate abortion-related information *and* the representation of abortion as choice become important, interrelated aims of reproductive justice activism. For instance, the #AbortTheStigma campaign of CREA and Youth Ki Awaaz is propelled by a twofold thrust against stigma and misinformation. The CREA website describes the campaign as an initiative to "normalise conversations about safe abortion" *and* also to "dispel myths and misconceptions about abortion services in India" (CREA n.d.).

Feminist representations: untangling abortion from sex-selection

Abortion rights activists have attempted to contest these misinterpretations, omissions and false equivalences between the MTP and PCPNDT Acts through multiple communication strategies. A recurrent feminist strategy of abortion representation is the deliberate emphasis on plurality and the avoidance of homogeneous stereotyping. However, such representations are not always unproblematic, especially when closely read. A graphic used by CREA and Youth Ki Awaaz in the #AbortTheStigma social media campaign has colourful, comics-style line drawings of six women from diverse identity intersections finishing the sentence "I had an abortion because ..." (Figure 13.1) (Dore 2015). Their answers range from decisions driven by compulsions, like financial inability, family planning, fetal disorder or contraceptive failure, to more autonomous and defiant choices, like, "I don't want children" and "Umm, I'm not obliged to tell you" (Dore 2015).

These women are depicted without any visible signs of pregnancy: this shifts the visual focus away from the fetus and towards the woman. The prominent speech bubbles – which articulate each woman's reason – de-silence abortion, reposition it as choice rather than sin and locate women at the centre of abortion discourse. The representation of the women opting for abortion with sombre – even pained – facial expressions, except the smiling woman identifying as mothering two children, is significant in multiple ways. On one hand, the sombre expressions may indicate the aggravated stigmatisation – and consequent trauma – that single or childless

Figure 13.1 #AbortTheStigma: normalising conversations around abortion. Graphic by CREA and Youth Ki Awaaz (2015).

Source: http://dz01iyojmxk8t.cloudfront.net/wp-content/uploads/2015/10/06065642/maitri-dore-abortion-abort-the-stigma.jpg.

women face when they decide to abort, which a married woman with children will not have to. This discriminatory cultural bias may have shaped their different expressions. The discriminatory stigmatisation revealed in the graphic representation mimics the biases of the MTP Act, which sanctions abortions only for married women. However, the replication of such generalised prejudices against single women – that abortion is more traumatic for them than it is for women with children – in a feminist graphic asserting the right to abortion may also undercut the radical agenda and reveal a subconscious seepage of prevalent cultural biases even into feminist representations.

In recent years, there have been several feminist activist projects, both offline and online, that attempt to reclaim the abortion agency and record the abortion experiences of women. When Rosalind Pollack Petchesky urged that women be restored to a "central place in the pregnancy scene," she suggested the need to contextualise women's abortions "through stories that give them mass and dimension" (1987, 287). Mass and dimension can be accumulated by breaking up monolithic stereotypes and by documenting a wide range of individual abortion experiences. This dual strategy of individualisation and inclusion undergirds the documentation of abortion stories by Indian women. For instance, the activist organisation Feminism in India (FII) has a YouTube podcast in which five women, aged between nineteen and twenty-seven, speak anonymously about their abortion/s (Feminism in India 2018). Aiming to create "judgement-free spaces" where women can talk about their "different experiences of abortion," the FII podcast includes oral testimonies where the women speak of feeling "relieved" and "triumphant" that they have been able to "exercise [their] choice"; or feeling "nothing really" as abortion "didn't change the person" they were; or feeling "stupid" at having an "unplanned pregnancy"; or feeling "pained" because it "hurts" to think of the unborn child (Feminism in India 2018). These testimonies resist the stereotyping and othering of abortion-choosing women as unfeeling murderers and insert a multiplicity of women's voices – ranging from apologetic to defiant – into the abortion discourse.

Such an often-conflicting range of emotions can also be found *within* individual narratives. Anwesha Arya's memoir about her teenage abortion experiences – included in a feminist anthology on mothering and motherhood – describes the internal, "intricate mental discussions" she continues to have "in the darkness of [her] room, to torture and confuse" herself, "without a solution or closure after a dozen years or more" (2006, 173). Although she emphasises that she "made the right decision," protests against the public silencing of abortion stories and has the support of her feminist mother and caring partner, Arya continues to judge herself as "'murderer' or 'irresponsible'" (Arya 2006, 181–3). Arya's persistent trauma and internalised guilt are rooted in her belief in fetal personhood. Her narrative compellingly returns to the refrain of Anne Sexton's poem, "The Abortion": "someone who should have been born is gone" (Arya 2006, 179). She concludes with an afterword about her later experience of giving birth to a stillborn daughter. This ending reifies the deep-rooted local beliefs – alluded to earlier in the memoir – that multiple abortions impact a woman's future ability to conceive healthy offspring. Significantly, Arya admits that her inability to "argue pro-choice" is caused by the "perfect 3D imaging" of the "growing embryo in clear images" (Arya 2006, 181). In spite of her feminist education, Arya is unable to resist the potent propaganda of such images. Although she recognises how "surveillance and potential social control" are embedded in ultrasound imaging, she continues to be deeply affected by the "level of fantasy or myth" coded therein (Petchesky 1987, 274). Despite asserting the need for de-silencing and de-stigmatising abortion, and despite voluntarily choosing abortion, Arya's – like many other Indian abortion memoirs – remains locked in an "apologist framework" (Thomsen 2013, 150). Fetal personhood is a powerfully felt reality and a lived loss for her, an experience that her feminist consciousness is unable to deny or rationalise. Arya's memoir opens up the risky, affective terrain of abortion guilt and grieving that is often unaddressed in feminist pro-choice agendas. Abortion guilt, which is socio-culturally pivoted on the belief in fetal personhood, is traumatic and persistently residual. The ending of Arya's memoir signifies her inability to find post-abortion closure, even after so many years. Instead of theorising or reducing fetal personhood or fetal materiality into abstractions, perhaps feminist reproductive justice activists and abortion providers need to understand and address such lived experiences of trauma and insist on the necessity of post-abortion counselling and care.[1]

Even though conflicted narratives like Arya's may tacitly or openly undermine feminist pro-choice abortion politics, Indian activists continue to engage with and archive a wide range of abortion stories. Recognising the autonomy of the abortion storyteller is an extension of respecting the autonomy of women's abortion choices. Surabhi Srivastava's *Voice Your Abortion* Facebook project adopts an "ethical storytelling framework": she puts the woman narrator "at the centre of the storytelling process," which enables them "to feel a sense of empowerment and ownership" about sharing their personal abortion stories in public, even though these stories "may not always align with" the "goals or motives" of "abortion rights activists" (2016). Thus, while women's decisions to undergo abortions may be located within a complex matrix of choices and compulsions determined by interlinked, subjugating power structures, these recent storytelling campaigns offer women bias-free spaces and support, if they choose to voice their abortion stories.

Feminist woman-centric politics can also re-imagine the creative visual representation of sex-selective abortions, which, in the Indian context, often tends to metaphorise the horrors of female feticide. The complex and nuanced representation of female feticide in Navjyot Altaf's *Palani's Daughters of Pieces* evokes the histories and contexts of the women who (are often compelled to) undergo sex-selective abortions (Figure 13.2).

Altaf's representation focuses on the embodied pain of abortion/s and she places the labouring, nude woman, Palani, at the centre. Female feticide is re-contextualised as an action enforced on the body of the mother, as indicated by Palani's supine position. The fetuses, Palani's daughters – scattered between Palani's spread legs – are de-personified and represented as vulva-shaped pods. This visual metaphor identifies the fetuses as female; and is also a commentary about how women are always essentialised to – and continue to remain locked in – their sexual/reproductive roles in patriarchal societies. In India, especially, son-producing mothers are culturally glorified, while mothers producing only daughters are vilified as failed mothers. The absence of class/caste identity markers on Palani universalises the aborting maternal body across classed and regional intersections. Although without choice, the powerful centrality of Palani's labouring body also implies a certain agency that uncovers the covert feticides she is forced to undergo and, literally, makes her trauma visible and no longer possible (for the viewer) to ignore. To see Palani's labouring body is to strip away the shame and

Palani's daughters : seven pieces 16x69x47 inches, 3x11x6 inches : acrylic paint on wood & a panel consisting of serigraphs on
paper & plexi glass : 60x30 inches : from series Images Redrawn : 1996
Installation view : Triveni Art Gallery New Delhi

Figure 13.2 Palani's Daughters. Wood sculpture by Navjvot Altaf, 1996.
Source: National Gallery of Modern Art, Mumbai. Used with permission of the artist.

secrecy associated with abortions. Altaf, thus, by rendering the labouring woman visible, critiques sex-selective abortion as an action performed *upon* the maternal body (rather than an abortion choice exercised *by* her), and also deploys this visible, agentic body to expose this discrimination.

The blurring of this distinction between coercive sex-selective abortion and voluntarily chosen abortion leads to problematic representations. Recent Indian government guidelines acknowledge this problem and suggest ways to represent abortion in less confusing, more just ways. In a booklet on safe abortion, the government focuses on "the overlap between abortion and sex selection" (Ministry of Health & Family Welfare 2015, 35). Instead of terms like "sin," "killing," "murder" or even "female feticide," the booklet suggests using the term *"gender-biased* sex selection" and advises that "violence against the fetus" be "positioned as violence against … women as a community" (Ministry of Health & Family Welfare 2015, 36–7; emphasis added). In a tabular list of "Do's" and "Don'ts" of abortion representation, the booklet promotes the use of "images that express joy and celebration linked to the birth of a girl child" and urges the discontinuance of images of "fetuses being crushed, stabbed or strangled," or fetal personification, like "a female fetus speaking from the womb," or even "imagery that selectively emphasizes the value of women only as brides" (Ministry of Health &

Family Welfare 2015, 38). These recent government guidelines attempt to shift from earlier punitive, often violent and confusing communication to new representation strategies which are more aligned to reproductive justice aims. This may be a tacit response to the continuing feminist demands to untangle the representations and receptions of the MTP and the PCPNDT Acts (ASAP 2015, 4). However, although the booklet demarcates between the MTP and the PCPNDT Acts, and emphasises the legality of abortion (while simultaneously emphasising the eradication of gender bias through misuse of sex-selection technology), it fails to centralise – or even to acknowledge – the primacy of women's choice in abortion. This is the significant absence that women's abortion narratives and activist campaigns are trying to address. By inserting a transformative focus on choice, as well as by exploring the multitudinous compulsions of abortion, these woman-centred and woman-voiced representations are necessary feminist interventions challenging abortion stigma and disablement and, also, the persistent omissions of official abortion laws and communication.

In conclusion, I consider the potential social impact of these emerging abortion representations. Surabhi Srivastava hopes that, in the "nascent" abortion activism discourse in India, "abortion storytelling can prove to be revolutionary in bringing about a change in the public understanding," while admitting "we have a long way to go, especially in terms of providing an enabling space for *women from all walks of life*" (2016; emphasis added). The dissemination of woman-centred abortion representations is a necessary step in resisting stigma and shame and in countering misunderstandings about abortion laws and rights. There are an estimated "ten million" Indian women who "undergo a secret abortion every year" (Mohta 2018). Although comparatively minuscule, the documented and accessible abortion stories can be valuable resources for other abortion-seeking or abortion-affected women. The persistence of gender-biased sex-selective abortions complicates the ethical/political resonances of abortion-as-choice assertions. This misogynistic cultural history that shapes abortion discourse in India is manifested in a visible "fear of celebrating abortion" (Thomsen 2013, 159). Although rarely celebratory, the new Indian representations and activism may collectively and eventually pressure the government into amending the existing MTP law to prioritise women's choice, include rights of non-married persons and expand legal abortion limits beyond twenty weeks.

However, most of these campaigns and artworks are accessible only to urban, English-speaking and digitally enabled persons. Surbhi Srivastava's *Voice Your Abortion* Facebook project aims to include "experiences of women that have traditionally been marginalised … like abortion accounts of sex workers, Dalit women, women incarcerated in prison, single women, etc.," but an archival search of her Facebook posts reveals that such marginalised abortion experiences are as yet undocumented there (Srivastava 2016). Urban–rural disparities and digital divides continue to limit the impact of online abortion representations. For instance, the ASAP safe abortion video has approximately 8,200 views, while the *Feminism in India* abortion stories podcast has only about 500 views (ASAP 2013; Feminism in India 2018; as accessed on 12 April 2019). Both are narrated or scripted mostly in English. On the other hand, a YouTube video by *Maa Tujhe Salaam* (Salute to You, Mother), a medical experts' collective, which uses a Hindi voiceover with Hindi/English captions to communicate information about abortion practices and laws, has over 238,500 views (Maa Tujhe Salaam 2018; as accessed on 12 April 2019). Although this video privileges the medical expert's voice over the woman's, its effective deployment of Hindi/vernacular language in reaching more viewers is a communication strategy that can be fruitfully adopted by feminist representations of abortion.

Thus far, the abortion stories documented, especially online, by Indian feminist activist organisations are mostly voiced by anonymous women from privileged identity intersections. Anonymity is sometimes necessary to construct safe spaces for storytelling. However, although radical headlines, like "Five Unmarried Indian Women Break the Silence around Abortion," transgress the unspeakable-ness of abortion, disclaimers stating that "the names of all the contributors have been changed to protect their identity" indicate the layers of stigma that continue to muffle abortion choices and testimonies (Mohta 2018). Across rural and even large parts of urban India, patriarchal practices like son-preference, daughter-discrimination, dowry giving, women's domestic subservience and woman blaming-and-shaming combine to blunt the implementation of both the MTP and the PCPNDT Acts. To counter this, abortion representations need to reach beyond linguistic, classed and locational barriers. There are researcher-activists who are working on abortion communication targeting low-literate rural women. For instance, the manual *Safai ki Jankari* (Information on Abortion) uses an easily understood "visual grammar" – "a black dot to represent pregnancy, an inverted 'u' to represent the uterus" – that de-personalises the fetus while promoting safe abortion choices among rural women in Rajasthan (Nidadavolu and Bracken 2006, 168–9). To dismantle the entrenched oppressions and silencing that permeate the abortion discourse across India, and to more accurately represent the socio-cultural diversity of Indian women's abortion experiences, the emerging online/offline feminist representations studied here will have to expand to – and work cohesively with – rural, vernacular, and intersectional activism and advocacy of abortion as a choice and right of all Indian women.

Note

1 See Hann and Ludlow's chapter in this volume on the necessity of not seeing the fetus as an undesired by-product. Ironically, though, in India, it is often the female fetuses that are culturally accepted as undesirable.

References

Anonymous. 2015. "Abortion May Be a Difficult Choice, but the Choice Is Mine." Youth Ki Awaaz. www.youthkiawaaz.com/2015/08/abortion-personal-story.

Aravamudan, Gita. 2007. *Disappearing Daughters: The Tragedy of Female Foeticide.* New Delhi: Penguin.

Arya, Anwesha. 2006. "The Mother Who Wasn't: Someone Who Should've Been Born Is Gone." In *Janani—Mothers, Daughters, Motherhood*, edited by Rinki Bhattacharya, 173–85. New Delhi: Sage Publications.

ASAP. 2013. *From Unwanted Pregnancies to Safe Abortion (New)*. ASAP. YouTube video, 9.02. www.youtube.com/watch?v=mwv81v96ick.

——— 2015. *Sex Selection and Safe Abortion Rights: Past Trajectories, Current Impact and Future Strategies.* ASAP and CREA. http://asap-asia.org/pdf/ASAP-CREA-Meeting-Report.pdf.

Bhatnagar, Rashmi Dube, Renu Dube, and Reena Dube. 2005. *Female Infanticide in India: A Feminist Cultural History.* Albany, NY: State University of New York.

CREA. n.d. "#AbortTheStigma." CREA World. Accessed on 12 December 2018. www.creaworld.org/abortthestigma.

Dore, Maitri. 2015. "No One's Decision but Mine." Youth Ki Awaaz. www.youthkiawaaz.com/2015/10/abortion-stigma-illustration.

Feminism in India. 2018. *Women Tell Their Abortion Stories: Feminism in India.* Feminism in India. YouTube podcast, 4.43. www.youtube.com/watch?v=XOcNaVk5FF0.

Maa Tujhe Salaam. 2018. *ABORTION in INDIA – Methods? At Home? When? Safety? (Hindi)*. YouTube video, 5.45. www.youtube.com/watch?v=xubg0UQW9t8.

MacPherson, Yvonne. 2007. "Images and Icons: Harnessing the Power of the Media to Reduce Sex-Selective Abortion in India." *Gender and Development* 15, no. 3: 413–23. www.jstor.org/stable/20461226.

Ministry of Health & Family Welfare. 2015. *Guidance: Ensuring Access to Safe Abortion and Addressing Gender Biased Sex Selection.* Government of India. www.nrhmtn.gov.in/guideline/SafeAbortionHandbook.pdf.

Mohta, Payal. 2018. "Five Unmarried Women Break the Silence around Abortion." Homegrown. 20 February. https://homegrown.co.in/article/802151/five-unmarried-indian-women-break-the-silence-around-abortion.

Nagpal, Ishmeet. 2018. "6 Bollywood Films That Mention Abortion, but It's Not What You Think." Feminism in India. 7 June. https://feminisminindia.com/2018/06/07/6-bollywood-films-mention-abortion/.

National Commission for Protection of Child Rights. 1994. *Pre-Conception and Pre-Natal Diagnostic Techniques (Regulation and Prevention of Misuse) Act.* Government of India. www.ncpcr.gov.in/view_file.php?fid=434.

Nidadavolu, Vijaya, and Hillary Bracken. 2006. "Abortion and Sex Determination: Conflicting Messages in Information Materials in a District of Rajasthan." *Reproductive Health Matters* 14, no. 27: 160–71. www.jstor.org/stable/3775862.

Petchesky, Rosalind P. 1987. "Fetal Images: The Power of Visual Culture in the Politics of Reproduction." *Feminist Studies* 13, no. 2: 263–92. www.jstor.org/stable/3177802.

Ravi, Aashika. 2018. "Zindagi ke Crossroads and the Stigmatisation of Abortion." Firstpost. 12 June. www.firstpost.com/entertainment/zindagi-ke-crossroads-and-the-stigmatisation-of-abortion-pressing-need-for-positive-portrayal-of-womens-issues-4506805.html.

Srivastava, Surabhi. 2016. "Abortion Storytelling and Story-Sharing: Keeping It Ethical." Feminism in India. 28 September. https://feminisminindia.com/2016/09/28/ethical-abortion-storytelling.

Subramuniyaswami, Sivaya. 1993. "Let's Talk about Abortion." Hinduism Today. January. www.hinduismtoday.com/modules/smartsection/item.php?itemid=995.

The Gazette of India. 1971. "The Medical Termination of Pregnancy Act." Ministry of Law & Justice. http://egazette.nic.in/WriteReadData/1971/E-1383-1971-0034-61647.pdf.

Thomsen, Carly. 2013. "From Refusing Stigmatization toward Celebration: New Directions for Reproductive Justice Activism." *Feminist Studies* 39, no. 1: 149–58. www.jstor.org/stable/23719304.

Visaria, Leela, Vimala Ramachandran, Bela Ganatra, and Shveta Kalyanwala. 2004. "Abortion in India: Emerging Issues from Qualitative Studies." *Economic and Political Weekly* 39, no. 46/47: 5044–5052. www.jstor.org/stable/4415809.

Whitney, William Dwight, trans. and Charles Rockwell Lanman, ed. 1905. *Atharva Veda Samhita*. Cambridge, MA: Harvard University Press.

Youth Ki Awaaz. 2015. *What Do Young Indians Think of Abortion? Youth ki Awaaz*. Youth Ki Awaaz. YouTube video, 3.58. www.youtube.com/watch?v=KOBk5evGGdo.

14 Underground Women's State

Polish struggles for abortion rights

Dagmara Rode

The abortion ban in Poland came into force in 1993. It is a symbol of the political transition of 1989, showing a tendency for the retraditionalisation of gender roles. After the ban, abortion has often been dismissed in public discourse as a distraction from "real" and "more important" topics. The pro-choice point of view, which accentuates women's rights, is rarely heard in popular debate. Conservative anti-choice rhetoric, grounded in religious terms, is dominant in public discourse and peppered with phrases like "conceived child," "murder of the unborn," or simply "life." As a consequence of the "lost battle over language" (Graff 2005, 121), women disappear from the discussion, as well as abortion as an experience and a routine medical procedure. The violent imagery present in films like *The Silent Scream* (1984), often screened during religious education classes, and drastic photos exhibited by anti-choice organisations on the streets have shaped common perceptions of abortion in Poland. Contemporary Polish films and television series either demonise and stigmatise abortion or do not mention it at all (Łaciak 2016; Wejbert-Wąsiewicz 2018).

The mixture of anti-communist rhetoric, Catholic principles, neoliberal values, and imported anti-abortion propaganda has proven very difficult for feminist activists to contest. There has been an obvious need for new language to talk publicly about abortion. In this chapter I analyse one of the attempts at formulating a new way of discussing and representing abortion – an independent feminist documentary, *Podziemne państwo kobiet* (*Underground Women's State*; Snochowska-Gonzàlez and Zdrojewska 2009), directed by two activist filmmakers and supported by the feminist fund MamaCash. The fact that the problem of the abortion underground was taken up by activists, not professional filmmakers (who tended to avoid contemporary "journalistic" subjects and, above all, a notion of engagement on the pro-choice side), is considered by Krzysztof Tomasik to be "a failure of the filmmakers' community" (2011, 153). *Podziemne państwo kobiet* circulated outside of official film distribution – most screenings were organised through leftist or feminist initiatives – and it was not shown on public television or any major private broadcaster, except for the documentary channel Planete (Tomasik 2011). The film's strategy is twofold, describing the contemporary reality of the abortion underground and asserting the continuity of women's struggles for abortion access. In this chapter, I first analyse the representation of the abortion underground as told by the subjects of documentary. Second, I concentrate on the role of historical context presented in the film, and finally, I argue that the documentary simultaneously failed to mobilise broader public while it influenced the trajectory of abortion activism in Poland.

Breaking the silence

When the film was released in 2009, abortion law was not a prominent political issue in Poland. Two years before the film's premiere, the proposed constitutional amendment banning abortion in all circumstances lost the parliamentary vote by a slight margin. Protests against the amendment were sparse in 2007. By 2008, the abortion bill appeared to be a stable element of Polish reality, leading to attacks on new areas of reproductive rights such as in vitro fertilisation (Chełstowska 2011). In 2011, feminist activists were unsuccessful in collecting 100,000 signatures to introduce a bill liberalising abortion law in parliament.

The ban did not reduce the number of procedures. It only caused many abortions, including those performed by qualified doctors, to go underground. Today abortion in Poland is legal in three restricted cases: when a pregnancy poses a threat to the health or life of the pregnant woman, when a pregnancy is a result of a criminal act, or when severe and irreversible fetal congenital anomalies are present. Access to legal procedures is further restricted by the common practice of doctors invoking the conscience clause or circumventing the rights of pregnant persons through misinformation, lack of access to prenatal testing, or ordering time-consuming and unnecessary tests and procedures that extend the pregnancy beyond the time limits for obtaining an abortion.

In 2009 "a resurrection of an abortion debate" was needed (Goll 2009). In order to reopen such discussion, the directors decided to give voice to those rarely represented: the women who undergo illegal procedures. Before the film's premiere, most abortion stories that circulated in public discourse concentrated on women who were refused access to healthcare; for example, the stories presented during abortion tribunals and speak-outs organised by The Federation for Women and Reproductive Rights (Girard and Nowicka 2002).[1] Snochowska-Gonzàlez and Zdrojewska made a different choice, by presenting women recalling their illegal abortion to create a "new space for women in which when they talk about abortion they are not presented as murderers" (Goll 2009). The directors looked for potential interviewees through online ads. They got responses from 20 people and, eventually, the testimonies of eight women were used in the film (Kula and Sadowska 2009).

The eight subjects are identified by their first names: Ela, Ewa, Jola, Julia, Karolina, Kasia, Magda, and Teresa. Teresa was the only person who underwent termination when it was still legal. At that time, she decided to undergo the procedure privately because it was faster and more comfortable. The same doctor terminated Teresa's second pregnancy after the ban. Teresa and Julia did not want children. Jola's and Magda's decisions to have an abortion were influenced by the lack of support from their partners, while Kasia's prior experience of abuse and fear led her to believe that, as a single mother, she would not have the means to raise two children. Some women did not clarify their motivations in the film. Contrary to common stories used to justify abortion, in *Podziemne państwo kobiet* there are no dramatic circumstances but mundane – and rare in the public debate – stories of unwanted pregnancies told by ordinary women.

Fragments of the testimonies are juxtaposed with interviews with activists and structured to show the step-by-step process of obtaining an illegal abortion. The first segment after the opening sequence is dedicated to language. As the interviewees explain, one cannot use the word "abortion" – the word used only reluctantly in everyday situations, since it is perceived as "too official, impersonal, and dangerous" – when talking to potential providers (Szczuka 2004, 21). Instead, women use indirect yet commonly understood phrases to code a request. The question of language returns when women reflect on their previous beliefs, like supporting women's right to choose but declaring that they would never have an abortion (Kasia and her high school friends thought they were "too sensitive"). The interviewees seemingly internalised popular liberal pro-choice arguments based on perceptions of abortion as a lesser evil. Karina Bugdal names it a "linguistic sabotage" and in a book that followed the film notes that "[n]owadays the only form of voicing support to legal abortion that is acceptable in public sphere is a statement connected with a simultaneous condemnation of abortion such as an obligatory declaration that one would never decide on abortion" (2011, 10). Such rhetoric has a similarly harmful effect as "safe, legal, and rare" argumentation that causes "reducing access to care, increasing stigma, justifying restrictions, and establishing unattainable goals" (Weitz 2010, 167). In hindsight, Kasia calls her views "youthful arrogance" and the "comfort of the privileged." The anti-abortion propaganda that permeates public discourse also complicates the decision-making process – Kasia recalls her fear of possible post-abortion depression.

Later the film gives us an overview of the contemporary abortion underground. It is relatively easy to find a doctor who performs pregnancy terminations through ads in newspapers or friends' recommendations. The stories in the film are consistent with research findings on the privatisation of reproductive health services (including criminalised abortions) in neoliberal Polish reality, conducted by Joanna Mishtal (2010). Explaining the lack of initiatives towards changing the law, Zdrojewska noted that "everything is reasonably well organised and reasonably safe" (Goll 2009). Nevertheless, the underground is full of traps waiting for a person not cautious enough. One could easily be hurt, like Karolina who was deceived and humiliated by anti-choice activists pretending to be abortion providers. At a meeting in a gynaecological clinic, an anti-choice activist named Ms Maria tried to persuade Karolina into giving birth, pointing at children accompanying their mothers and publicly asking whether she wanted to kill such a child.

Another obstacle is the high cost of illegal abortion that, as Julia says, "segregates" women. Some pay in instalments, like Kasia, or get a bank loan, like Magda. The prices vary; Teresa mentions highly qualified doctors who perform expensive illegal abortions and, because of their position in the medical community, do so almost openly. *Podziemne państwo kobiet* addresses the fundamentally important and often forgotten issue of class: restrictions in reproductive health services were, and still are, foremost a class issue. As Mishtal explains: "[c]ircumventing the ban was easier for women with money than those on low income ... the poor often turn to less skilled practitioners or self-induce, thereby exposing themselves to greater health risks" (2010, 62–3).

Illegal abortion is emotionally difficult because of the necessity to mask true feelings, intentions, and experiences. The women describe painful and humiliating moments. Magda recalls a nurse staging the situation to look like a spontaneous miscarriage; Kasia describes how she felt forced to show enthusiasm during ultrasonography to avoid suspicion. Gynaecologists in the film are presented as lacking respect for their patients or their ability to perform the procedure seems questionable. Viewed against the recollection of the procedure that opens the film, where Karolina assists her own doctor by holding tools after receiving anaesthetics, the dangers of illegal abortion are foregrounded.

The potentially harmful character of the underground is confirmed by two descriptions of the procedure in the film. Kasia recalls that her doctor was in visible distress. The procedure lasted around 40 minutes, after which Kasia was forced to leave even though she was not fully awake. Unable to take a taxi, she had to lay down for 15 minutes at the nearby tram stop. Julia's story is similar; she had to park the car at a distance and come to the doctor's office late in the evening. Both the gynaecologist and anaesthesiologist were nervous; the anaesthesiologist left when Julia was waking up, because she did not want to be remembered or recognised. Significantly in the film, no procedures are shown, which is typical for feminist documentaries on abortion, and only three women share their abortion experience (Warren 2015). Abortion as a medical procedure is still a taboo subject.

The horrors of the underground stand in sharp contrast to the vision of women's solidarity in Ela's story. During the healing process after her abortion she began to write about her experience on the internet. Together with some other participants she decided to start a secure internet forum dedicated to obtaining medical abortions. She states that more than 1,000 women got support through her forum and recalls talking to three women undergoing their medical abortions in one day – numbers showing the reality of the abortion ban. Ela notes that the most common feeling after the procedure is relief. The protagonists stress that their decision was good and they would make the same choice again. The silence, however, seems only partially broken: women feel they cannot speak about their abortions and if they do, they confide in their mothers. Stories reveal the power of stigma: Karolina found out about her mother's abortion only when she told her about her own. But stories also reveal women's solidarity: Julia remembers the "human face" shown by her conservative Catholic mother. Finally, we hear Ewa's remarks on humiliation, being deprived of dignity, and the nature of the "underground women's state" as an unwritten deal between women.

Reclaiming the past

This unwritten deal between women, based on silent circumvention of the law, has a long history. Women know who to ask and how to find an abortion provider. We also know the dangers of botched procedures and stories of women dying without help, as well as feelings of deception, exploitation, and humiliation. The arguments used in contemporary discussions are strikingly similar to arguments from the 1950s (Grabowska 2018, 17). It comes as no surprise that the cases reported in today's newspapers or in the film bear resemblance to the stories from the past.

The liberal abortion law was introduced as early as 1956 during the post-Stalinist thaw, and after 1959, abortion was available officially on social grounds and practically on demand until 1993. Given the lack of sex education and access to effective contraception at the time, abortion was often used as a basic means of family planning. During the parliamentary debate in the 1950s issues of class as well as social and economic factors were emphasised rather than women's rights or equality (Czajkowska 2012; Grabowska 2018). As part of the medicalisation of reproductive health, the bill was directed against women who performed abortions without any medical qualifications ("granny midwives") and was introduced to protect the health of women (Kuźma-Markowska 2017). The popular perception of abortion was ambiguous and its stigmatising vision was perpetuated by official family planning organisations (Klich-Kluczewska 2015; Ignaciuk 2014). The fact that the new law was "handed over" made it "easier for Catholic fundamentalist groups to contest it" (Heinen and Portet 2010, 1012). The 1956 act was met with fierce opposition by the Polish Catholic Church. This reaction gained in strength in the 1980s, especially after the democratic transition, resulting in restrictions in access to abortion and a rapid decrease in the number of legal procedures (Wejbert-Wąsiewicz 2011, 77; Chełstowska 2011, 101). The anti-communist argument viewed the liberal abortion law and women's rights in general as a totalitarian idea – Pope John Paul II considered the abortion ban in terms of freedom from the totalitarian past (Chełstowska *et al.* 2013, 91).

After 1989, the anti-communist stance was also popular among prominent feminists. It resulted in the "broken genealogy" of Polish feminism – a radical discontinuity in the women's movement before and after transition (Grabowska 2018). This stance also complicates discussion of the legacy of state socialism, which introduced liberal abortion law but also perpetuated abortion stigma. Therefore, historical knowledge is instrumental in preventing the spread of stereotypes concerning abortion (especially those based on a false vision of abortion in state socialism) and the distorted image of the current abortion bill as a "compromise" that ignores the fact that the law was imposed by right-wing politicians under the influence of the Catholic Church, despite mass protests.

The second narrative line in *Podziemne państwo kobiet* consists of interviews with feminist activists of different generations, who explain the historical contexts of the abortion law, the process that led to the ban, and the contemporary situation. The directors recall recent moments in Polish abortion history, like the 2003 visit of the *Langenort*, the Dutch "abortion ship" on which women could obtain an abortion on international waters, which Rebecca Gomperts discusses in her interview. Kazimiera Szczuka comments on the role of the Catholic Church in the 1980s, the abortion ban as instrumental in "seal[ing] certain division of power," and the willingness of democratic opposition to "pay this price." The filmmakers also included some scarcely remembered facts from the socialist past and transition period, such as the story of the Women's Section of Independent Self-Governing Trade Union "Solidarity," disbanded when its members questioned the support of the anti-abortion bill provided by the union's authorities after 1989, told by Section's coordinator Małgorzata Tarasewicz. Ewa Dąbrowska-Szulc recollects early protests against the ban in May 1989 and the first infamous "anti-abortion exhibition" consisting of graphic and manipulated photographs of abortion, which she saw in a church in 1980. Such imagery fell on fertile soil. Polish society was prudish and heavily influenced by the Catholic Church, and the women's movement was unable to contest the popular perception of abortion as a violation of traditional ideals of womanhood and a messy, unhealthy procedure sought by irresponsible women – a vision that serves as a foundation of abortion stigma (Norris *et al.* 2011). The filmmakers also interviewed the late Maria Jaszczuk, forgotten co-author of the 1956 act. She recalled the circumstances of writing the bill and almost unanimous support for the liberalisation.

To show the historical context in which the ban was imposed, directors incorporated archival footage of early pro-choice demonstrations, marches of "Solidarity," and religious processions used as a tool of pressure on the state authorities. A prominent image from the archival footage shows women behind bars, a clear symbol of the detrimental effects of the transition on women and a perspective rarely present in the public debate. The activists recall their disbelief that the abortion law could be changed even in light of the enormous anti-abortion campaign of the Church, and the feeling of powerlessness when mass protests failed to prevent the law from coming into force.

Mobilising a movement

Because of its limited distribution, the documentary reached and inspired mainly feminist audiences. The screenings were often followed by discussions – the directors "organised almost the whole movement around the film" (Tomasik 2011, 156). *Podziemne państwo kobiet* resonated powerfully in feminist groups because it presented the reality of the abortion underground – a taboo subject in public discourse. For example, activists used the film's title while organising the annual International Women's Day demonstration in 2010 in Łódź. Outside of feminist circles, the film was rather unsuccessful. For example, Magdalena Rek-Woźniak has used the documentary in sociology classes and comments that her students are unmoved by the film and say that "it does not concern us" (discussion during conference *Społeczeństwo a płeć – problemy, wyzwania, perspektywy badawcze*, Łódź, October 11–12, 2018).

The abortion underground is a lonely place – the sentiment of a third narrative line of the film. In silence, a figure named "A Woman" by the film goes through the process of obtaining an illegal abortion. She meditates looking through the window, speaks to someone over the phone, walks through corridors and streets, reads newspaper ads, waits at the tram stop, passes advertisements for bank loans and a cross towering over the area, and browses internet forums. She personifies all women who wander alone through the maze of the abortion underground, creating the impression that despite all the differences between the stories, there is one pattern of experience. It may make the documentary narrative easier to follow and offer the possibility to show certain aspects of the stories (as newspaper ads or internet forums), yet the presentation of a universal woman's experience is clearly inconsistent with the diversity of experiences portrayed in the film. Moreover, the narrative stresses the strictly individual character of the experience – there is no community offering support. This is consistent with remarks made in the film by Nowicka, who stated that women do not organise or fight the bad law but learn how to circumvent it, and Katarzyna Bratkowska, who added that it would not lead to forming a movement. Gomperts highlighted another aspect – that although Polish abortion law does not criminalise pregnant women seeking abortions, it criminalises those helping women access illegal abortion, "cut[ting] off the support lines around these women which makes them even more vulnerable."

The overall loneliness is foregrounded in the way the subjects of the documentary are portrayed: they are also presented alone. We do not hear or see the interviewers; the women are filmed separately and are unidentifiable (with the exception of Teresa), according to their wishes to stay anonymous (Goll 2009). Often, we see close-ups of parts of their bodies, like their eyes or hands. Sometimes the women are filmed from a distance and the image is out of focus or otherwise distorted. The activists are shown in a more conventional documentary frame, as talking heads with their names and affiliations beneath them on the screen. The contrast is clear. The close-ups may make the viewer feel an intimate connection to the subjects. At the same time, presenting them in this way may suggest that they have something to hide or that they are ashamed of their deeds or guilty of a crime. It also constructs, at least to some extent, a hierarchy, given that the activists do not share personal details (only Dąbrowska-Szulc mentions that her life had been dedicated to children and family before she got involved in protests in 1989). Instead they comment on abortion through their own engagement in the pro-choice movement, revealing growing personal frustration, but not their individual experience.[2]

Podziemne państwo kobiet was not rooted in practices of the Polish pro-choice movement, where sharing personal abortion stories was rare (Chełstowska 2010). The film does not grant its subjects an expert status, as some feminist documentaries do (Juhasz 1999; Warren 2015). It does not create a common pattern of oppression or treat women's stories as the sources of knowledge, as American feminist documentaries of the second wave structured by consciousness-raising principles did (Lesage 1978). The testimonies of the protagonists of *Podziemne państwo kobiet* do not compose the knowledge of the abortion underground; rather, they serve as illustrations of what we learn from interviews with activist-experts, who explain statistics, mechanisms, and political processes that affect "average women."

Of course, the fact that *Podziemne państwo kobiet* does not easily fit into schemes of western feminist documentary does not necessarily mean that it is a failed attempt. Instead, it inspires us to look for new strategies and tactics rooted in local experience. Zdrojewska commented on how speaking publicly about abortion through the process of making the film led to multiple stories of abortion experiences:

> A lot of women told us that when they confided in someone after the procedure, they opened the theme – it turned out on the spot that this woman also [had an abortion], and her mother, and suddenly a chain of similar experiences was created around them. Before making the film I could only say that I heard about someone third-hand, it did not seem to me something close and common. I perceived the battle over a right to decide on abortion as a struggle for democratisation of the society. I did not see the drama of individual women. Working on the film has opened my eyes.
>
> (Goll 2009)

As I already mentioned, the film's premiere was accompanied by a series of activities. After making the film, the directors started a blog under the same title (https://podziemnepanstwokobiet.blogspot.com) as a place for publication of personal stories of abortion. The stories featured on the blog covered a wider set of perspectives than in the film. We learn, for instance, a story of a woman filled with remorse after the procedure, as well as stories of medical abortions, legal abortions, or abortions performed abroad. Some of the stories were reprinted in *A jak hipokryzja* (*A Like Hypocrisy*), a book edited by Snochowska-Gonzàlez and published in 2011, together with articles written by activists and researchers. The book – "ahead of its time," as Natalia Broniarczyk, co-founder of Aborcyjny Dream Team (Abortion Dream Team), puts it – takes up subjects of, among others, "linguistic sabotage," social justice, and reproductive justice as new frames for abortion activism, and new possibilities for the pro-choice movement connected with medical abortion, the abortion underground, and abortion tourism, or the concept of the "spiral of silence" (Broniarczyk 2018).

In 2013 Snochowska-Gonzàlez analysed different arguments used by Polish pro-choice activists in search of a "good strategy" that would be able to both connect and mobilise diverse groups. During the post-screening discussions the filmmakers explored the film's main argument: that a law which is commonly violated is a dead law. These discussions proved the inability of this argument to mobilise women, since the law is commonly recognised as serving only the privileged in Poland. Therefore Snochowska-Gonzàlez stated that a strategy based on the idea of reproductive justice would be more efficient, not as divisive, and effective for mobilisation efforts (Snochowska-Gonzàlez 2013). Chełstowska suggested that reproductive justice offered "a chance for a broader and stronger movement" (2010). Reproductive justice is connected to social justice and refers to a wider set of issues, such as sex education, contraception, infertility treatment, child care, and child support – "it is more in tune with our life experience. Our life does not consist of separate fragments" (Chełstowska 2010). Commenting on debates surrounding the film, Chełstowska stressed the importance of discussing "abortion as an experience, not an issue" and not avoiding the emotional aspects of the experience (2010).

To conclude, *Podziemne państwo kobiet* was an important intervention in Polish abortion discourse. The film concentrated on everyday experiences of women who had to learn how to break the law. Though their lives are different, the subjects of the documentary tell stories that have a lot in common. The focus on the lack of social justice paved the way to new forms of abortion activism. The film also reclaims the history and resilience of women's struggles for equality. It shows the importance of dismantling myths, remembering women who fought for the 1956 Act, and knowing the strategies and tactics used previously to question the status quo. Otherwise, we will be "reinventing feminist wheel to fight yet again for our rights," as Alexandra Juhasz warns (1999, 192).

Changing Polish abortion discourse is a long and difficult process. Recent protests against proposals for further restrictions brought much-needed transformation. As Elżbieta Korolczuk observed, the argument against further restrictions was presented from women's position, and the legal and medical consequences of the ban, as well as the threatened dignity of women, were explicitly named (2019). Also the ideas and practices of self-help and solidarity profoundly changed abortion activism in Poland. This is visible in, for example, the work of Aborcyjny Dream Team, a group that propagates knowledge on medical abortion in workshops and publications and foregrounds the need for destigmatisation and normalisation of abortion. The abortion law imposed in 1993, however, is still a stable element of Polish reality.

Notes

1 Some of these stories, as well as footage of pro-choice events and demonstrations, were included in another feminist documentary that was important and representative of the discourse of the time, Ewa Pytka's *Przełamując ciszę. Prawa kobiet w Europie Środkowo-Wschodniej* (*Breaking the Silence: Women's Rights in Central and Eastern Europe*, 2007).
2 Kinga Jelińska is filmed in front of a computer monitor with a sticker saying "I had an abortion" attached to it. She also explains the abortion procedures in detail, naming the substance used in medical abortion.

References

Broniarczyk, Natalia. 2018. "Być albo nie być matką. Rozważania o aborcji są częścią naszego życia." *Codziennik Feministyczny*, September 9, 2018. http://codziennikfeministyczny.pl/broniarczyk-byc-albo-nie-byc-matka.
Bugdal, Karina. 2011. "Jestem za prawem do aborcji, ale sama bym jej nigdy nie zrobiła. O sabotażu językowym." In *A jak hipokryzja. Antologia tekstów o aborcji, władzy, pieniądzach i sprawiedliwości*, edited by Claudia Snochowska-Gonzàlez, 9–10. Warszawa: Wydawnictwo O Matko!
Chełstowska, Agata. 2010. "Stawiam na sprawiedliwość reprodukcyjną." *Lewica.pl*, January 9, 2010. http://lewica.pl/?id=20714.
——— 2011. "Stigmatisation and commercialisation of abortion services in Poland: turning sin into gold." *Reproductive Health Matters* 19, no. 37: 98–106. DOI: 10.1016/S0968-8080(11)37548-9.
Chełstowska, Agata, Małgorzata Druciarek, Jacek Kucharczyk, and Aleksandra Niżyńska. 2013. *Relacje państwo – kościół w III RP*. Warszawa: Instytut Spraw Publicznych.
Czajkowska, Aleksandra. 2012. "O dopuszczalności przerywania ciąży. Ustawa z dnia 27 kwietnia 1956 i towarzyszące jej dyskusje." In *Kłopoty z seksem w PRL. Rodzenie nie całkiem po ludzku, aborcja, choroby, odmienności*, edited by Marcin Kula, 99–186. Warszawa: Wydawnictwo Uniwersytetu Warszawskiego.
Girard, Françoise and Wanda Nowicka. 2002. "Clear and compelling evidence: The Polish tribunal on abortion rights." *Reproductive Health Matters* 10, no. 19: 22–30. https://doi.org/10.1016/S0968-8080(02)00023-X.
Goll, Monika. 2009. "Czarny rynek aborcyjny. Wywiad z Claudią Snochowską-Gonzàlez i Anną Zdrojewską." *Wysokie Obcasy*, October 13, 2009. www.wysokieobcasy.pl/wysokie-obcasy/1,96856,7125691,Czarny_rynek_aborcyjny.html?disableRedirects=true.

Grabowska, Magdalena. 2018. *Zerwana genealogia. Działalność społeczna i polityczna kobiet po 1945 roku a współczesny polski ruch kobiecy*. Warszawa: Wydawnictwo Naukowe Scholar.

Graff, Agnieszka. 2005. *Świat bez kobiet. Płeć w polskim życiu publicznym*. Warszawa: Wydawnictwo W.A.B.

Heinen, Jacqueline and Stéphane Portet. 2010. "Reproductive rights in Poland: When politicians fear the wrath of the Church." *Third World Quarterly* 31, no. 6: 1007–21. https://doi.org/10.1080/01436597.2010.502735.

Ignaciuk Agata. 2014. "'Ten szkodliwy zabieg.' Dyskursy na temat aborcji w publikacjach Towarzystwa Świadomego Macierzyństwa/Towarzystwa Planowania Rodziny (1956–1980)." *Zeszyty Etnologii Wrocławskiej* 1, no. 20: 75–97.

Juhasz, Alexandra. 1999. "They said we were trying to show reality – all I want to show is my video: The politics of the feminist realist documentary." In *Collecting Visible Evidence*, edited by Jane M. Gaines and Michael Renov, 190–215. Minneapolis, MN and London: University of Minnesota Press.

Klich-Kluczewska, Barbara. 2015. *Rodzina, tabu i komunizm w Polsce 1956–1989*. Kraków: Wydawnictwo LIBRON – Filip Lohner.

Korolczuk, Elżbieta. 2019. "Odzyskiwanie języka, czyli jak zmieniła się debata o aborcji w kontekście Czarnych Protestów i Strajków Kobiet." In *Bunt kobiet. Czarne Protesty i Strajki Kobiet*, edited by Elżbieta Korolczuk, Beata Kowalska, Jennifer Ramme, and Claudia Snochowska-Gonzàlez, 119–53. Gdańsk: Europejskie Centrum Solidarności. https://ecs.gda.pl/library/File/nauka/e-booki/raport/ECS_raport_buntkobiet.pdf.

Kula, Klaudia and Agnieszka Sadowska. 2009. "Chcemy skończyć z podziemiem aborcyjnym! (Interview with Claudia Snochowska-Gonzàlez and Anna Zdrojewska)." *WP Kobieta*, November 5, 2009. https://kobieta.wp.pl/chcemy-skonczyc-z-podziemiem-aborcyjnym-5983058079061121g.

Kuźma-Markowska, Sylwia. 2017. "Walka z 'babkami' o zdrowie kobiet: medykalizacja przerywania ciąży w Polsce w latach pięćdziesiątych i sześćdziesiątych XX wieku." *Polska 1944/45–1989. Studia i Materiały* XV: 189–215. DOI: http://dx.doi.org/10.12775/Polska.2017.10.

Lesage, Julia. 1978. "The political aesthetics of the feminist documentary film." *Quarterly Review of Film Studies* 3, no. 4: 507–23.

Łaciak, Beata. 2016. *Aborcja w polskich serialach. Tabuizacja i poprawność polityczna*. Warszawa: Instytut Spraw Publicznych.

Mishtal, Joanna. 2010. "Neoliberal reforms and privatisation of reproductive health services in post-socialist Poland." *Reproductive Health Matters* 18, no. 36: 56–66. https://doi.org/10.1016/S0968-8080(10)36524-4.

Norris, Alison, Danielle Besset, Julia R. Steinberg, Megan L. Kavanaugh, Silvia De Zordo, and Davida Becker. 2011. "Abortion stigma: A reconceptualization of constituents, causes, and consequences." *Women's Health Issues* 21, no. 3, Supplement: S49–S45. https://doi.org/10.1016/j.whi.2011.02.010.

Pytka, Ewa, dir. 2007. *Przełamując ciszę. Prawa kobiet w Europie Środkowo-Wschodniej*. Python Studioss for The Federation for Women and Reproductive Rights, 2007.

Snochowska-Gonzàlez, Claudia, ed. 2011. *A jak hipokryzja. Antologia tekstów o aborcji, władzy, pieniądzach i sprawiedliwości*. Warszawa: Wydawnictwo O Matko!

———— 2013. "O zarodkach, ludziach i dobrej strategii pro-choice." *Bez Dogmatu* 4, no. 98. www.iwkip.org/bezdogmatu/98.

Snochowska-González, Claudia and Anna Zdrojewska, dir. 2009. *Podziemne państwo kobiet.* Kobieca Grupa Filmowa Entuzjastki.

Szczuka, Kazimiera. 2004. *Milczenie owieczek. Rzecz o aborcji.* Warszawa: Wydawnictwo W.A.B.

Tomasik, Krzysztof. 2011. "Podziemne państwo kobiet Claudii Snochowskiej-Gonzàlez i Anny Zdrojewskiej, czyli aborcja – temat, którego nie ma." In *Polskie kino dokumentalne 1989–2009. Historia polityczna,* edited by Agnieszka Wiśniewska, 147–56. Warszawa: Wydawnictwo Krytyki Politycznej.

Warren, Shylah. 2015. "Abortion, abortion, abortion, still: Documentary show and tell." *South Atlantic Quarterly* 114, no. 4: 755–79. https://doi.org/10.1215/00382876-3157122.

Weitz, Tracy A. 2010. "Rethinking the mantra that abortion should be 'safe, legal, and rare'." *Journal of Women's History* 22, no. 3: 161–72.

Wejbert-Wąsiewicz, Ewelina. 2011. *Aborcja. Między ideologią a doświadczeniem indywidualnym. Monografia zjawiska.* Łódź: Wydawnictwo Uniwersytetu Łódzkiego.

———— 2018. "Problematyka niechcianej ciąży i aborcji w polskim filmie. Ideologia, polityka, rzeczywistość." *Sztuka i Dokumentacja* 25: 259–72. DOI: 10.32020/ARTandDOC/18/2018/25.

Part IV

Representations for new arguments

Reproductive justice activists and scholars have long called for an expanded vision of abortion access that exceeds the liberal notion of "choice," premised on an idealised autonomous decision-maker whose choices are not constrained by misogyny, racism, colonialism, ableism, and/or classism. One provocation that inspired this volume was Rosalind Pollack Petchesky's call for feminists and pro-choice activists to resist "ced[ing] the visual terrain" (1987, 264) to anti-abortion discourse, and to generate new images that "recontextualized the fetus" within a social, political, and historical context (1987, 287). And indeed, chapters in the first three parts of this book have demonstrated why new representations are urgently necessary for countering the misinformation and stigma that is born of silence and invisibility; for demystifying the physicality of abortion, especially the fetal body; and for developing new understandings of abortion that can encompass a wide range of responses to abortion and embed abortion within a wider political field. Part IV – Representations for new arguments is the last section of this book, and its chapters invite deeper reflection on Petchesky's appeal, now over 30 years old, as well as creative energy towards envisioning what kinds of representations can expand arguments and activism that aim to expand safe and legal abortion access and oppose the encroachment of religious and right-wing influence on legislation.

The contemporary anti-abortion movement in Canada and the United States is shrewd and responsive in its public relations efforts, as Kelly Gordon and Paul Saurette demonstrated in their analysis of RightNow in Chapter 6. The vitriolic misogyny that infused the anti-abortion representation of the pregnant woman's body as an "inhospitable waste land, at war with the 'innocent person' within" described by Carol Stabile in 1992 (179) is no longer palatable for the public-facing anti-abortion movement, which instead aligns the interests of the pregnant woman with the fetus in its discourse and positions women in leadership roles. Jennifer Scuro's "'What you do hurts all of us!': when women confront women through pro-life rhetoric" proposes that pro-life politics, rhetoric, and ideology articulate as a system of confrontation between women. Beginning from a disquieting moment of confrontation that she experienced personally (analysed in her

The Pregnancy ≠ Childbearing Project: A Phenomenology of Miscarriage (2017)), Scuro critiques the apparently earnest concern for pregnant women expressed by women engaged in anti-abortion work through crisis pregnancy centres and interventions outside of abortion clinics. She argues that such concern is a technique of passive coercion aiming to manipulate women who are ambivalent or vulnerable into carrying the pregnancy to term, satisfying pro-life politics, without any consideration or support for the woman's life after she gives birth. Through an analysis of her own experience of confrontation, represented through graphic narrative, Maisie Crow's documentary *Jackson* (2016), and the fictional reproductive politics in Margaret Atwood's *The Handmaid's Tale* (1998), Scuro examines the harm that is wrought through confrontations between women, which expunge all possibility for solidarity between pregnant persons.

Several chapters in this volume have expressed a need for more robust prochoice understandings of the embodied and emotional meanings of abortion that do not minimise its impact on the lives of people who have abortions (see Ludlow, Ludlow and Hann, and Latimer). A common argument against embracing this complexity is that it is easily manipulated by anti-abortion rhetoric to support specious diagnoses like "post-abortion trauma syndrome" as well as the increasingly resonant argument that abortion is harmful to women. Within this political field, pro-choice discourse is compelled to publicly depict abortion as an uncomplicated decision, a depiction that does not honour the multiplicity of positions and experiences held by people who have abortions. Melissa Huerta's chapter, "'This is how I was born on the operating table of an abortion clinic': *Coatlicue* State and reproductive decision-making in Teatro Luna," is a meditation on ambiguity as a legitimate position in relation to making reproductive choices. Focusing on Maria Vega's "Trapped" from Teatro Luna's play *Déjame contarte* [*Let Me Tell You*] (2002), Huerta argues that Teatro Luna enunciates a Latina analysis of the politics and individual experience of reproductive decision-making, one that allows for a larger range of responses to an abortion. Gloria Anzaldúa's conceptualisation of *Coatlicue* State – explaining the ambivalent and ambiguous experience of inhabiting an identity position that is "othered," producing an incongruence between one's identity and stereotyped perceptions of that identity as a Latina woman (2007, 68) – is central to Teatro Luna's representation of a space entered by the character considering abortion, and to representing abortion as a site of transformation and the creation of new knowledge.

Creating more complex abortion politics and arguments for expanded abortion access requires a refusal of the binary between life and choice, a theme that has been taken up by reproductive justice scholars and abortion providers (see, for example, Ludlow 2008 and Smith 2005). Reproductive justice approaches note that the polarisation of abortion debates does particular harm to those who are oppressed on the basis of colonialism, race, class, sexuality, and ability, as neither position (at least in their most mainstream versions) recognises the multifaceted process of reproductive decision-making for oppressed people. "Abortion and the ideology of love in Kathy Acker's *Blood and Guts in High School* and *Don Quixote, Which Was a Dream*" re-envisions abortion as a site of resistance and liberation through tracing the role of abortion in Kathy Acker's novels. Yoonha Shin argues that Acker dismantles heteronormative ideals of love through her representations of abortion in *Blood and Guts in High School* (Acker 2017) and *Don Quixote, Which Was a Dream* (Acker 1986), informed by second-wave feminist critiques of love as possessive and patriarchal; these ideals of love indirectly support men's control over women's reproductive bodies. Acker imagines abortion as a locus of connection between marginalised subjects to resist heteropatriarchal capitalism as well as of queer love, and Shin argues that the radical potential for these novels to undermine the biopolitical nation-state of neoliberalism continues to be salient in the present day.

References

Acker, Kathy. 1986. *Don Quixote, Which Was a Dream*. New York: Grove Press.
—— 2017. *Blood and Guts in High School*. Anniversary edition. New York: Grove Press.
Anzaldúa, Gloria. 2007. *Borderlands/La Frontera, Third Edition*. San Francisco, CA: Aunt Lute Books.
Atwood, Margaret. 1998. *The Handmaid's Tale*. New York: Anchor Books.
Crow, Maisie, dir. 2016. *Jackson*. New York: Girl Friday Films, 2018. DVD video.
Ludlow, Jeannie. 2008. "Sometimes, It's a Child and a Choice: Toward an Embodied Abortion Praxis." *NWSA Journal* 20, no. 1: 26–50.
Petchesky, Rosalind Pollack. 1987. "Fetal Images: The Power of Visual Culture in the Politics of Abortion." *Feminist Studies* 13, no. 2: 263–292.
Scuro, Jennifer. 2017. *The Pregnancy ≠ Childbearing Project: A Phenomenology of Miscarriage*. London: Rowman & Littlefield International.
Smith, Andrea. 2005. "Beyond Pro-Choice Versus Pro-Life: Women of Color and Reproductive Justice." *NWSA Journal* 17, no. 1: 119–140.
Stabile, Carol. 1992. "Shooting the Mother: Fetal Photography and the Politics of Disappearance." *Camera Obscura* 10, no. 1: 178–205.
Vega, Maria. 2002. "Trapped," in *Déjame contarte* by Teatro Luna. Unpublished script.

15 "What you do hurts all of us!"

When women confront women through pro-life rhetoric

Jennifer Scuro

The affective harm of confrontation[1]

More than a decade ago, I was 19 weeks pregnant and had been haemorrhaging for weeks, confined to my bed or in the hospital. I had felt myself as no more than an incubator desperately trying to hold onto a pregnancy that was going to kill me. When the ultrasound specialist viewed the pregnancy and the tremendous clot that was crushing everything in my abdomen, he gave me a panicked look and said, to paraphrase: "You have to terminate immediately before you bleed out. You might not wake up in the morning." The only doctor qualified and experienced enough to terminate a pregnancy this advanced was one that would only do the procedure in his office, with his team. The hospital admitted me only to transfuse blood in preparation for the procedure. The doctor picked me up in the morning from the hospital and drove me in his own car through the back entrance of his clinic.

After the procedure, in the recovery chairs, I sat next to a woman who had just terminated her pregnancy and she confessed her situation to me (Figure 15.1). Hers was an unwanted pregnancy and, although mine had been wanted, our situation was fundamentally no different. An overwhelming feeling of solidarity came over me and surprisingly relieved some of my grief. There was no real choice once pregnant; rather, I knew that there were a limited number of options such that she and I were blameless no matter what decision we needed to make. There was no moral culpability in what brought us to this situation. In fact, one of the outcomes of my own experience with miscarriage and abortion – a product of the labour of having to confront those experiences and the corresponding trauma – is what I have come to claim in my book, *The Pregnancy ≠ Childbearing Project* (Scuro 2017): there is a deep and urgent need for a democratic solidarity among women who have been pregnant regardless of it leading to a successful or healthy childbirth, whether it is wanted or unwanted, aborted or miscarried, including freedom from moral culpability.

After my recovery – and to be clear, I would return to the clinic hours later haemorrhaging again from the D&E procedure – my husband was to pick me up. He had been waiting for me in the reception area and when

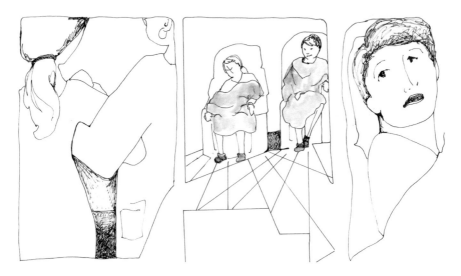

Figure 15.1 Left panel: me and the nurse as she brings me to recovery chairs. Middle
　　　　　panel: a woman talks to me while we recover from our procedures.
　　　　　Right panel: she asks me how I am and tells me her story.

Source: Inked panels by J. Scuro, 2017. *The Pregnancy ≠ Childbearing Project: A
Phenomenology of Miscarriage*. London: Rowman & Littlefield International.

I came out to meet him, he clearly said, "Wait here," while he went to get
the car. I didn't listen because I didn't realise where I was. For me, I was
recovering from a medical procedure and did not think of it as an abortion
clinic. And that's when an older woman approached me while I leaned
against the railing of the clinic stairs:

　　You know what you did hurts all of us.

It was such a shock. The woman had said it so quietly and politely and it
took me a few moments to register what she was saying to me. It felt like
a threat and a verbal assault. She did not know me or my situation. I then
responded:

　　Get away from me! Stop talking to me!

She wouldn't step away but got closer. As my husband pulled up, she
attempted to hold the door open for me as if to gesture care or concern for
my wellbeing. I could not speak at that point, but my husband continued in
my place: "Get away from her, you cunt!" I thought: "He never says stuff
like that to anyone." As I recollected and sketched out these experiences
many years later in graphic novel form, my memory initially held the woman

Figure 15.2 Left panel: the woman who approached me. Right panel: me, entering the car as the woman attempts to hold the door open for me.

Source: Inked panels by J. Scuro, 2017. *The Pregnancy ≠ Childbearing Project: A Phenomenology of Miscarriage*. London: Rowman & Littlefield International.

who confronted me as if she had been shouting these words, "*What you do hurts all of us!*" Her holding open the door of my car for me as a gesture of feigned solicitude I knew was just a way to further insert herself and aggress against me (Figure 15.2).

This kind of solicitous gesture is neither care nor benign intent; it is a strategy built into pro-life rhetoric delivered to vulnerable women by other more privileged and protected women. It is a demonstrated harm as I will argue it here such that, as it was in my case, *performatively*, this woman might have been soft-spoken and grandmotherly, but *affectively*, she added a depth and complexity to the trauma already built into my liminal experience. This was a pregnancy that had almost killed me, and the post-partum effects of this pregnancy loss would later make it barely survivable.

How does this confrontation harm? Pro-life ideologies are anti-feminist and yet they are inherited by women and girls as truths by which they are meant to abide by and not deviate, operating like a misogynistic plot of entanglement in which *all* pregnancies must lead to the birth of a child.[2] This script transfers from mothers and grandmothers to daughters, from counsellors and doctors to clients and patients. So, can we or ought we trust the women who care about us in our particular situatedness, whatever their biases and inherited ideologies, even when all the suspicion is burdened on women and girls who are pregnant yet are ambivalent, anxious, without resources and support, and/or simply unable to carry to term? This disproportionate burden begs for scrutiny and needs challenge if any future solidarity among women is possible.

Using Maisie Crow's documentary *Jackson* (2016) and the narrative of a young, Black pregnant woman, April Jackson, as an anchor, I want to examine the subversive rhetoric of advocacy and care by the paternalistic and patronising beliefs of women who lead pro-life organisations or subscribe to their agenda. As de Beauvoir in *The Ethics of Ambiguity* argues it:

> The notion of ambiguity must not be confused with that of absurdity. To declare that existence is absurd is to deny that it can ever be given a meaning; to say that it is ambiguous is to assert that its meaning is never fixed, that it must be constantly won.
>
> (1949, 48)

Ambivalence according to an existential feminist ethics, although not the same as ambiguity, is an important instruction and starting point for scrutiny against any moral certitude. Caroline Lundquist uses de Beauvoir to describe how the social status that comes with pregnancy creates a feeling of value that "is an illusion" (2008, 143). She adds: "Cultural attitudes toward ambivalence do a great disservice to pregnant women, who find themselves discouraged from expressing feelings about pregnancy in their full richness and complexity" (Lundquist 2008, 151).

So, is feminist solidarity possible when the intention to care among women is duplicitous? When women who offer to help other women carry their pregnancy to term not out of friendship and care, but as an attempt to manipulate women to perform their duty to "bear children"? Robin May Schott clarifies that the ambiguity de Beauvoir reveals is a "complexity of oppression," the "double-mask of a survival strategy" (2003, 244). De Beauvoir gives insight into how the controlling mechanisms of moral judgement confine women to their roles and how zealous commitments to pro-life ideology – as if haunted and terrorised by the idea of murdered babies – betray more the consciousness of the zealot than of the truth and urgency of the perceived situation represented by the aborting mother. The phantasm of a free-floating fetus becomes representative of crisis, shame, and murder.

Our scrutiny here needs to include the so-called activism of the pro-life protest in front of clinics, as it is not to be confused with advocacy. Advocacy requires solidarity among competing and concomitant life experiences and democratic engagement, yet the performance of care and the gentleness of concern in pro-life activism mask the more epistemological and existential mechanisms of control over the meaning of pregnant embodiment.

When confrontation is not care

> There's nothing life-affirming about abortion.
>
> Women are made to die for their babies, not their babies die for them.
>> (Barbara Beavers, Director of the Center
>> for Pregnancy Choices; Jackson 2016)

> We have got to take shame out of the word abortion. And until we stop being ashamed of who we are … and what we believe to be right, we are going to continue to have these issues.
>> (Shannon Brewer, Director of Jackson Women's
>> Health Organization; Jackson 2016)

The pro-life pregnancy center profiled in Crow's documentary, *Jackson*, operates as a facility posing as support and resource to pregnant women, yet the mission of this care centre is to undermine the idea of site-specific care and in its place find opportunity to persuade women to be childbearing – equating pregnancy with the inviolable responsibility of a "Precious One." These plastic figures (racialised white fetus figurines; see Figure 15.3) and corresponding aphorisms are meant to relieve situations fraught with conflict and ambiguity. This is the heart of the existential untruth when it comes to the situation of pregnant embodiment – manipulative and strategic in creating a harmful false narrative, and misrepresenting the meaning of pregnancy through the lens of a theocratic ideology.[3]

There are several forms of confrontation by women to other women narrated in the documentary, each bearing a special kind of perniciousness about the one-who-is-pregnant and the context by which she comes to bear an exceptional situation.[4] It is my claim here that pro-life rhetoric is fundamentally ideological and theocratic, substituting the language of blame and moral culpability with care and concern for the wellbeing of women. These, I argue, are forms of confrontation meant to mask the highly political agenda of right-wing, white Christian groups *as if* they were not confrontational; *as if* they are only careful and caring.

Confrontation as mentorship

At the Center for Pregnancy Choices, April is offered a mentor, a young black woman they call "Miss Sonja" who states how she is "a friend" to April in a "Mommy & Me" counselling session.[5] This counsellor questions April on her attempt at self-aborting her first pregnancy and then follows with, "What's your take on forgiveness, April?" (Jackson 2016). When she replies with "I don't know," Miss Sonja takes the opportunity to provide counsel through the code of theocratic ideology, "The only way you can get through life, to survive life, is by leaning and depending on Him."[6] April responds with a steady ambiguity: "I just stopped believing in God."

Figure 15.3 "Precious One" fetus models featured in the documentary *Jackson*, directed by Maisie Crow, 2016.

Source: Image courtesy of Maisie Crow.

A key aspect of these contrived mentoring and counselling sessions is that, on the condition these classes are attended, some necessary goods are provided – diapers, clothes – and after the session, April goes through used clothes for her one-year-old daughter. Contrast this with advice given to a young girl in the Jackson Women's Health Organization Facility as she completes a termination procedure, with the hope of de-shaming the experience: "You make sure you're okay. You make sure you love yourself more than anybody else, okay? And if they can't do that, then you got no business getting with no one. And that's the truth" (Jackson 2016).

Confrontation as selective information sharing

When the goal of the rhetoric is compliance, the greater and more democratic concern is the prevalence of acquiescence bias.[7] There is a subordination to moral certitude with which April is expected to comply. When the counsellor ("I am not a doctor or a nurse and so I cannot diagnose or confirm what I am finding today," she states to April) offers to "turn on the big screen" to provide an ultrasound image of her pregnancy, April responds, "Not really 'cause … Yeah, I guess. I don't know" (Jackson 2016). At this moment of ambiguity, instead of yielding to April's ambivalence and without her clear consent, the technician declares: "This is your baby" (Jackson 2016).

This is a confrontation with ambivalence without direct consent as if consent is already forfeited out of April's moral failure of being pregnant. When she is asked if she wants a printout of the image, April clearly states, "I really ain't that happy about [the pregnancy], but I guess if I look at it I'll be," then, additionally, the counsellor adds, "Do you want me to put 'Hi Mom' on it?" which is met with silence (Jackson 2016). Then April states, "I cannot believe I am pregnant. ... That little old worm." The counsellor inserts a "HI MOM" on the corner of the ultrasound image, unambiguously aggressive in her intention to caption for April what she thinks that image represents.

April, living with her mother and four brothers, with four children already, when showing the ultrasound image to someone, ignores the demand of "MOM" and states cautiously, "It ain't even a baby yet" (Jackson 2016).[8] When April describes her attempt to terminate her first pregnancy by drinking Clorox so that she would "bleed through," and when she is asked why it is she will have five children at age 24, tells about how most people would say she would be like her mom and "amount to nothing," but that only her grandmother would say she would do and be better. April attributes the passing of her grandmother as to why she stopped caring and got pregnant again because her grandmother was the only one who thought more of her (Jackson 2016).

Compare this to the illusory grandmotherly posture of Barbara Beavers, the Center's Director, towards April, evident when she is asked by someone off camera if April should be on birth control despite the ideological implications. Beavers implicitly admits her disdain for April, responding that it is "ultimately about [her] self-control" and that "our real issue with abortion is our sexual immorality" (Jackson 2016). Beavers' misappropriated kindness is highly constricted power over the conditions which crystallise poverty with an anti-black, systemic intergenerational racism. As she says in the car once she drops off a baby gift for April to clear her conscience, "Bless her heart. She needs help" (Jackson 2016).

Confrontation through policy and political influence

One indication of the complexity of this form of confrontation is in the soft prohibitions, like withdrawal of funding for abortion care or the arbitrary procedural obstacles for clinics, all in order to meet the goal of an abortion-free state. In the documentary, Crow adds a clip from *The Rachel Maddow Show*, with Maddow explaining the complex strategy of TRAP [Targeted Regulation of Abortion Providers] laws, meant to shut down clinics and facilities through procedural non-compliance.

Hospitals and health insurance companies are complicit in these soft prohibitions of reproductive care, implicitly supporting sanctioned care through the ideology of pro-life rhetoric in lieu of a more rigorous, anti-racist, and anti-biased humanising health care. When pregnant women must find the money to pay for the termination, even if they have health care coverage, it is a contrived confrontation with what seems to be circumstantial, as if an abortion were an elective procedure. In *Jackson*, we see a discussion between care providers narrating how they sometimes need to ask patients: "Can you pawn something?" "Do you have any jewelry you can sell?" (Jackson 2016).

Additionally, as the abortion-free state policies get instituted and normalised, we see an added threat of direct prosecution: jail time for the few doctors who know how to do these complicated procedures or even for women who miscarry.[9]

Advocacy towards solidarity and against ideology

> We would like to conceive of Serena Joy as a classical villain – someone who has her own, self-determined (but evil) motivations. But that's the patriarchal vision of the villain. Serena Joy is something else entirely. Having negated any concept of her own capacity to self-determine, she becomes the empty vessel, a machine through which to enact the visions of others (Gilead).
>
> (Elsby 2019, 65)

Margaret Atwood's *The Handmaid's Tale* is a useful fictional narrative in describing what can happen when the democratic is replaced by the theocratic. The theocratic engenders present and future sites of confrontation among women in which women are not only confined to their reproductive function *by other women* – in all the ways in which medicine is already a projection of racist, ableist, and classist ideologies rather than functioning as infrastructure for health and wellbeing – but where this also does not work in service to women as they might self-determine. It is control over the potential and futural sense of self as well as a gendered and heteronormative version of social control. What complicates this further is the white saviourism that infects the narrative of pro-life discourse.

In Crow's documentary, *Jackson*, we get the image of that state's Governor preaching for an abortion-free Mississippi with (again) an imagined "she" who is not-yet-born as he questions the status of her right: "The Child in the Womb ... doesn't *she* have a right to life?" (Jackson 2016; emphasis added).[10] It is easy to analogise the state of Gilead in Atwood's *The Handmaid's Tale* to the real-world Governor's vision of an abortion-free Mississippi. Serena Joy or Aunt Lydia both easily figure as analogues to a woman like Barbara Beavers – with her scripted good intention and preachy, white-washed solicitude towards April Jackson.

De Beauvoir again provides instruction through the ethics of ambiguity in challenging the myth of women as either pure and innocent or evil and villainous. De Beauvoir suggests a greater confrontation with social or ontological evils and oppressions through this feminist ethics.[11] I suggest utilising the narrative weight of marginalised pregnant experience offering an epistemological and pedagogical defence in order to rally against the preconditioned certitude of faith-based and conservative pro-life agendas. Why haven't we listened to the women as they experience this ambiguity, without shame, without judgement? What and who are we trying to "save" in these confrontations?

What is saved by the confrontation? The claims made by the pro-life protestor are most often theocratic, which also means there is a whitewashing of ideology as apolitical. As theocratic, there is no genuine appeal to science or medical authority. These metaphysical and often outright fantastic claims are not based on pragmatic concerns or philosophical tensions.[12] These ideological claims transfer affectively with slogans either shouted in an explicit and aggressive confrontation, as in: "Mommy, mommy, please don't kill me!" or as passive-aggressive pleas, as in: "Ma'am, do the right thing, please. Please do the right thing" (Jackson 2016). The goal is to find any which way to affectively impact the complex situatedness of pregnant embodiment in favour of an illusory and harmful moral certitude.

To further this inquiry: *who* is saved by the performance of concern and care for the unborn? As a white woman talking to fellow white legislators, actively lobbying to restrict abortion in any way possible, Barbara Beavers, Director of the Center for Pregnancy Choices (CPC), admits, "I makin' a stump speech ... Ya know, I have to tell them why we have to have CPCs ... and I'm raisin' money" (Jackson 2016). She also references an unnamed enemy, representing her concern with images of violence: "We are not going to solve the problem by killing *our* babies" (Jackson 2016; emphasis added).

This rhetoric begs the question: Who is the "our" here? Khiara Bridges in *Reproducing Race* underscores the "fundamental and inherent ambivalence of a power that is simultaneous in its productivity and repression" (2011, 255). The advocacy is not for the women, but in the projection it makes women disposable. The phantasm of the murdered unborn stands in for all unsuccessful pregnancies. Again, Beavers states with urgency: "These are *our* children, *our* Mississippi babies" (Jackson 2016; emphasis added).

If we understand and perhaps prioritise the quality of threat, especially when it poses as neutral but is in fact an assumption granted and permissible in the context of white supremacy, we could see that the script is edited when needed. Upon meeting with April in the CPC Center, Beavers disturbingly says, as if seemingly playfully in regards to April's fifth and unwanted pregnancy, "Listen, one of thems going to have to be a big ol' football player and make mama lots of money!" Beavers then bursts into laughter and looks directly at the camera (Jackson 2016).[13] Here, Beavers promotes the trope of racialised poverty and, arguably, the natural talent myth.[14] This kind of solicitude overtly includes racist, somatophobic, and ableist tropes. Beavers, I argue, cares nothing for April; rather, it isn't about April at all. This is the most harmful effect of this feigned care: it impoverishes April of the capacity for her own self-determination. Beavers, similar to Atwood's Serena Joy, is merely "a machine through which to enact the visions of others."

At a follow-up ultrasound in the Maternal Fetal Clinic of the local hospital, April would again encounter a white female tech who asks her with a polite lilt to her voice about her daughter:

TECH: Is this little one yours? How old is that one?
APRIL: She'll be one on Tuesday.
TECH: Oh my gosh! Are you crazy?

(Jackson 2016)

If only that it is documented on film, these micro-exchanges exemplify how the confrontation with women by other women does its most harmful work.

The maternal mortality rate for women of colour in a developed nation is and ought to be a moral outrage.[15] Organisations like "Americans United for Life" and "Operation Save America" are – simply stated – in it for the long game. The strategy is twofold: not only to withhold sex education so that there is a high rate of teen pregnancy, but at the same time to create impossible obstacles to eliminate clear and private access to reproductive care. As one nurse at the last clinic in Mississippi states it: "This is an issue that affects predominantly poor, black women in this state" (Jackson 2016).

The effort here is to excite a somatophobia – a fear of the body – making women suspicious of their own bodies and distrust themselves as they may be ambivalent, as well as using the ambiguities of pregnant embodiment against any possible future solidarity.

CPC COUNSELLOR: (*to April*) Do you trust yourself?
APRIL: I trust myself a whole lot.
CPC COUNSELLOR: What mistakes have you made?
APRIL: Having kids. You know that's what I'm getting at. Even though I love my kids, there is so much I could be doing right now. ... I could be pursuing my dreams right now.
BEAVERS: It's healthier not to have sex until we find somebody to father all of these babies.
APRIL: We don't need no father to all these babies, I am.

(Jackson 2016)

The groups utilising pro-life rhetoric profiled in *Jackson* were predominantly white organisations, operating under an ideology populated with white, heteronormative, middle-class interests. If we ask about whether black lives matter in the United States, we still find the answer that some women's lives matter more than others.[16] If we take these confrontations to also operate in the context of an underlying race politics, as not neutral but active and aggressive misogynoir, then every attempt at the care and concern for the life of the unborn is truly race-based, causing systemic and invisible harms. This was never just a debate about beliefs.

A final note

> Many of the poor, pregnant women I have encountered do not pas-
> sively accept state regulation of their bodies. Nor do they watch the
> vanishing of their privacy rights with disinterest. Nor do they submis-
> sively accept conscription into a biomedical model of pregnancy and the
> concurrent construction of their bodies as unruly. ... As the figure of the
> wily patient makes clear, the poor, pregnant women I have encountered
> loudly, passionately, and eloquently articulate their anger and dissatis-
> faction with the order of things.
>
> (Bridges 2011, 254)

In this chapter, I've used my own personal experience, a documentary
narrative, and a fictional hypothesis to best describe the specific problem of
confrontation I raise and the scrutiny required to resist and challenge these
forms of confrontation for the sake of a future, democratic solidarity. In
articulating how the feigned care and solicitude through pro-life rhetoric and
ideology is a kind of harm, I am hoping to return to the dilemma and demand
I first argued in *The Pregnancy Project ≠ Childbearing Project*: where is the
solidarity among women as they are pregnant, independent of the outcomes

Figure 15.4 Campaigners stage a protest to demand more liberal abortion laws in
Dublin, Ireland, March 8, 2017. The protest sign reads, "Trust Women."
Source: REUTERS/Clodagh Kilcoyne.

or expectations of childbearing? It is a question that I think is essential to grapple with if not also to urgently reconcile.

My best but tentative response to this larger question is that advocacy and resistance can make for future solidarity because the repeal of the 8th amendment in Ireland was possible (Figure 15.4).[17] One of the most powerful strategies to move the needle on cultural perception about abortion was a Facebook group named In Her Shoes – Women of the Eighth, started by Erin Darcy; it provides a catalogue of narratives speaking to the complexity and indeterminacies of pregnant embodiment (2018).[18] What gave me permission to narrate and publish my own experience was the #ShoutMyAbortion social media campaign, but through these narratives, I was able to represent what I knew and had experienced even though I found it all painfully idiosyncratic. If we listen to women, *trust women* as credible knowers, and yield to the ambiguity and ambivalence that comes with the possibility of future self-direction, I would argue solidarity and cultural shift is not just possible but plausible and urgently necessary.

Notes

1 Thank you to Bertha Alvarez Manninen, Alisa Jahns, Clara Fischer, and Abbie Perrault for their assistance in accessing the materials referenced in this chapter, and to Victoria Browne and Maisie Crowe for their support for this work.
2 Schouten argues that those who defend the moral status of the fetus are not necessarily anti-feminist: "One goal of my project is to show that theorists who have minimized the importance of determining fetal moral significance have been wrong to do so. I do not know what moral status fetuses have, if any" (2017, 638); this idea of a misogynistic "plot" is in reference to my argument in *The Pregnancy ≠ Childbearing Project*.
3 See Iris Marion Young's "Pregnant Embodiment: Subjectivity and Alienation" from *On Female Body Experience: "Throwing Like a Girl" and Other Essays*.
4 The "she-who-is-pregnant" is how I refer to pregnant embodiment in *The Pregnancy Project*. It is worth noting that the gendering of pregnancy generally ("she") is normative and contingent; not all who are pregnant identify as women. An "exceptional situation" is in reference to my existential analysis of pregnancy in *The Pregnancy Project*.
5 April Jackson will be referred to as "April" so as not to confuse the title of the film with her last name.
6 This is not dissimilar to what Atwood develops in *The Handmaid's Tale* as a mandatory code of compliance: "Under His Eye" and "Blessed Be the Fruit."
7 See Rapley and Antaki, "A Conversation Analysis of the 'Acquiescence' of People with Learning Disabilities," on the complexity of the "yes-bias."
8 By the end of the film, we discover that April would later have twins – seven children in all.
9 As reported: "State prosecutors, for example, might be able to charge women whose pregnancies end in miscarriage with second-degree murder … if they can prove the miscarriage was a result of the woman's own conduct, like drug or alcohol use" (Panetta 2019).

10 As an object of care, she is always a gendered object – the "she" who needs "saving" – a "damsel-in-distress" narrative in pro-life rhetoric.
11 Following Schott's reading of de Beauvoir (2003, 242).
12 See S. Finn, "Bun or Bump?"
13 More than once in the documentary, April despairingly refers to being pregnant again as a "dream" and that she doesn't believe it can be real.
14 See R. Whitmire, "Emphasizing Sports Over Academics Sets Up Black Boys to Lose."
15 See A. Roeder, "America Is Failing Its Black Mothers."
16 See Khiara Bridges, *Reproducing Race: An Ethnography of Pregnancy as a Site of Racialization*, on this point.
17 Another site of confrontation not developed here is through social media with prolife groups as it may be used for political targeting. See J. Murdock reporting for *Newsweek* (2018).
18 Clara Fischer, "Abortion and Reproduction in Ireland: Shame, Nation-Building, and the Affective Politics of Place," develops a critical context for how this grassroots movement was able to shift the vote on the 8th Amendment.

References

Atwood, Margaret. 1998. *The Handmaid's Tale*. New York: Anchor Books.
Bridges, Khiara M. 2011. *Reproducing Race: An Ethnography of Pregnancy as a Site of Racialization*. Berkeley, CA: University of California Press.
Crow, Maisie, dir. 2016. *Jackson*. A Girl Friday Films Production in association with Reel Peak Films, Last Clinic Film, LLC. Film.
Darcy, Erin. 2018. "In Her Shoes – Women of The Eighth." Facebook [Community], January 14, 2018. www.facebook.com/InHerIrishShoes.
de Beauvoir, Simone. 1949. *The Ethics of Ambiguity*. Translated by Bernard Frechtman. Citadel Press. Reposted by Webster University Philosophy Department. www.marxists.org/reference/subject/ethics/de-beauvoir/ambiguity/index.htm.
Elsby, Charlene. 2019. "Serena Joy, Miserable, Despicable." In *A Womb of One's Own: The Handmaid's Tale and Philosophy*, edited by R. Robison-Greene, 65–75. Chicago, IL: Open Court Press.
Finn, Suki. 2017. "Bun or Bump?" *Aeon* Magazine, July 17, 2017. http://aeon.co/essays/is-the-mother-a-container-for-the-foetus-or-is-it-part-of-her.
Fischer, Clara. 2019. "Abortion and Reproduction in Ireland: Shame, Nation-Building, and the Affective Politics of Place." *Feminist Review* 122, no. 1.
Lundquist, Caroline. 2008. "Being Torn: Toward a Phenomenology of Unwanted Pregnancy." *Hypatia* 23, no. 3: 136–55.
Murdock, Jason. 2018. "American Pro-Lifers are Using Facebook to Sway Ireland's Abortion Debate." *Newsweek*, April 26, 2018. www.newsweek.com/american-pro-lifers-are-using-facebook-sway-irelands-abortion-debate-902355.
Panetta, Grace. 2019. "Women Could Get Up to 30 Years in Prison for Having a Miscarriage Under Georgia's Harsh New Abortion Law." *BusinessInsider.com*, June 10, 2019. www.businessinsider.com/women-30-years-prison-miscarriage-georgia-abortion-2019-5.
Rapley, Mark and Charles Antaki. 1996. "A Conversation Analysis of the 'Acquiescence' of People with Learning Disabilities." *Journal of Community & Applied Social Psychology* 6, no. 3: 207–27.

Roeder, Amy. 2019. "America Is Failing Its Black Mothers." *Harvard Public Health Magazine*, Winter. www.hsph.harvard.edu/magazine/magazine_article/america-is-failing-its-black-mothers.

Schott, Robin May. 2003. "Beauvoir on the Ambiguity of Evil." In *The Cambridge Companion to Simone de Beauvoir*, edited by C. Card, 228–47. Cambridge: Cambridge University Press.

Schouten, Gina. 2017. "Fetuses, Orphans, and a Famous Violinist: On the Ethics and Politics of Abortion." *Social Theory and Practice* 43, no. 3: 637–65.

Scuro, Jennifer. 2017. *The Pregnancy ≠ Childbearing Project: A Phenomenology of Miscarriage*. London: Rowman & Littlefield International.

Whitmire, Richard. 2010. "Emphasizing Sports Over Academics Sets Up Black Boys to Lose." *Education Week*, December 13, 2010. www.edweek.org/ew/articles/2010/12/13/15whitmire.h30.html.

Young, Iris Marion. 2005. *On Female Body Experience: "Throwing Like a Girl" and Other Essays*. New York: Oxford University Press.

16 "This is how I was born on the operating table of an abortion clinic"

Reproductive decision-making and *Coatlicue* State in Teatro Luna[1]

Melissa Huerta

Women of colour writers and theorists expand our thinking about reproductive decision-making by articulating that choice does not exist in a
vacuum: there are systemic and structural difficulties limiting the options for
individuals and communities. For example, writers like Ntozake Shange and
Migdalia Cruz represent women of colour characters and include themes of
abortion or unwanted pregnancy in their texts.[2] In Chicana/Latina theatre
and performance, Teatro Chicana (Teatro Raíces) represented abortion as
lived experience on the page and stage as early as 1970. In the summer of
2000, Teatro Luna, the only all-Latina theatre collective still in existence in
the US, was founded in Chicago, Illinois by Coya Paz and Tanya Saracho
as a consciousness-raising ensemble focused on bringing twentieth-century
Latina stories and experiences onto Chicago stages. In 2014, the ensemble
formed Teatro Luna-West (Los Angeles, CA) to continue the ground-
breaking and resistance work started in Chicago, IL.

Representations about reproductive decision-making and abortion in
Teatro Luna's work, specifically in "Trapped" from "Déjame contarte"
(Vega 2002), explicate the theme of ambiguity in reproductive decision-
making, through the character's journey into *Coatlicue* State. For this edited
collection's goal of making representations about abortion more nuanced,
I propose that the protagonist in "Trapped" draws on ambivalence in her
decision and finds power and agency in her choice. Informed by Gloria
Anzaldúa's state of ambiguity – *Coatlicue* State – this chapter will demonstrate how through "Trapped" Teatro Luna builds a space for Latina artists
to share their stories about reproductive decision-making, as reproductive
justice artivists (blending art and activism). In this respect, Teatro Luna's
storytelling is used as a consciousness-raising tool within their respective communities. For Teatro Luna, "authentic storytelling," including expressions of
story in the body, in images and sound, is one of their core beliefs in practice
and theory, especially as a source of strength (Meda and Acosta 2015, 156).
In sharing their reproductive decision-making experiences, Teatro Luna's
work builds on the work of other women of colour writers who use writing
and performing to tell their stories. As Loretta J. Ross explains, "storytelling
is a crucial part of reproductive justice theory, an act of reclamation and

resistance, because our theories grow from our activist locations" (Ross *et al.* 2017, 203). Teatro Luna's storytelling allows for healing and reclamation as a way to mobilise reproductive justice on stage, by building a creative space to advance a reproductive justice movement.

"Déjame contarte" dramatises the results of the US 2000 Census by defining "Latina/Hispana" at the onset of the twenty-first century (Kent 2011). The varied vignettes demonstrate diversity in Latina lives, indicative of a wide range of experiences. In the case of "Trapped," the main character reveals to the audience that she was raped and became pregnant. The protagonist embarked on a painful journey of self-empowerment. As the title of this chapter suggests, she felt and verbalised relief once she found an abortion clinic. Her journey opens with female figures, "Shadows," wearing black wings on their sleeves, ominously repeating "una senorita [sic] que no es virgencita, no sirve pa nada (a young woman who is not a virgin is worthless)"; she sits up and says, "I was good for nothing because I had lost my virginity/although I hadn't really lost it/it had been stolen from me" (Vega 2002). This is a powerful statement because it challenges mainstream ideas about abortion and expands our understandings of abortion access. This character's story documents and stages the experience, history, thoughts, and emotions of Latina women and other women of colour like current social media movements such as #YouKnowMe and #ShoutYourAbortion.

Representations of abortion are not exclusive to theatre and performance or simply determined by cultural or ideological contexts. Given the current political climate where many Planned Parenthood clinics have closed because of a lack of funding, and many US states have restricted access to abortion, representations of abortion are of a peculiar resonance. Most recently, the *New York Times* reported on a decrease in abortions in the US, mostly due to contraceptive use and fewer pregnancies overall (Belluck 2019). Nevertheless, abortion is more than just a personal matter, and it has historically been linked to ways of controlling both women and nations.[3] Teatro Luna's work on the matter emphasises second-wave feminism's adage of "personal is political," by bringing to the stage compelling Latina stories that interrogate reproductive decision-making. In this chapter, I contribute to the consideration of rethinking Teatro Luna's work as reproductive justice artivism, grounded in Chicana/Latina theories of representations of abortion in "Trapped."

The next section briefly surveys theoretical approaches to ambivalence, Teatro Luna's work, and *Coatlicue* State, followed by a close reading of the vignette "Trapped." I include a brief description of Teatro Luna's creative practices that speak to broad-reaching reproductive justice. By reproductive justice, I rely on Loretta J. Ross' definition:

> a theoretical paradigm and model for activist organising centring on three interconnected human rights: the right not to have children using safe birth control, abortion, or abstinence; the right to have children

under the conditions we choose; and the right to parent the children we have in safe and healthy environments.

(Ross et al. 2017, 14)

Teatro Luna's work as resistance theatre attests to the demanding social problems women of colour and their communities face, and to the effect-iveness of Latina storytelling as agents of change, centred on reproductive justice. In doing so, Teatro Luna's theatricalisation of reproductive decision-making and abortion provides insight into the role of a reproductive justice approach. On the one hand, it enables artists to represent reproductive decision-making beyond notions of "choice" and, on the other, it provides readers and audiences with an opportunity to think through reproductive choice-making as ambiguous and ambivalent.

Theoretical approaches to ambiguity perceived in pregnancy and mother-hood capture both positive and negative emotions, beliefs, or thoughts. In the work of psychoanalytic theorists like Sigmund Freud, love and hate in mother–child relationships are rooted in the unconscious and coexist (Holloway and Featherstone 1994). Contemporary psychotherapist Rozsika Parker extends this understanding and addresses the significance of ambiva-lence for maternal psychological development (1995). Ivana Brown, in her study on the ambivalence of motherhood, shifts from psychoanalytic approaches and looks at both psychological and social components shaping and defining a woman's life (2010). Sociologists have argued that environ-mental contexts and not personality, connected to contrasting expectations, attitudes, beliefs, and behaviours, make ambiguity more apparent in indi-viduals (Kaplan 1992). As such, ambiguity does not occur in a vacuum, but derives from the social definitions of roles and statuses along with their conflicting demands, and as discourse. Jennifer Scuro's chapter in this volume is also grounded in a nuanced consideration of ambiguity, through an analysis of Maisie Crow's documentary *Jackson*. Scuro's work highlights the use of ambiguity in facilities that deem themselves supportive of and a resource to pregnant women seeking to terminate their pregnancy. Scuro argues that these groups impose a right-wing political agenda masked as sympathetic, meant to persuade women to comply and keep the child, thus exercising patriarchy and racism through ambivalence.

Moving beyond these approaches, different perspectives on ambiguity in potential motherhood and reproductive decision-making have shown a continuous evolution in the various approaches: from psychology and soci-ology, to feminist theory and feminist of colour theory. Scholars such as Patricia Hill Collins, Evelyn Nakano Glenn, Gloria Anzaldúa, and Cherríe Moraga question the notion of maternity connected to lived experiences of women of colour where dominant ideologies and representations of mater-nity and sexuality reinforce and complicate women's experiences that do not fit the ideal.[4] Nuyorican playwright Migdalia Cruz noted in an interview about sexuality in her plays,

I think part of where it comes from is that the one thing women always own is our bodies. ... I think women use their bodies differently than men do. Men always feel entitled to their bodies; women think they're supposed to act certain ways with their bodies, do certain things [and] [t]he body is the only concrete thing you have.

(Arrizón and Manzor 2000, 212)

Latina theatre and performance scholars such as Alicia Arrizón have argued that theatre oriented towards change, produced by women of colour, reclaims their stories and power, the right to self-determination, and the right to construct self and communal identities (2000). If, as Cruz asserts, the body is the only concrete thing we have, then it serves as a vital foundation and a bridge that communicates racial, gendered, and sexual interconnectedness of histories.

Coatlicue State and Teatro Luna

Cherríe Moraga and Gloria Anzaldúa's theory in the flesh is useful to explicate the role of lived experiences and empowerment. "A theory in the flesh is where the physical realities of our lives – our skin colour, the land or concrete we grew up on, our sexual longings – all fuse to create a politic born out of necessity. Here, we attempt to bridge the contradictions in our experience" (Anzaldúa and Moraga 1983, 21). Their theorisation connects to *Coatlicue* State in explaining how consciousness rises from, is informed by, and is radically altered by others' perceptions of Chicana/Latina bodies, identities, and self-understanding. I understand Anzaldúa's consideration of *mestiza* consciousness as a state of being derived from individual and collective identifications; for example, being a woman and a Latina. Furthermore, Anzaldúa's *Coatlicue* State is fundamental in examining representations of ambiguity in reproductive decision-making and abortion. She defines *Coatlicue* State as one of ambivalence and contradiction, where old knowledges struggle to resist emergent new knowledges, and redefines the Aztec goddess of creation and destruction as a metaphor of strength to challenge patriarchal binaries.[5] Anzaldúa's work emphasises that cultural and institutional frictions are caused by navigating multiple and contradictory spaces. It is a state of "psychic unrest" but it is also one of transformation, a "prelude to crossing," towards *mestiza* consciousness. For Anzaldúa, consciousness is a particular type of "spiritual inquiry," demanding action and a space for change (Anzaldúa and Keating 2002, 542). In "Trapped," the character enters *Coatlicue* State by navigating her decision to have an abortion, releasing the power of *Coatlicue*'s ambiguity to empower herself, and possibly opening a space to rehearse social change.

In thinking through *Coatlicue* State as one of empowerment and change, I find the work of Edwina Barvosa and Mariana Ortega useful because they argue through Anzaldúa's theories of self-hood that a *mestiza* autonomy is made possible, grounded on conflicting social relationship and experiences (Barvosa 2007, 3). For Barvosa, subjects are socialised through conflicting social relationships, and by practising autonomy through ambivalence, where its productive nature can be a useful site for thought and action (2007). Barvosa's perspective is in line with understanding how in "Trapped" the character navigates conflicting relationships shaping her decision-making once she finds out she is pregnant. For scholars like Barvosa, the *mestiza* subject's ability to tolerate ambiguity and ambivalence in everyday life is productive and can lead to "*mestiza* autonomy" (Barvosa 2007, 2). In the case of the character in "Trapped," Anzaldúa's claims that the *mestiza* continuously engages with conflicting worlds inform her identity which apply to her experiences of entering and exiting ambivalent spaces.

Mariana Ortega's work on Anzaldúa's theorisation of in-betweenness explores the possibilities of world-building and solidarity through ambiguity and living on the borderlands. Ortega's innovative philosophical work draws on Anzaldúa's work to better understand how lived experiences shape and reveal a sense of being for *mestiza* subjects (Ortega 2016). Ortega's work draws on Anzaldúa and other Chicana/Latina theorists and puts them in conversation with the work of philosophers like Martin Heidegger. Ortega argues that Anzaldúa makes a case for the state of *nepantla* as one that is unstable and precarious, yet rich with possibilities (Ortega 2016, 26). In this liminal space, the *mestiza* experiences *Coatlicue* States: moments of ambivalence whereby the subject encounters fear and moments of trans-formation. For Barvosa and Ortega, Anzaldúa's *Borderlands/La Frontera* draws on lived experiences and on the relationship between history and social relations to forge a distinct definition of Chicana/Latina embodiment.

Artists like Anzaldúa and Teatro Luna speak about their reproductive bodies, not only psychologically, but also through cultural experiences, revealing stories of oppressive social structures by incorporating ambiguity in their embodied narratives. Specifically, Teatro Luna's body of work since 2000 demonstrates a commitment to telling nuanced stories emerging from their lived experiences as Latinas in the twentieth century. Joanna Mitchell argues that autobiographical representation in Teatro Luna demystifies Latina sexuality and the female body, and allows for conversations about sexual abuse, body image, and reproductive rights (2011).

Teatro Luna's current work emerges from the early ensemble members' commitment to writing for and staging stories beyond traditional and stereotypical notions of the Latina experience. While Teatro Luna's history is beyond the scope and detail of this chapter, a brief presentation of two milestones illuminates the relationship between their work, *Coatlicue* State, and a broad-reaching reproductive justice movement.

Coya Paz and Tanya Saracho appear to have exhibited movement in and out of *Coatlicue* State, including the capacity to navigate ambiguity. Paz and Saracho navigated through predominantly white-dominant performance spaces in Chicago. In a 2005 interview, Saracho comments:

You could count the ones [Latino actors] that were working all the time with two hands. Most of them were men, too. Finally, I was thinking this is not going to work if I write mostly for women and Latina women.

(Sobeira and Mitchell 2006, 26)

Following her initial experience with a lack of Latina representation in Chicago theatre, she met Paz, and Teatro Luna was born. Despite the differences between the two, Teatro Luna grew quickly, eventually including diverse ensemble members.

In 2015, Teatro Luna wrote and published a Manifesto, delineating their approach to theatre-making. In this Manifesto, Teatro Luna shares with readers their core beliefs on how to live and practise ensemble work. In the Manifesto, Teatro Luna looks to the past, present, and future to remain a theatre of resistance, one that uses and articulates a sense of Latina identity, community, and experiences as core elements in their storytelling (Meda and Acosta 2015). Furthermore, Teatro Luna's work sheds light on the potential of ambiguity to create stories from lived experiences as Latinas, like pregnancy and motherhood. In both theatrical practice and in their creative work, Teatro Luna employs a reproductive justice framework.

These two examples demonstrate Teatro Luna's mission to create Latina-centred stories and their commitment to grounding their work in their community. Teatro Luna theatricalises *Coatlicue* State, one that moved past and present ensemble members to create stories as a way to make sense of their experiences off stage. In this state, Teatro Luna as an artivist group confronts oppressive ideologies that have inhabited and splintered Latina bodies on and off stage, and they work towards transforming their consciousness, allowing for a more nuanced representation of their experiences.

Coatlicue's daughter

Ambiguity in pregnancy as the result of rape is represented in the vignette "Trapped." *Coatlicue* State informs my reading of the character, staging, and dialogue/monologue. Davida Bloom's observation about rape, feminism, and theatre extends to the importance of Latina feminist stories on stage since these stories provide insight into lived experiences serving as consciousness-raising tools for audiences and performers alike (2016). In the context of pregnancy caused by rape, abortion is widely accepted as a recourse because of the violent nature of the act. However, there is stigma attached to rape and to abortion, especially in women from more conservative backgrounds. Furthermore, in legal exceptions made in the US, there can be undue burden on women to prove they were raped, subsequently encountering unnecessary red tape in the process of accessing an abortion (Ely and Dulmus 2010). Also, some of the waiting periods implemented in several US states, regardless of the woman's reason, could further intensify the rape survivor's trauma. Expanding our understanding of the complicated nature of abortion because of rape in Teatro Luna's work like "Trapped" further illuminates nuanced representations of abortion beyond restrictive notions of choice.

From the beginning of the vignette, the character describes powerlessness and shame because she lost her virginity and became pregnant. The character's *Coatlicue* State is brought on by the crisis she experienced, thus the contradictory parts of her identity encounter each other: loss of agency and virginity (Vega 2002). Inherent in what she mentions is the internalisation of the gendered patriarchal concepts of sexuality often related to how Chicanas/Latinas should behave: "[i]n patriarchy, a woman's sex is the site of her deepest power (creation, which must be controlled and monitored at all times) and her deepest weakness (penetration, which must be punished)" (Gaspar de Alba 2014, 74).

The vignette makes use of the Shadows to enact ambiguity and serve as mirrors for the character. The material aspects of the vignette such as the Shadows and red ribbons used to tie the woman become intelligible symbols for female readers and viewers who have encountered moments of gender- and class-based oppressions. On the surface, the Shadows may appear chorus-like, reminiscent of Greek tragedies. However, they propel the character into *Coatlicue* State, becoming the mirrors Anzaldúa references: "The mirror is an ambivalent figure. Not only does it reproduce images … it contains and absorbs them" (2007, 64). The potentially empowering story along with the staging equips Teatro Luna's audience to retell their painful stories and recognise contradictory parts of the self. In this aspect of their work, Teatro Luna centres on acknowledging the importance of Latina lived experiences around reproductive decision-making. As the character narrates her story, the Shadows begin to embody other characters, such as the police and the abortion provider. In these moments, the Shadows allow the audience and readers to reflect upon moments of ambiguity, where contradictory parts of life come into contact and make us question and possibly rebel against dominant expectations. The disempowering experiences the character felt early in the vignette are further amplified using red ribbons on stage. The stage directions note that after the first ribbon is placed, the other Shadows approach her to tie her up, "pulling at part of her: her feet, her torso, her neck" (Vega 2002).

The strain of feeling powerless and angry after rape further emphasises ambiguity and her journey into *Coatlicue* State in the aftermath. The character embodies La Malinche, the *mestiza* mother-figure, deemed the "traitor" of the Mexican people because of her involvement with a Spanish conquistador, Hernán Cortés. She symbolises the traitor after serving as a translator for Cortés and giving birth to the first *mestizo*, representing the whore, the sell-out (Paz 1985). Accepting the patriarchal history of La Malinche reinforces a misogynistic reading of her story and therefore perpetuates the virgin/whore dichotomy. Many Latina/Chicana writers and theorists have reimagined La Malinche's story to redefine her as a source of strength

(Moraga and Rodriguez 2011). Nevertheless, the character expresses anger and guilt, confirming Malinche narratives of shame and self-blame. As the character navigates through the shame of her rape, she faces more restrictive barriers: since she did not report the rape immediately, she is unable to press charges. As such, the violated Chicana/Latina woman's body and her "lack of responsibility" become sites of shame symbolised by the virgin and whore (Castillo 1995, 116–18).

From the beginning, cultural forces such as her Latina identity and cultural expectations make the character feel powerless, reinforce victim blaming, and are further physically intensified: "I feel sick/I don't feel human" (Vega 2002). Her feelings and perceptions are not uncommon, but within the (virgin) mother/whore dichotomy, she subverts the most traditional role for women: the overjoyed pregnant woman. Chicana feminists such as Ana Castillo have argued against and re-appropriated these attributes in their work:

> [i]n modern man's schema woman must choose between two polarised roles, that of mother as portrayed by the Virgin Mary vs. that of whore/ traitor as Eve ... by refusing to submit to a man/god, the way Lilith/Eve/ La Llorona did, woman, according to myth, is to be punished forever.
>
> (Castillo 1995, 116–18)

Feeling and representing ambiguity because of rape is particularly relevant in Latina cultural production where authors have consciously critiqued Latino culture's demand for the virgin spouse and the suffering mother. The fact that the character describes her pregnancy as invasive echoes Shulamith Firestone's assertion: "[p]regnancy is barbaric [and] [p]regnancy is the temporary deformation of the body of the individual for the sake of the species" (1997, 188–9).

The character's journey in *Coatlicue* State intensifies when she is thrust into immobility:

> [w]e need *Coatlicue* to slow us up so that the psyche can assimilate previous experiences and process the changes ... Our greatest disappointments and painful experiences – if we can make meaning out of them – can lead us toward becoming more of who we are.
>
> (Anzaldúa 2007, 68)

As a result of the painful experience, the character intimates: "I was suspended in air watching the days pass in slow motion" (Vega 2002). In the subsequent comments, access to abortion becomes economically inaccessible, placing emphasis on social and individual circumstances. This immobility coupled with powerful moments of self-hatred and her shift towards reproductive decision-making gives the reader a deeper insight into the complicated notion of "choice" for women of colour. This interrogation is present throughout the remainder of the vignette and is akin to "*mestiza* autonomy," whereby *mestizas* act as agents while keeping the contradicting notions of their identities in mind through "their critical reflection on the array of values and norms that are given to them socially as part of their different social and personal identities" (Barvosa 2007, 2).

Similarly, the character exercises *mestiza* autonomy and refuses to be silenced or conform to how she should express her pain. She acknowledges her anger and fears but internalises self-hate because she cannot pay for the abortion. Dominant narratives of individual responsibility and individualism resonate in her words: "what's wrong with you? ... maybe I deserve to die" (Vega 2002). Thus, she is further thrust into *Coatlicue* State, in a dark space, systemically pointing to the individual devoid of any collectivity or community. The character navigates darkness to find her sister, weaving a complex counter-narrative surrounding reproductive decision-making and the Latina female collective. This aspect illustrates Teatro Luna's artivist work by theatricalising female collectivity on stage, mirroring the ensemble's creative storytelling approach – focused on drawing from their lived experiences and those of women they know, such as their mothers, grandmothers, friends, etc. As in the vignette, Teatro Luna ensemble members' stories shed light on narratives seldom shared in public, let alone on stage.

The character comes to a crossroads after confronting and surpassing cultural, symbolic, and economic barriers; she now faces a legal obstacle: she is too far along in the pregnancy. Faced with the impossibility of terminating her pregnancy, she falls deeper into *Coatlicue* State: "[h]ad I not been a good daughter? ... my mother's nightmare had become my reality/I wanted so much for myself" (Vega 2002). This is significant because in the majority of cases, rape is one of the reasons for allowing abortions; however, the character's experience with her pregnancy progression speaks to the complicated and ambiguous nature of abortion bans and laws restricting access after a certain number of weeks. The self-doubt and fear imbedded in her words echo Emily Klein's analysis of Latina representations of pain through resistance whereby staging allows the bodies to be visually represented as contested sites, written and rewritten by society and Latina women themselves (2011). In other words, by focusing on Latina stories of pain and resistance, "Trapped" reframes Latina reproductive decision-making as part of the larger reproductive justice movement, revealing the intersections of race, class, and other markers of difference that affect individual and collective notions of reproductive decision-making (Ross *et al.* 2017).

Throughout the remainder of the vignette, the character is deeply immersed in her experience and comes face to face with her fears, with societal demands, and with psychic and physical wounds: "I was trapped/ raped/tied up/just another pregnant teenager/just another statistic" (Vega 2002). She finally locates an abortion clinic that will terminate the pregnancy, but for more money. Freeing the powerful duality of *Coatlicue* State through the body, as represented in the falling red ribbons, her power was released: "[m]y life had been given back to me" (Vega 2002). Her empower-ment and newfound strength serve as a source of increased consciousness of the self, challenging traditional constructs of being a Latina woman beyond constraining notions of womanhood steeped in the virgin/whore binary.

Conclusion

The character's personal shame and social stigma over her rape, loss of vir-ginity, and abortion are themes in "Trapped," by Teatro Luna. The distortion of what those things mean or represent for the character came into conflict, forcing her into *Coatlicue* State. Anzaldúa's concept is useful in representing reproductive decision-making as ambiguous, further permitting the char-acter to inhabit contradictory psychic and physical spaces, leading to healing, self-awareness, and a journey towards *mestiza* consciousness. Ambiguity is a component of reproductive decision-making because it threatens dominant understandings of reproductive "choice" both in pro-choice communities and in women of colour communities. By linking ambiguity to reproductive decision-making, Teatro Luna's work in "Trapped" challenges dominant modes of representing abortion by giving voice and agency to the woman's experience. Similarly, current US and internationally based social media movements such as #YouKnowMe and #ShoutYourAbortion have shed light on the stigma felt by women who have had abortions, providing public platforms to share their stories, across a range of intersectional identities and across generations of women.

The possibility of change and renewal after the character's experience opens a space for those Latina readers and viewers to rehearse social change in their own lives. At a time when access to reproductive health and abortion is under attack, the work of Teatro Luna as resistance theatre stages social problems women of colour and their communities face, and their work speaks to the effectiveness of Latina storytelling as a powerful agent of change, centred on reproductive justice.

Notes

1 Maria Vega, "Trapped," in "Déjame Contarte." Performed and arranged by Teatro Luna (Chicago, IL), 2002. Unpublished script.
2 See Ntozake Shange, *For coloured girls who have considered suicide/when the rainbow is enuf* and Migdalia Cruz, *The Have-Little: Contemporary Plays by Women of Colour.*
3 See Trinh T. Minh-ha, *Woman Native, Other* and Inderpal Grewal and Caren Kaplan, *Scattered Hegemonies: Postmodernity and Transnational Feminist Practices.*
4 See Suzanne Bost, *Encarnación*; Evelyn Nakano Glenn *et al.*, *Mothering, Ideology, Experience, and Agency*; see Norma Alarcón, Ana Castillo, and Cherríe Moraga, eds., *The Sexuality of Latinas*; Cherríe Moraga, *Waiting in the Wings: A Portrait*

of a Queer Motherhood; Audre Lorde, *Sister Outsider* and Lisa Hagen, *Examining the Use of Safety, Confrontation and Ambivalence.*
5 In Aztec mythology, Coatlicue is "Serpent Skirt" (Nahuatl) and the symbol of creation and destruction. See Encyclopedia Britannica, "Coatlicue" and Gloria Anzaldúa, *Borderlands/La Frontera*, 68–9.

References

Alarcón, Norma, Ana Castillo, and Cherríe Moraga, eds. 1993. *The Sexuality of Latinas*. Berkeley, CA: Third Woman Press.

Anzaldúa, Gloria. 2007. *Borderlands/La Frontera*. San Francisco, CA: Aunt Lute Books.

Anzaldúa, Gloria, and Cherríe Moraga, eds. 1983. *This Bridge Called My Back: Writings by Radical Women of Colour*. New York: Kitchen Table: Women of Colour Press.

Anzaldúa, Gloria, and Analouise Keating. 2002. *this bridge we call home*. New York: Routledge.

Arrizón, Alicia, and Lillian Manzor, eds. 2000. *Latinas on Stage*. Berkeley, CA: Third Woman Press.

Barvosa-Carter, Edwina. 2007. "Mestiza Autonomy as Relational Autonomy: Ambivalence and the Social Character of Free Will." *The Journal of Political Philosophy* 15, no. 1: 1–21.

Belluck, Pam. 2019. "America's Abortion Rate Has Dropped to Its Lowest Ever." *New York Times*, September 18, 2019. www.nytimes.com.

Bloom, Davida. 2016. *Rape, Rage and Feminism in Contemporary American Drama*. Jefferson, NC: McFarland.

Bost, Suzanne. 2010. *Encarnación*. New York: Fordham University Press.

Brown, Ivana. 2010. "Ambivalence of the Motherhood Experience." In *Twenty-First Century Motherhood: Experience, Identity, Policy, Agency*, edited by Andrea O'Reilly, 121–39. New York: Columbia University Press.

Castillo, Ana. 1995. *Massacre of the Dreamers: Essays on Xicanisma*. New York: Plume.

Cruz, Migdalia. 1996. *The Have Little: Contemporary Plays by Women of Colour*. Edited by Kathy A. Perkins and Roberta Uno. New York: Routledge.

Ely, Gretchen E., and Catherine N. Dulmus. 2010. "Abortion Policy and Vulnerable Women in the United States: A Call for Social Work Policy Practice." *Journal of Human Behavior in the Social Environment* 20, no. 5: 658–67.

Encyclopedia Britannica. 2016. "Coatlicue." Encyclopedia Britannica, January 28, 2016. www.britannica.com/topic/coatlicue.

Firestone, Shulamith. 1997. "The Dialectic of Sex." In *The Second Wave: A Reader in Feminist Theory*, edited by Linda J. Nicholson. New York: Routledge. 188–9.

Gaspar de Alba, Alicia. 2014. *[Un]Framing the "Bad Woman": Sor Juana, Malinche, Coyolxauhqui and Other Rebels with a Cause*. Austin, TX: University of Texas Press.

Grewal, Inderpal, and Caren Kaplan. 1994. *Scattered Hegemonies: Postmodernity and Transnational Feminist Practices*. Minneapolis, MN: University of Minnesota Press.

Hagen, Lisa. 2010. *Examining the Use of Safety, Confrontation and Ambivalence.* New York: Edwin Mellen Press.

Holloway, Wendy, and Brid Featherstone. 1994. *Mothering and Ambivalence.* New York: Routledge.

Kaplan, Ann E. 1992. *Motherhood and Representation: The Mother in Popular Culture and Melodrama.* New York: Routledge.

Kent, Mary. 2011. "First Glimpses from the 2000 Census." Population Reference Bureau, June 1, 2011. www.prb.org/firstglimpsesfromthe2000censuspdf22mb.

Klein, Emily. 2011. "Spectacular Citizenships: Staging Latina Resistance through Urban Performances of Pain." *Frontiers,* 32, no. 1: 102–24.

Latorre, Sobeira, and Joanna L. Mitchell. 2006. "Performing the 'Generic Latina': A Conversation with Teatro Luna." *Meridians: feminism, race, transnationalism* 7, no. 1: 19–37.

Lorde, Audre. 1984. *Sister Outsider.* New York: Crown Publishing.

Meda, Alexandra, and LizaAnn Acosta. 2015. "Teatro Luna Manifesto." *Gestos* 60: 151–60.

Minh-ha, Trinh T. 1989. *Woman Native, Other.* Bloomington, IN: Indiana University Press.

Mitchell, Joanna L. 2011. "Teatro Luna: Bodies That Matter on the Chicago Stage." *Gestos* 51 (April): 115–28.

Moraga, Cherríe. 1997. *Waiting in the Wings: A Portrait of a Queer Motherhood.* Ann Arbor, MI: Firebrand Books.

Moraga, Cherríe, and Celia H. Rodriguez. 2011. *A Xicana Codex of Changing Consciousness: Writings, 2000–2010.* Durham, NC: Duke University Press.

Nakano Glenn, Evelyn, Grace Chang, and Linda Rennie Forcey. 1994. *Mothering, Ideology, Experience, and Agency.* New York: Routledge.

Ortega, Mariana. 2016. *In-Between: Latina Feminist Phenomenology, Multiplicity, and the Self.* Albany, NY: SUNY Press.

Parker, Rozsika. 1995. *Torn in Two: The Experience of Maternal Ambivalence.* London: Virago Press.

Paz, Octavio. 1985. *The Labyrinth of Solitude.* New York: Grove Press.

Ross, Loretta, Lynn Roberts, Erika Derkas, Whitney Peoples, and Pamela Bridgewater Toure. 2017. *Radical Reproductive Justice: Foundation, Theory, Practice, Critique.* New York: Feminist Press at CUNY.

Shange, Ntozake. 1977. *For coloured girls who have considered suicide/when the rainbow is enuf.* Basingstoke: Macmillan Publishing.

Vega, Maria. 2002. "Trapped" in *Déjame contarte* by Teatro Luna. Unpublished script, Chicago, IL.

17 Abortion and the ideology of love in Kathy Acker's *Blood and Guts in High School* and *Don Quixote, Which Was a Dream*[1]

Yoonha Shin

"[*Roe v. Wade*] has fundamentally altered the legal, medical, and political landscape of [the United States]," said the then-president of the Planned Parenthood Federation of America Gloria Feldt in 1998 (Greenberg 1998). *Roe v. Wade* was indeed a landmark decision in 1973 that disallowed many state and federal restrictions on abortion during the first trimester. It recognises the abortion rights by taking an individualist approach that interprets the right of privacy as "broad enough to encompass a woman's decision" to terminate pregnancy (410 U.S. 113 (1973)). The idea of negative liberty behind the ruling, however, soon ignited controversy since women's reproductivity has always been a domain of state intervention. Many feminists and scholars, while welcoming the decision, have thus shown concerns about the right to privacy that formed the basis of the constitutional right to abortion. Catharine MacKinnon, for example, contends that personal liberty for women is not guaranteed because women's experience is shaped by the public (1987): the male-dominated social relations and legal systems.

The Supreme Court's definition of the fetus's viability provoked even more controversy. The ruling states that "the 'compelling' point is at viability. This is so because the fetus, then, presumably has the capability of meaningful life outside the mother's womb" (410 U.S. 113 (1973)). The term *viability* conveys a sense of ambiguity since it does not define birth as the beginning of personhood. Fetal rights advocates, as a result, have focused on the potential human life and promoted the idea of fetal personhood, which has largely framed the choice vs. life debate. As Mary Poovey puts it, "A woman's right to terminate her pregnancy is not absolute, and may to some extent be limited … [to protect] potential human life" (Poovey 1992, 244). As such, despite the precedent it has set for the protection of women who seek abortions, *Roe v. Wade* in many ways has generated the antagonism between pro-choice and pro-life activisms and reaffirmed the governmental regulation of the female body.

Choice is an ironic term in the abortion discourse, especially within the framework of choice vs. life. It evokes the rhetoric of neoliberalism, a policy that takes market economy as a principle and sees each individual as "capital-ability," to borrow Michel Foucault's term (2008, 225). In a neoliberal nation state, the activities of its population are considered as voluntary choices to pursue maximum profit. The neoliberal rhetoric of choice displays the absurdity of abortion as a personal decision because, as Drucilla Cornell remarks, "no woman *chooses* to have an unwanted pregnancy" (1995, 246). What is equally important is that the anxiety of white Anglo-Saxon Protestants over the rise of immigration played a pivotal role in criminalising abortion in the nineteenth-century US. According to Nathan Stormer, it was the reinforcement of the "white bourgeois culture" via medically institutionalised power that regenerated the anti-abortion campaign (2002, 32). Seen in this light, reproductive rights are not so much a matter of choice or entitlement as a biopolitical tool of the government. Roughly understood as the politicisation of bare life, biopolitics focuses on the management of a modern sovereignty's population by controlling the human body as well as any random events that may affect the control, i.e. by "[making] live" and "[letting] die" (Foucault 2003, 239–49). More significantly, because the state exercises its power to regulate through permanent surveillance, sex and sexuality become a "field of vital strategic importance." As Foucault writes, "Sexuality exists at the point where body and population meet. And so, it is a matter for discipline, but also a matter for regularisation" (2003, 251–2). Reproductive rights, especially abortion rights, thus lie at the centre of governmental interests as the decriminalisation of abortion necessarily involves a compromise of its institutional power.

Interestingly but not surprisingly, fictional representations of abortion as well as literary criticism in the US have closely followed the choice vs. life dichotomy.[2] It is only recently that scholars have started to read literary texts outside of the choice vs. life debate, with Heather Latimer as a notable example (Latimer 2013). In conjunction with the recent shift in criticism and with other essays in this edited collection, I argue that moving beyond the antipodes of choice and life is significant to understand the neoliberal and biopolitical system of the contemporary nation state. In particular, I focus on Kathy Acker's two novels, *Blood and Guts in High School* (1978/1984; *Blood and Guts* hereafter)[3] and *Don Quixote, Which Was a Dream* (1986; *Don Quixote* hereafter), to examine her unique and compelling perspectives on abortion. Acker problematises heterosexual love as a capitalist patriarchal ideology and envisions abortion as a site of symbolic resistance in these works of fiction. Her fictional representations of abortion demonstrate the connection between her novels and the feminist discourses since the 1970s that politicise love but further this critique as she examines the neoliberal atmosphere of the 1980s.

In *Blood and Guts* and *Don Quixote*, the two protagonists, Janey Smith and Don Quixote, are already marked as women faced with the implications of the male-controlled world but continuously attempting to establish new subjectivities. Such an effort is, predictably, not always successful as far as neoliberal and biopolitical sovereignty is concerned; nevertheless, as the death of the two protagonists leads to rebirth, both texts performatively request a readerly engagement by calling the readers out and asking them to carry out radical social critique and praxis. In so doing, abortion serves as a reminder of the socially constructed relations of class, race, and gender, as well as the beginning point of new subject formation outside the dominant ideological framework.

At first glance, *Blood and Guts* reads like a list of violent and abusive encounters that Janey has with men. After breaking the relationship with a Father, Janey struggles financially in New York City while meeting a number of men; later, she is abducted by two men and then sold to a Persian slave holder for prostitution. More troublingly, even though the men in *Blood and Guts* only see physical values in women, Janey provides those values in the hope of reciprocal love: "I was desperate to fuck more and more so I could finally get love" (Acker 2017, 35). This particular scene embodies a fictional imagination of what Shulamith Firestone calls love in its "diseased state" in *The Dialectic of Sex* (2003). The phenomenon of love according to Firestone is based on the desire for a mutual exchange of selves, but the unequal balance of power between men and women makes love "complicated, corrupted, or obstructed" (Firestone 2003, 116–19). Janey is desperate to find love but is always abandoned by men whose diseased love takes advantage of her, and her pursuit of love results in two abortions.

Since the power imbalance directly influences the practices of love, abortion becomes "the symbol, the outer image, of sexual relations in this world" (Acker 2017, 34). The staff in the abortion clinic ironically reiterate the neoliberal rhetoric of choice by saying, "It's all up to you girls. You have to be strong. Shape up. You're a modern woman. These are the days of post-women's liberation" (Acker 2017, 32). In *Blood and Guts*, Acker carefully intertwines the issue of gender with those of class and race to reflect the reproductive policies of the biopolitical nation state. As a young, underprivileged woman and possibly a woman of colour ("Since I'm dark enough to pass for Moroccan" (Acker 2017, 127)) who has to financially support herself, Janey needs to save a substantial amount of money to have an abortion. When Acker was writing the novel in 1976, the Hyde Amendment was passed and barred the use of federal funds for abortion except under certain conditions, mostly affecting Medicaid and women with limited resources. Indeed, as Jerome S. Legge points out, even after *Roe v. Wade*, African-American women reportedly had a greater risk of death than their white counterparts since their lower socioeconomic status affected the accessibility of a timely abortion as well as post-surgery nutrition (1985, 24). In other words, classism and racism work closely with the biopolitics of reproduction to the extent that the state selectively chooses whom to make live and whom to let die by distinguishing the abortion rights of the governing from those of the governed.[4] The subsequent scene of the abortion clinic in *Blood and Guts* epitomises the intersection of class and race with gender in the abortion discourse:

> The women in my line were handed long business forms: at the end of each form was a paragraph that stated she gave the doctor the right to do whatever he wanted and if she ended up dead, it wasn't his fault. We had given ourselves up to men before. That's why we were here. All of us signed everything. Then they took our money.
>
> (Acker 2017, 32)

> She couldn't say anything. Whether she wanted a local or not. A LOCAL means a local anaesthetic. They stick large hypodermics filled with novocaine in your cunt lips and don't numb where it hurts at all. A general anaesthetic costs fifty dollars more and fills you up with synthetic morphine and truth serum. All of us gathered around her, held her hands, and stroked her legs. Gradually she began to calm down.
>
> (Acker 2017, 33)

The clinic where more than fifty young women who have paid their "one-hundred-ninety stolen, begged-for, and borrowed dollars" and wait on the "factory line" to leave their bodies – and sometimes their lives – in the male doctor's hands does not seem to guarantee safety at all even if these women pay an additional cost, not to mention that their pain is ignored or dismissed at best (Acker 2017, 32). Acker's critique clearly aims at the capitalised medical institutions and their effort to further regulate safe access to abortion depending on the purchasing power of each individual.

Similarly, the termination of pregnancy in *Don Quixote* is described as an experience of ultimate objectification and dehumanisation:

> When a doctor sticks a steel catheter into you while you're lying on your back and you do exactly what he and the nurses tell you to; finally, blessedly, you let go of your mind. Letting go of your mind is dying. She needed a new life. She had to be named.
>
> (Acker 1986, 9–10)

The anonymous female protagonist in the novel, who soon names herself Don Quixote, becomes an object to be displayed and manipulated on the table before a male doctor and a number of nurses. Abortion in this regard particularly marks a shift in female subjectivity since she symbolically dies in the course of the operation and then is reborn to create a new sense of self. At the same time, it serves as a moment to defy the (male-defined) Cartesian split as she realises "the mind is the body. This ... is why [she's] got a body. That's why [she's] having an abortion" (Acker 1986, 10). Borrowing Annette Schlichter's words, Don Quixote's abortion "[transforms] the suffering that results from the mind-body dualism into resistance to normalization" (2007). Compared to the abortion scenes in *Blood and Guts* in which the surgery symbolises the existing class, race, and gender relations of the world, the meaning of abortion in *Don Quixote* is distinctly extended to a starting point for resistance as the female knight re-establishes herself beyond the male-dominant social system. As she proclaims later, abortion "[refuses] normalcy which is the capitulation to social control" (Acker 1986, 17–18). Acker's fictional imagination here is aligned with Carly Thomsen's conception of abortion as "liberatory and painful, devastating and empowering, all at the same time" (2013, 151).[5] For Acker, abortion is not only a political issue but also a rebellious and even celebratory action.

Reading and writing are significant means for Janey and Don Quixote to redefine and re-establish their subjectivities. The two characters read and appropriate male writers and their works because women's writing is situated outside of the canon and is thus unavailable for them. After being confined to a room by the Persian slave trader, Mr. Linker, Janey starts to write by copying and parodying male texts including Nathaniel Hawthorne and Propertius. While doing so, she realises that "culture stinks: books / and great men and the / fine arts" (Acker 2017, 73). Her awareness once again parallels *The Dialectics of Sex* as Firestone argues that "love is tied to culture in much deeper ways" and that the power imbalance has barred women from thinking, writing, and creating while men create culture (2003, 113). Likewise, in her knightly quest to find love, Don Quixote turns to male authors such as Andrei Bely and Frank Wedekind, in addition to borrowing the narrative framework from Cervantes: "BEING BORN INTO AND PART OF A MALE WORLD, [DON QUIXOTE] HAD NO SPEECH OF HER OWN. ALL SHE COULD DO WAS READ MALE TEXTS WHICH WEREN'T HERS" (Acker 1986, 39). This process of developing subjectivities is inevitably gendered because both Janey and the female knight have to define themselves *as opposed to* men. Furthermore, Acker's unique writing style of plagiarism plays a critical role. As Martina Sciolino puts it, Acker's intentional plagiarism suggests a "plastic" identity of the protagonists (1990, 441). By decontextualising and recontextualising passages from essays, poems, and letters of other artists as well as her own, Acker alludes to a collaged female subject, a subject that is always interpellated by different ideological apparatuses but strives for deconstruction and reconstruction regardless.

The male texts that Janey and Don Quixote rewrite repress female sexual desire and accentuate love as an institutional unification. By appropriating these writings, Acker denounces the ideology of love that regenerates compulsory heterosexuality. Compared to *Blood and Guts* in which she centres her critique upon love as a symbol of unequal balance of power, Acker's criticism targets a broader system of heteronormativity especially in *Don Quixote*. A typical heterosexual love relationship ends with marriage that implies future procreation and the subsequent formation of a nuclear family. Since this paradigm of love defines heterosexuality as hegemony and reinforces gender norms and hierarchies, many feminists and scholars have shared Acker's concerns. For instance, Firestone criticises the power structure in a patriarchal nuclear family (2003, 67); Michael Hardt and Antonio

Negri call the family unification a form of "corrupt love" that closes a couple in a unit and bars them from forming a community (2011, 183). Among these thinkers, Gilles Deleuze and Félix Guattari directly connect to Acker's politicisation of love as she refers to *Anti-Oedipus* (1972) in both novels.[6] Deleuze and Guattari contend that the nuclear family as a functioning principle of society oppresses its members, which in turn creates the "incestuous familial drives" that symbolically show what is repressed within the "daddy-mommy-me" structure (2009, 119). Not only does Acker describe a similar familial drive of Janey towards a Father, but she also plagiarises a passage from *Anti-Oedipus* in which desire is reconsidered as a positive force in *Blood and Guts* (2017, 125). Moreover, the following scene in *Don Quixote* instantly recalls the image of the daddy-mommy-me familialism of psychoanalysis.

> "You've come back to prison of your own free accord," my mother barked when I returned from the bathroom.
>
> "You're my property," daddy amended. "From now on, you will do whatever I woof you to do and, more important, be whoever I order you. This is a safe unit."
>
> My father further barked that since the US prisons had become privatized so that, in accordance with NBC, electrocutions could be televised, my family was going to strap me into a leather chair. They strapped me. They left the room. On a TV set in its bedroom, my father watched me be electrocuted.
>
> (Acker 1986, 116–17)

In this passage, Acker's anthropomorphised canine family is docile and domesticated, feeling that the nuclear household is a safe entity. Within this unit, the father is a patriarch-authority who can claim the possession of the rest of the family and exercise control over their identities. The house-prison is a repressive site of surveillance that references the Foucauldian notion of house as an "extended network of carceral system," as well as the prison industrial complex of the Nixon administration (Foucault 1979, 301). As Acker aptly calls it, this "Portrait of an American Family" provides a powerful critique of the normative and normalising institutions of heterosexual love (Acker 1986, 115).

Abortion as a counterhegemonic force against the heteronormative system of power becomes evident in this respect since a woman's right to terminate pregnancy rejects the surveillance of the biopolitical nation state. It also challenges the governing power of the state because an unmarried woman's abortion repudiates the possible establishment of a nuclear household that is enforced by the state. Acker embodies this idea more clearly in *Don Quixote* by naming Ronald Reagan as one of the female knight's evil enchanters (1986, 102). Defending traditional family values and emphasising the importance of family in the functioning of neoliberal capitalism, Reagan's

New Right administration attempted to overturn many achievements of feminists from the 1970s, with the right to abortion as a major target. In 1984, he aligned the pro-life campaign with the Civil Rights Movement and eventually succeeded in cutting funds for abortions (Houen 2012, 176). In such an atmosphere, abortion serves not only as a counterattack against the administration's heterosexual family ideology but also as a nonconforming and radical means of resistance. As Don Quixote contemplates,

> A man who controls political power does whatever he likes. It's natural for him to do whatever he likes because that's what having power means and is: the power to do. A man who controls other people steals their souls. Therefore, when the poor or soulless steal, they are acting unnaturally, they're redressing through unnatural means the proper balance of human power. This is why women have to get abortions.
>
> In humans, human sexuality is closely tied to power. What are the sexualities of those white men who have almost complete political control?
>
> (Acker 1986, 178)

The group of white men that holds political control wields heterosexuality as the main source of power. Abortion, as an unnatural means to redress the unequal balance of power, thus enables women to at least partly regain their autonomy as it gives them *the power to do* what they want to do with the unwanted pregnancy. As such, whereas Janey rejects corrupt love and endeavours to reclaim her repressed desire, the female knight renounces institutional love, marriage, and reproduction, and by so doing, queers the ideology of love. Lauren Berlant argues that love is queered not when one resists all its known forms but when one does not admit it "as a principle of living" (2001, 443). Indeed, realising that "as soon as [she's] married, [she'll] be a prisoner; [she'll] be normal," Don Quixote decides not to accept love as a principle of living by not loving at all (Acker 1986, 202).

Notably, queering love for the female knight is achieved by refusing to love, not by practising the diverse aspects of love outside the established rules and norms. In her biography of Acker published in 2017, Chris Kraus explains that *Don Quixote* seriously deals with the "limits and possibilities of a same-sex relationship" for the first time in Acker's career (2017, 213). However, as a heterosexual woman, Don Quixote defines herself as a freak and remains an ally to the sexually marginalised; homosexuality and queerness as well as the resistant power they entail are examined by St Simeon, the knight's genderqueer sidekick. Throughout the novel, St Simeon's identity constantly changes from a male human to a male dog and then to a female dog. In a section ironically entitled "HETEROSEXUALITY," St Simeon and their partner are referred to with two gender pronouns together – *he(she)* or *her his* – as no one can "get sexual genders straight" (Acker 1986, 159). In the next section, St Simeon's queerness blurs what Judith Butler characterises as the binary between "normalized heterosexuality and abject homosexuality" (2011, 103–4) since St Simeon is ostracised from their family for not fitting into any of the gender categories:

> They don't hug me cause I'm unlike other people: I'm neither male nor female. My nurse likes my sisters and brother unlike me, because they, unlike me, 're normal. I'm weird. I love the river because it isn't human and I'm not human.
>
> (Acker 1986, 142)

Completely excluded from the genealogy of a normal or normative family and not conforming to any specific gender representations, St Simeon is an *under*dog of the society that disrupts the heteronormative notions of gender divisions and renders all genders unstable.

As both protagonists die at the end of the novels, Janey, Don Quixote, and St Simeon ultimately fail to demolish the fortified system of power by means of their unnatural and radical resistance. However, Acker heralds continuous action through the possible rebirth of the two characters. In *Blood and Guts*, after being abandoned by Mr. Linker, Janey goes to Tangier and meets Jean Genet, who leaves her as she dies.[7] The novel soon moves onto the afterlife stories entitled "The Journey" and "The World."[8] These stories, based on *The Egyptian Book of the Dead* and Tantric images, centre upon the idea that desire creates pain; nevertheless, Kathryn Hume argues, Janey comes back to the mundane world of desire because "withdrawal and detachment do not lead to political action" (2000, 434). Likewise, *Don Quixote* alludes to the knight's reawakening when the novel ends with "I closed my eyes, head drooping, like a person drunk for so long she no longer knows she's drunk, and then, drunk, awoke to the world which lay before me" (Acker 1986, 207). Such a narrative structure of circular return defies linearity or the male-centred notion of coherence while also suggesting women's constant fight against the neoliberal and biopolitical nation state.[9] In this respect, the two novels do not end with the defeat and despair of the underprivileged. As Marjorie Worthington succinctly puts it, these endings show that "resistance is only possible through the effort, not the result" (2000, 252). In a world where the hegemonic power of white heterosexual men is too strong to be overturned overnight, the defiance carries weight when the marginalised endlessly and relentlessly tries.

The textual level of constant and continuous resistance of the discriminated would be actualised if the readers translated the message into action in reality. Acker's performative writing style acknowledges the significance of praxis by addressing the readers and asking for their participation. As Christina Milletti discusses, Acker's novels are "uniquely designed to arouse readers (to action)" (2004, 358). The corrected text of *Blood and Guts* ends with a set of questions that calls for a response: "Shall we look for this wonderful book [on human transformation]? Shall we stop being dead people?

Shall we find our way out of all expectations?" (Acker 2017, 165). In *Don Quixote*, the female knight speaks to her fellow freaks outside the text ("It is for you, freaks my loves, I am writing and it is about you" (Acker 1986, 202)) and proposes a communal and radical act: "Since dualism's no longer a usable logical model ... anarchy and collectivity can work hand-in-hand" (Acker 1986, 204). Seeking an anarchist counterattack that overthrows the social expectations or dualisms of mind/body, personal/political, and choice/life, the request for political awakening and action – to *stop being dead people* – is directly connected to Acker's problematisation of the abortion discourse and the ideology of love. According to Acker, writing inevitably entails social consciousness as it engages in the "constructing of the political, economic, and moral community in which [the] discourse is taking place" (Acker 1997, 4). The performativity of her texts, then, is a powerful attempt to create a public sphere, a bonding community of its own where readers can critically reflect on the problems raised and act accordingly.

Abortion policies have further undergone significant changes since *Roe v. Wade* in the US. Most notably, *Gonzales v. Carhart* in 2007 rekindled the debate on abortion trauma; the forty-fifth president targeted women's health legislation immediately after his inauguration; and recently in 2019, a number of states including Georgia and Ohio passed bills that would ban abortion after the detection of a "fetal heartbeat." These regressive movements in reproductive politics at least manifest one thing: the termination of pregnancy has never been solely a matter of personal choice. Considering the current political climate, the representations of abortion in *Blood and Guts* and *Don Quixote* are strikingly resonant and relevant even after more than three decades since their publication. Revisiting Acker's works and exploring her political engagement, in this sense, may be timelier than ever.

Notes

1 An earlier version of this chapter was published in 2017 as part of the author's doctoral dissertation.
2 See, for instance, Judith Wilt, *Abortion, Choice, and Contemporary Fiction* and Meg Gillette, "Modern American Abortion Narratives and the Century of Silence."
3 Although copyrighted in 1978, *Blood and Guts* was first published in 1984 because of negotiation issues.
4 A few scholars have recently delved into the connection between race and the biopolitics of reproduction. See Rosalyn Diprose and Ewa Plonowska Ziarek, *Arendt, Natality, and Biopolitics*, for example.
5 Explaining that abortion is considered as a negative decision even among reproductive rights activists, Thomsen suggests a celebration of abortion while acknowledging the diverse experiences of women.
6 Acker also explains the influence of Deleuze and Guattari's theory on *Don Quixote* as well as her admiration for their political engagement in an essay (Acker 1997, 85).

7 Interestingly, Genet's works have been reviewed positively by feminist scholars. Kate Millett, for example, comments in *Sexual Politics* (2000) that Genet recognises women as an oppressed group and identifies with them (Millett 2000, 356); Hélène Cixous writes in "The Laugh of the Medusa" (1976) that Genet's writing is exemplary of *écriture feminine* (Cixous 1976, 885). Genet in *Blood and Guts*, however, is depicted as abusive and possibly sadist. Considering Janey's remark that "Sex in America is S & M" (Acker 2017, 99) in the sense that sadistic men and masochistic women – at least superficially – represent conventional sexual hierarchy, the unfavourable characterisation of Genet likely intends to reiterate the power imbalance of the society. Acker also plagiarises Genet's *The Thief's Journal* (1949) and *The Screens* (1961) and Mohamed Choukri's *Jean Genet in Tangier* (1974) in the novel.

8 The two sections had been misplaced until it was finally corrected in the 2017 anniversary edition. Given that Janey comes back to the world ("The World") after finding enlightenment ("The Journey"), the originally intended order of "The Journey" and then "The World" is more convincing.

9 See Gayle Greene, *Changing the Story* for a feminist narrative theory and its discussion on the circular pattern.

References

Acker, Kathy. 1986. *Don Quixote, Which Was a Dream*. New York: Grove Press.
———— 1997. *Bodies of Work: Essays by Kathy Acker*. New York: Serpent's Tail.
———— 2017. *Blood and Guts in High School*. Anniversary ed. New York: Grove Press.
Berlant, Lauren. 2001. "Love, a Queer Feeling." In *Homosexuality and Psychoanalysis*, edited by Tim Dean and Christopher Lane, 432–51. Chicago, IL: University of Chicago Press.
Butler, Judith. 2011. *Bodies That Matter: On the Discursive Limits of Sex*. New York: Routledge.
Cixous, Hélène. 1976. "The Laugh of the Medusa." Translated by Keith Cohen and Paula Cohen. *Signs* 1, no. 4: 875–93.
Cornell, Drucilla. 1995. *The Imaginary Domain: Abortion, Pornography, and Sexual Harassment*. New York: Routledge.
Deleuze, Gilles, and Félix Guattari. 2009. *Anti-Oedipus: Capitalism and Schizophrenia*. New York: Penguin Books.
Diprose, Rosalyn, and Ewa Plonowska Ziarek. 2018. *Arendt, Natality, and Biopolitics: Toward Democratic Plurality and Reproductive Justice*. Edinburgh: Edinburgh University Press.
Firestone, Shulamith. 2003. *The Dialectic of Sex: The Case for Feminist Revolution*. New York: Farrar, Straus and Giroux.
Foucault, Michel. 1979. *Discipline and Punish: The Birth of the Prison*. Translated by Alan Sheridan. New York: Vintage Books.
———— 2003. *Society Must Be Defended: Lectures at the Collège de France 1975–76*. Translated by David Macey. New York: Picador.
———— 2008. *The Birth of Biopolitics: Lectures at the Collège de France 1978–1979*. Translated by Graham Burchell. New York: Picador.
Gillette, Meg. 2012. "Modern American Abortion Narratives and the Century of Silence." *Twentieth Century Literature* 58, no. 4: 663–87.

Greenberg, Jan Crawford. 1998. "*Roe vs. Wade* at 25: America's Great Divide." *Chicago Tribune*, January 19, 1998. chicagotribune.com/news/ct-xpm-1998-01-19-9801190133-story.html.

Greene, Gayle. 1992. *Changing the Story: Feminist Fiction and the Tradition.* Bloomington, IN: Indiana University Press.

Hardt, Michael, and Antonio Negri. 2011. *Commonwealth.* Cambridge, MA: Belknap Press.

Houen, Alex. 2012. *Powers of Possibility: Experimental American Writing since the 1960s.* Oxford: Oxford University Press.

Hume, Kathryn. 2000. "Books of the Dead: Postmortem Politics in Novels by Mailer, Burroughs, Acker, and Pynchon." *Modern Philology* 97, no. 3: 417–44.

Kraus, Chris. 2017. *After Kathy Acker: A Literary Biography.* South Pasadena, CA: Semiotext(e).

Latimer, Heather. 2013. *Reproductive Acts: Sexual Politics in North American Fiction and Film.* Montreal: McGill-Queen's University Press.

Legge, Jerome S. 1985. *Abortion Policy: An Evaluation of the Consequences for Maternal and Infant Health.* New York: State University of New York Press.

MacKinnon, Catharine. 1987. *Feminism Unmodified: Discourses on Life and Law.* Cambridge, MA: Harvard University Press.

Millett, Kate. 2000. *Sexual Politics.* Chicago, IL: University of Illinois Press.

Milletti, Christina. 2004. "Violent Acts, Volatile Words: Kathy Acker's Terrorist Aesthetic." *Studies in the Novel* 35, no. 3: 352–73.

Poovey, Mary. 1992. "The Abortion Question and the Death of Man." In *Feminists Theorize the Political*, edited by Judith Butler and Joan W. Scott, 239–56. New York: Routledge.

Schlichter, Annette. 2007. "'I Can't Get Sexual Genders Straight': Kathy Acker's Writing of Bodies and Pleasures." *Postmodern Culture* 17, no. 2. pmc.iath.virginia.edu/text-only/issue.107/17.2schlichter.txt.

Sciolino, Martina. 1990. "Kathy Acker and the Postmodern Subject of Feminism." *College English* 52, no. 4: 437–45.

Stormer, Nathan. 2002. *Articulating Life's Memory: U.S. Medical Rhetoric about Abortion in the Nineteenth Century.* Lanham, MD: Lexington Books.

Thomsen, Carly. 2013. "From Refusing Stigmatization toward Celebration: New Directions for Reproductive Justice Activism." *Feminist Studies* 39, no. 1: 149–58.

Wilt, Judith. 1990. *Abortion, Choice, and Contemporary Fiction: The Armageddon of the Maternal Instinct.* Chicago, IL: University of Chicago Press.

Worthington, Marjorie. 2000. "Posthumous Posturing: The Subversive Power of Death in Contemporary Women's Fiction." *Studies in the Novel* 32, no. 2: 243–63.

Index